The Ecology of Pre-Primary Foreign Language Learning

EARLY LANGUAGE LEARNING IN SCHOOL CONTEXTS

Series Editors: **Janet Enever**, *Umeå University, Sweden* and **Annamaria Pinter**, *University of Warwick, UK*

The early learning of languages in instructed contexts has become an increasingly common global phenomenon during the past 30 years, yet there remains much work to be done to establish the field as a distinctive area for interdisciplinary investigation. This international research series covers children learning second, foreign and additional languages in educational contexts between the ages of approximately 3 and 12 years. The series will take a global perspective and encourage the sharing of theoretical discussion and empirical evidence on transnational issues. It will provide a platform to address questions raised by teachers, teacher educators and policy makers who are seeking understanding of theoretical issues and empirical evidence with which to underpin policy development, implementation and classroom procedures for this young age group. Themes of particular interest for the series include: teacher models and teacher development, models of early language learning, policy implementation, motivation, approaches to teaching and learning, language progress and outcomes, assessment, intercultural learning, sustainability in provision, comparative and transnational perspectives, cross-phase transfer issues, curriculum integration – additional suggestions for themes are also most welcome.

All books in this series are externally peer-reviewed.

Full details of all the books in this series and of all our other publications can be found on http://www.multilingual-matters.com, or by writing to Multilingual Matters, St Nicholas House, 31-34 High Street, Bristol, BS1 2AW, UK.

EARLY LANGUAGE LEARNING IN SCHOOL CONTEXTS: 9

The Ecology of Pre-Primary Foreign Language Learning

Joanna Rokita-Jaśkow

MULTILINGUAL MATTERS
Bristol • Jackson

DOI https://doi.org/10.21832/ROKITA7854
Library of Congress Cataloging in Publication Data
A catalog record for this book is available from the Library of Congress.
Names: Rokita-Jaśkow, Joanna, author.
Title: The Ecology of Pre-Primary Foreign Language Learning / Joanna Rokita-Jaśkow.
Description: Bristol; Jackson, TN: Multilingual Matters, [2025] | Series: Early Language Learning in School Contexts: 9 | Includes bibliographical references and index. | Summary: "This book synthesises research on very early language learning in pre-primary organised instruction settings, using a framework of ecological development to investigate the nested systems in which very young learners operate and the influence of other agents on children's foreign language learning"-- Provided by publisher.
Identifiers: LCCN 2024029637 (print) | LCCN 2024029638 (ebook) | ISBN 9781800417847 (pbk) | ISBN 9781800417854 (hbk) | ISBN 9781800417878 (epub) | ISBN 9781800417861 (pdf)
Subjects: LCSH: Second language acquisition. | Language and languages--Study and teaching (Early childhood) | Bilingualism in children.
Classification: LCC P118.2 R65 2025 (print) | LCC P118.2 (ebook) | DDC 372.65--dc23/eng/20240925
LC record available at https://lccn.loc.gov/2024029637
LC ebook record available at https://lccn.loc.gov/2024029638

British Library Cataloguing in Publication Data
A catalogue entry for this book is available from the British Library.

ISBN-13: 978-1-80041-785-4 (hbk)
ISBN-13: 978-1-80041-784-7 (pbk)

Multilingual Matters
UK: St Nicholas House, 31-34 High Street, Bristol, BS1 2AW, UK.
USA: Ingram, Jackson, TN, USA.

Website: https://www.multilingual-matters.com
X: Multi_Ling_Mat
Facebook: https://www.facebook.com/multilingualmatters
Blog: https://www.channelviewpublications.wordpress.com

Copyright © 2025 Rokita-Jaśkow.

All rights reserved. No part of this work may be reproduced in any form or by any means without permission in writing from the publisher.

The policy of Multilingual Matters/Channel View Publications is to use papers that are natural, renewable and recyclable products, made from wood grown in sustainable forests. In the manufacturing process of our books, and to further support our policy, preference is given to printers that have FSC and PEFC Chain of Custody certification. The FSC and/or PEFC logos will appear on those books where full certification has been granted to the printer concerned.

Typeset by Deanta Global Publishing Services, Chennai, India

To those who, with a good word and thoughtful advice, have inspired and supported me in my academic career.

Contents

Acknowledgement		ix
Abbreviations		xi
Introduction		1
1	The Child's Biosystem: How Children Learn to Communicate in Their First and Foreign Languages	9
	1.1 Learning to Communicate in the First Language	9
	1.2 Children's Ways of Learning	13
	1.3 How First Language Development Impacts Early Foreign Language Learning	15
	Summary	30
2	Microsystem: The Educational Institution	31
	2.1 Children's Attitude to and Motivation for FL Learning	31
	2.2 Defining Quality in Very Early FL Instruction	34
	2.3 Organisation of Instruction, Institution Type and Curriculum	35
	2.4 Methodology	38
	2.5 The Teacher	48
	2.6 The Role of Peers in FL Instruction	57
	2.7 Teacher Agency	58
	Summary	59
3	Mesosystem: Family Environment	60
	3.1 Parental Involvement in Child FL Education	60
	3.2 Factors Affecting Parental Involvement	73
	3.3 Parental Agency	77
	Summary	78
4	Exosystem: The Affordances of the Linguistic Landscape	79
	4.1 Globalisation, Englishisation and Neoliberalism as Drivers of Early FL Education	79
	4.2 Affordances of Linguistic Landscapes	84

	4.3 Affordances of Screen Media	88
	4.4 Agency and the Linguistic Landscape	94
	Summary	94
5	Macrosystem: Early Language Learning Policy and Planning	96
	5.1 An Early Start in a FL in European Language-in-Education Policy	96
	5.2 Early Language Learning Policies Outside Europe	104
	5.3 Early Language Learning Policy Implementation	111
	5.4 Access Policy and Equity	115
	5.5 Evaluation Policies	118
	5.6 Agency and Policy	121
	Summary	123
6	The Chronosystem	124
	6.1 A Very Early Start in an FL as Utilising 'a Window of Opportunity'	124
	6.2 FL Learning Continuity From Pre-Primary to Primary School	131
	6.3 Agency and Time	132
	Summary	133
	Concluding Remarks	134
	References	142
	Subject Index	165
	Author Index	168

Acknowledgement

I wish to thank the series editors Janet Enever and Annamaria Pinter and an anonymous reviewer for careful reading of the text and valuable comments.

Abbreviations

AoO	Age of Onset
BICS	Basic Interpersonal Communication Skills (Cummins, 1979)
CALP	Cognitive Academic Language Proficiency (Cummins, 1979)
CEFR	Common European Framework of Reference for Languages
CLIL	Content and Language Integrated Learning
CPH	Critical Period Hypothesis
DLL	Dual Language Learners (bilingual)
EAL	English as an Additional Language
ECEC	Early Childhood Education and Care
ECML	European Centre for Modern Languages
ELA	English Language Area
ELP	European Language Policy
EMI	English-Medium Instruction
EU	European Union
FL	Foreign Language
FLP	Family Language Policy
L1, L2	First Language, Second Language
LAD	Language Acquisition Device
LL	Linguistic Landscape
MA	Metalinguistic Awareness
MALL	Mobile-Assisted Language Learning
NEST	Native English-Speaking Teacher
NNEST	Non-Native English-Speaking Teacher
SES	Socioeconomic Status
SLA	Second Language Acquisition
TEYL	Teaching English to Young Learners
TPR	Total Physical Response (Asher, 1969)
VYL	Very Young Learner
WM	Working Memory
YL	Young Learner
ZPD	Zone of Proximal Development

Introduction

Without doubt, teaching and learning foreign languages to young (aged approx. 7 up to 12/14 years) and very young (i.e. below 7) learners has become a global phenomenon, being an outcome of both parental aspirations and policy measures. Despite the lack of linguistic evidence, as children who start language learning earlier are often surpassed by those who start later but more intensively (e.g. Muñoz, 2006), the trend of teaching languages to children is flourishing worldwide, embracing younger and younger learners. This popularity may signify parental demand arising from a concern for their children's future; alternatively, it may signify a gap in the educational market which can be filled with a multitude of courses, teaching and teacher education solutions, educational materials and so on. Needless to say, it also provides new research opportunities.

Language teaching to young learners is not a novel issue. It is over 40 years since the first seminal publication on how to teach this age group was first published, edited by Reinhold Freudenstein, titled *Teaching Foreign Languages to the Very Young* (1979). This publication was followed by a number of TEYL (teaching English to young learners) methodology guidebooks, which include, among others, volumes by Broomfit et al. (1991), Cameron (2001), Brewster *et al.* (2002), Pinter (2006, 2011) and Szpotowicz and Szulc-Kurpaska (2009). As a result, the principles and techniques of teaching young learners are generally well known. In the last decade, due to lowering the age of starting foreign language (FL) instruction to pre-primary years, we can observe an increased interest in teaching very young learners, that is, those who start learning a FL before the onset of compulsory school instruction, which is in most countries around the age of six, but can also be at seven or five years of age. These children do not possess literacy skills in their first language (L1), which restricts their FL learning opportunities to mainly oral input and interaction.

In response to this growth of interest in teaching and researching very young learners, an increase in the number of publications dedicated to this age group has been observed, which include stand-alone methodological resource books (e.g. Mourão & Ellis, 2020) as well as sections within reference books on teaching young learners (e.g. Bland, 2015; Garton & Copland, 2019; Murphy, 2014). The edited collections by Mourão and Lourenço (2015), Murphy and Evangelou (2016), Schwartz (2020), Cortina-Pérez *et al.* (2022) and Otto and Cortina-Pérez (2023) focus on policy and attitudes towards teaching such young learners, including learning in multilingual and content and language integrated learning settings. Early and very early FL learning has been a central topic of special issues of the Spanish journal *Porta Linguarum* (Cortina-Pérez, 2022) and the Greek journal *Research Papers in Language Learning and Teaching* (Alexiou, 2021). These publications indicate a surge of interest into researching very young learners, yet, as Pinter and Kuchah (2021) argue, there is sufficient research *on* very young learners but still little *with* them, partly due to the ethical and methodological constraints of doing research with them. A recent overview of studies on pre-primary learners (Nikolov & Mihaljević Djigunović, 2023) features various studies conducted within the last 20 years across the globe, often published locally, which provide insight into the processes and outcomes of such early teaching of FLs. However, as the authors highlight, there are still some research gaps yet to be filled.

The goal of this monograph is to contribute to this abundant area of research with a holistic look at the process of learning a FL by very young learners by surveying up-to-date research findings. By a FL, we mean a language that is not spoken in the public sphere in a country. Thus, the majority of the exposure to the FL comes from formal instruction, sometimes enhanced by additional exposure or practice at home.

In Poland, as in many other Central European countries (such as Hungary, Croatia, Serbia and Slovenia) early and very early FL learning has been practised widely since the early 1990s, although initially largely on a private basis (cf. Nikolov & Mihaljević Djigunović, 2006, 2011; Rokita, 2007; Rokita-Jaśkow, 2013a). This was mainly due to the widely held belief that FL competency facilitates access to well-paid jobs and enables upward social mobility. For this reason, and due to limited access to the L2 input, an early start, and consequently a prolonged period of language learning, was regarded to be key to attaining proficiency. It seems nowadays that similar motives lay behind introducing early and very early start policies in other contexts across the globe, most notably in East Asia (cf. Butler, 2015a; Enever, 2018; Murphy & Evangelou, 2016). This appears to be a widespread phenomenon, not always regulated by policy but arising in response to parental desires and boosted by the educational market.

Why the Ecological Approach?

I have adopted van Lier's (2004) ecological approach and Bronfennbrenner's (1979) theory of human development as the major theoretical framework for this book. The two theories complement each other and emphasise that no individual grows in a vacuum but in an environment (i.e. ecology/ecosystem), in which one's development is impacted by various social agents and sociopolitical contexts. Likewise, in the case of child language development, be it first or second, it is nowadays widely accepted from research evidence (e.g. Nikolov & Mihaljević Djigunović, 2023; Pearson *et al.*, 1997) that language outcomes, such as richness of vocabulary, complexity and accuracy of syntactic structures and pragmatic use, depend on the quantity and quality of child interactions with significant others, such as caregivers and teachers, as well as the visibility of the language in the semiotic landscape (Javorsky & Thurlow, 2010). This view challenges the Chomskyan view that language development is the result of the innate predispositions of the child and that it is static, prescriptive and unanimous. Conversely, van Lier's (2004) ecological theory takes into account the whole ecosystem of the child's growth and posits that it is 'an approach that focuses primarily on the quality of learning opportunities, of classroom interaction and of educational experience in general' (van Lier, 2010: 2). He also pinpointed and characterised features of a flourishing ecosystem, such as: *relationships* (rather than objects), *context*, *emergent patterns*, *quality*, *value*, *critical perspective*, *variability*, *diversity* and *agency* (van Lier, 2004, 2010).

Relationships are established between different elements of the ecosystem, which can be physical (trees, ponds, etc.), social (families, schools, etc.), 'sociocultural world of artefacts' (e.g. elements of the landscape, such as signposts, classrooms, etc.) and symbolic (e.g. ideas, belief systems, stories) (van Lier, 2010: 2). These relationships constitute *affordances*, that is, possibilities for interaction between the language user and an object. Clearly, FL learning by a child learner will result from the quantity of available relationships, which will not be restricted to the immediate social environment but also the larger semiotic landscape as well as values and beliefs held by the society one lives in, as well as the perception of early language learning being key to success.

The saliency of context in ecological learning is emphasised as it defines the type and register of language that is used. Language is seen as an emerging system of 'patterns that connect' (van Lier, 2004: 5). For these reasons language development takes place in an unpredictable and dynamic way. Similarly, a child's FL learning performance fluctuates, depending on the frequency of contact hours, quality of teacher input. Therefore, overall levels of competence are not just the sum of smaller learning elements, like words, grammar and so on, but 'emergence happens when relatively simple elements combine together for a higher-order system' (van Lier, 2004: 5), through which one is able to convey thoughts, negotiate meanings, analyse language patterns and make inferences about language rules.

Education quality is often measured by standardised tests, and thus quality equals accountability. Yet, van Lier (2010) critiques such an approach as it does not take into account the 'all-important notion of the quality of the educational experience, of learning opportunities, and the wellbeing of the learners, the wellbeing of participants or the process of education' (van Lier, 2010: 3). Therefore, for the purpose of building meaningful relationships, it is the quality of the learning experience that matters. In order to assess this, one needs to look inside the language classroom in order to observe the type of input provided to the children via various language learning techniques and teacher discourse strategies.

Having recognised the prominence of quality and value, an ecological approach takes a critical stance to reality. Ecological learning also makes the point that unlike 'pure' science, 'critical and moral enterprise' should be taken into account (van Lier, 2004: 6). Thus, ecological learning often challenges the sociopolitical contextual macro order. In view of social phenomena such as migration and social inequalities, ecological learning regards language learning as a human right. It further strives towards 'a constant evaluation of what is actually happening (what we are doing...) with what we think (in line with our principles, moral values, and so on) should be happening' (van Lier, 2010: 8). As van Lier further argues, 'it is a call to critical thinking and critical acting, based on well-articulated principles and personal convictions' (2010: 8). From this perspective, early language learning should not be seen as elitist, restricted only to the privileged classes. Thus, it is a frequent goal of equitable politics to introduce such policies that provide equal opportunities to all children and counteract possible negative outcomes of neoliberal forces in the educational market.

Recognition of variability in education takes into account individual differences between learners. It also assumes that the good language teacher is able to take these differences into account and appropriately support the child in the teaching process while working towards similar levels of achievement among all learners. Equity, understood as expectation to meet identical educational goals irrespective of the child's background and ability, is thus perceived as a fairer approach to learning than just providing equal opportunities.

Finally, diversity emphasises 'the value of having different learners and teachers in a class (or school)' (van Lier, 2004: 7). In the same manner as in the biological ecosystem, the more varied the educational ecosystem, the richer it becomes, through the amalgam of learners' gender, personalities, race, ethnicity, mother tongue languages, cultures and so on. Exposing children to language output of diverse learners prepares them to face diversity in the out-of-school ecology and for the fact that language use in reality is far from being homogenous. Early FL learning should thus encompass children from various socioeconomic backgrounds, children with special educational needs and so on. It must also be recognised that due to migration trends, language classes comprise more and more frequently learners with diverse mother tongues. In response, teachers should recognise this diversity of learners and learn to treat it as an added value, not as an obstacle to the attainment of educational goals.

Finally, a salient concept in the ecological theory is *agency* (or activity), which can be understood, as Emirbayer and Mische (1998) put it, as 'the capacity of actors to critically shape their own responsiveness to problematic situations' (Emirbayer & Mische, 1998: 971). Cole (2024: n.p.) refines this definition by saying that 'agency refers to the thoughts and actions taken by people that express their individual power'. Agency should thus be seen as a dynamic construct distinct from structure which describes stable characteristics of society, that is, one's position in that structure as manifested by one's socioeconomic status, place of living, race, gender and so on. Agency is the activity of an individual pursued to change one's position despite the obstacles. It is the driving force that stands behind the motivation to strive. Agency can be manifested by all individuals in any learning situation, such as teachers who continue to teach enthusiastically despite an unfavourable sociopolitical climate. Agency is practised by immigrants who with effort learn the language of school instruction, thanks to which they upgrade their professional skills, achieve vocational success and integrate into society. Agency is also related to one's *identity* in the sense that it is one's current and future vision of Self that can motivate an individual to undertake action to change one's position in society. Language learning can be seen as key to an individual's repositioning. Similarly, a goal of classroom teaching can be the provision of 'an agency-promoting curriculum [that] can awaken learners' agency through the provision of choices and the opportunity to work as a member of a learning community on interesting and challenging projects and puzzles' (van Lier, 2010: 4).

Are very young learners of a FL capable of such agency? Schwartz (2018) argues that successful early language learning is the outcome of child, parent and teacher agency, yet she mainly relates this to bilingual children learning the dominant language of the society in kindergarten. It is more doubtful whether very young learners of a FL can show similar agency if the language they are learning is mainly learnt for fun and not so much for communication. If all children in the group as well as the teacher share the same mother tongue, the children do not feel the need to make the cognitive effort to attempt communication in an L2, as it is mainly social strategies, such as a desire to join other children's games, that foster L2 development in natural contexts (Wong Fillmore, 1979). The question then arises, whose agency is it that underpins early FL learning in an instructed setting? This question will permeate throughout the book, only to be answered in the final pages.

The book revolves around Bronfenbrenner's (1979) model of human development, regarded to be generic in its character and thus suitable for adaptation. The chapter titles correspond to the names of the nested systems in which the very young learner of L2 operates and which together impact the child's FL learning. Within each chapter, available research evidence is outlined in relation to each element of the child language learner's ecosystem. As van Lier (2010: 8) argues:

> research often isolates particular pieces of the complex puzzle in order to study them in detail. However useful this may be, it obscures the dynamism of the actual teaching and learning work that goes on, and cannot show the emergent and contingent nature of that work.

Stemming from this criticism, this book aspires to combine available research results to provide a holistic and state-of-the art picture of the FL learning process in early years. Following from the model the book consists of six chapters:

The goal of Chapter 1 is to describe the biosystem of a child, that is, the cognitive and biological propensities that make them capable of acquiring a language, be it first, second or foreign. It draws on findings in psycholinguistics by first briefly describing how children acquire their mother tongue and formulate conceptual representations for newly learnt phenomena in their mind, and secondly, how this process may impact FL acquisition. The mutual interaction of languages at the conceptual level is addressed, following the Linguistic Coding Differences Hypothesis (Sparks, 2022; Sparks et al., 2019). The role of implicit and explicit mechanisms in relation to language exposure is highlighted with emphasis on the development of metalinguistic awareness. Furthermore, this chapter draws attention to the cognitive propensities of a child that may bear particular relevance to instructed learning and account for differences in learning outcomes, such as executive functions and their relation to working memory and aptitude. Finally, the issue of child agency is addressed, identifying that in contrast to naturalistic language learning it does not drive children's learning in a similar manner, as it does not stem from the learner themselves but must be generated by the environment.

Chapter 2, titled 'Microsystem: The Educational Institution', looks at the educational institution in which FL learning takes place (nursery, kindergarten, afternoon classes, etc.) and the quality of offered instruction, as defined by its organisation (frequency and length of classes), setting (decor), available teaching resources and last but not least, teacher competencies and applied age-appropriate teaching methodology. With reference to the latter two, efficiency of different pedagogical solutions will be presented in the light of available research data. Finally, the agency of teachers is emphasised, as they should be willing and competent to work with very young learners.

Chapter 3, titled 'Mesosytem: Family Environment', characterises the proximal and distal characteristics of the young learner's family. By the former I consider socioemotional ties within the family which result from spending time together and catering for the socioemotional and cognitive growth of the whole child. This stance will resonate in the amount of parental involvement in child FL education at home, that is, providing opportunities for additional language input, revision of class material, joint play and so on, as well as communicating and cooperating with the educational institution. It will also point to parental aspirations in reference to future child FL achievement and the treatment of early FL learning as an investment. As regards distal variables, it is mainly the socioeconomic status of the family that is addressed, together with the parental level of (language) education, as this mediates access to educational resources, the quality of instruction accessed and opportunities for intercultural encounters. The conclusion is that parental agency in early FL education is of high importance for setting models as language users, for inspiring and motivating the child, providing opportunities and resources, as well as liaising with the educational institution.

Chapter 4, titled 'Exosystem: The Affordances of the Linguistic Landscape', looks at the general social climate that generates favourable conditions for early language teaching, either because of the historical past or because of the current sociopolitical situation of a country, marking the value and status of FL learning. This climate manifests itself in the semiotics of the linguistic landscape, in media discourse, in the mission of educational institutions and so on, which arise from and influence the beliefs of the general public, including heads of educational institutions, and provide opportunities for exposure to language beyond the classroom.

Chapter 5, titled 'Macrosystem: Early Language Learning Policy and Planning', aims to present the forces that impact early language learning at the macro level. First of all, this is language education policy, which is shaped by both political decisions and parental aspirations which may promote or inhibit the learning of particular languages. In this respect, attention is drawn to the European language policy as a model for shaping language education policies in other countries globally, a trend known as 'policy borrowing'. Secondly, neoliberal trends in early language education are addressed, which promote early FL education, of English as a lingua franca in particular, as a necessary investment and a distinctive feature of belonging to global society. These trends are also evident in the buoyant educational market, in which FL educational institutions compete for prospective customers with innovative, yet not always research-based, offers. Finally, the commoditisation of education is discussed as a means of creating social inequalities. High quality pre-primary education is usually fee-paying and thus restricted to the few, whereas low-quality FL education will not advantage the child in either further education or in the job market.

The last chapter, titled 'The Chronosystem', refers to the last element of the Bronfenbrenner model, that is, the role of key time moments in child language development. Such moments comprise the moment of joining a FL class and the moment of transition to primary education. The moment of beginning to learn a FL is discussed as utilising a 'window of opportunity' or a critical period for language learning. The transition to primary education will raise issues of continuity and consistency of teaching programmes as well as the potential benefits to early starters.

The book finishes with a section on 'Concluding Remarks' that briefly recapitulates the key findings of the research presented in the book, highlighting that the effectiveness of early FL learning should be seen in the enacted agency of the various agents involved in the learning ecosystem, that is, educators, parents, public space, language policy decision-makers. Additionally, it will be emphasised that very early FL education provides a head start for ongoing education in the years to follow.

It is hoped that the book will be of interest to all those involved in the process of planning and implementation of early language learning policies in a variety of settings as well as to professionals (teachers, teacher educators, researchers) involved in early language learning and thus stimulate further research in this field.

1 The Child's Biosystem: How Children Learn to Communicate in Their First and Foreign Languages

The goal of this chapter is to describe the biosystem of a child, that is, the cognitive predispositions that make them capable of acquiring language, be it their first (L1), second (L2) or foreign language (FL). First, the chapter briefly outlines the process of acquiring the mother tongue as a frame of reference for the subsequent acquisition of an L2 and FL, explicating possible similarities and differences. Cognitive factors that may impact the process of acquiring the FL in instructed settings in early childhood are then highlighted, such as metalinguistic awareness (MA), executive functions, working memory (WM) and aptitude. The chapter then considers how much language the learners can actually acquire at such an early age, considering the cognitive limitations of the child. Finally, the issue of child agency is addressed, specifying that in contrast to naturalistic language learning, language instruction does not stimulate children's learning in a similar manner as motivation does not stem from the learner themselves but must be generated by the environment.

1.1 Learning to Communicate in the First Language

All normally developing children learn to speak their mother tongue by the age of 3;0, that is, 36 months. They acquire the language to which they are exposed in their surroundings from birth, from their parents, siblings and other caregivers. There exists the so-called natural order in which children acquire different language subsystems, starting from phonology, through lexis, syntax and finally pragmatics, which is mastered by approximately nine years of age, when the child begins to understand metaphorical functions of language use, such as jokes, irony and also different registers of politeness (Ratner & Gleason, 1993).

Newborn babies first learn to discriminate the phonemes of a particular language, distinguish between voiced and voiceless phonemes and become aware of phonotactic regularities of the language, that is, they are able to distinguish which sound clusters are associated with their language and which are not (Coady & Aslin, 2004). They are also able to distinguish between the phonemes of their and other languages. This perceptual ability is, however, lost by age eight to ten months, that is, when the child starts to say its first words. It seems as if the child selects which phonemes are present in their surroundings and eliminates those which appear to be meaningless in a given context.

It is in the prelinguistic phase that communicative development starts. Children start using communicative gestures, usually showing that they want to get something. This shows that reception precedes production and that before the child says their first word, they develop a meaning for it in the mind. The child first learns to understand certain concepts, such as objects, actions, causality and space relations, and only when the communicative need appears does the child seek appropriate linguistic forms to encode their thoughts. Therefore, in the cognitive view, the initial development of lexis, syntax and morphology is the process of mapping meaning onto previously acquired concepts. The acquisition of concepts, in turn, allows the child to generalise new words onto novel contexts of use (Bowerman & Choi, 2003).

The strategy that babies apply, called phonological (prosodic) bootstrapping strategy, consists in using prosodic cues, such as pitch, rhythm, amplitude, tempo, intonation and contour, to identify words from the stream of connected speech. That is also why caregivers' speech exhibits exaggerated tone, high amplitude, slower pace and so on when directed at infants. This shows how adult speakers indirectly 'teach' children the language; that is, by making distinct pauses, they allow infants to observe clause boundaries or draw attention to a word spoken distinctly while labelling an object (Stoel-Gammon, 2011).

Since the meanings of particular words are largely arbitrary, the babies need to learn to associate the particular cluster of sounds with a particular meaning. This process is called *semantic mapping* and consists of three stages: labelling, packaging and network-building (Aitchinson, 2003). *Labelling* refers to the stage in which the child learns to single out a word from the stream of speech and associates it with an object in the situation at hand. For example, when a caregiver points to a bottle of milk and names it 'milk', the baby learns that the liquid inside refers to milk. However, some mapping errors can occur, that is, the child may refer the word 'milk' to the bottle (*semantic mismatch*) or to all liquids in a bottle (which is a more likely error to appear, called *overextension*). Such semantic errors usually appear as a result of single exposure to the object, which sometimes is sufficient for a word to be acquired. However, with time and more frequent exposure to the referent, the child learns to label a given object correctly. The acquisition of lexicon is initially very slow: two to three words per week. The child initially learns onomatopoeic words and concrete nouns that relate to their surroundings. Only after the child has acquired approximately 50 words does the so-called vocabulary spurt take place. It seems that once the baby has acquired a certain threshold level, they discover a strategy for mapping new meanings. Subsequently, the acquisition of new words proceeds much faster.

In the next stage, *packaging*, the child learns to apply a new word to a whole class of similar-looking objects, on the grounds of sharing similar features, for example, to milk in a bottle, milk in a bowl or milk spilt on the table. *Network-building* denotes the ability to connect novel words into larger chunks or pairs with those already existing in the mental lexicon. The earliest and simplest links created by children concern collocational links, for example, the children will respond to the word 'milk' with 'drink' or to the word 'table' with 'eat'. It seems links are built between coordinates as a consequence of acquiring syntax and more extensive vocabulary, which later on enables faster word retrieval (Aitchison, 2003). Obviously, it may take many months, if not years, until the child first encounters a word and is able to build links to other items in the mental lexicon, which depends on the frequency of word reoccurrence in the language input.

These stages of vocabulary acquisition show that children learn the meanings of words by both associationist (known from behavioural psychology) and cognitive learning processes. The former means that the children learn the meaning a word by associating it with its referent, that is, an object or action the word refers to. Current computational models of language acquisition, for example connectionism, also rely on associationist learning in the sense that word labels and images are fed through distinct sensory pathways into a network, and the network is trained to associate the two (e.g. Elman, 1993). Successful production occurs when the network generates the appropriate label in response to an image; successful comprehension occurs when an appropriate image is generated in response to a label. Thus neural connections are created in response to the stimuli. Learning in general, and not only of words, proceeds in the manner of imitation and memorisation of these connections.

Clearly, one can easily replicate this way of learning in the FL classroom when a child is taught new words by means of flashcards or objects and is trained to associate this meaning with a word label, and subsequently to respond to an object stimuli with a memorised word. Memorisation of words in the instructed setting relies then to a large extent on repetition and rote learning of the learning material (lexis, chunks, simple sentences) that has been presented explicitly (Clark, 1993).

However, children do not only repeat the words they hear in their surrounding environment, they also appear to interpret the potential meanings of words by understanding the thoughts of themselves and of others, an ability referred to as Theory of Mind (Premack & Woodruff, 1978). Bloom (2000) reports on an example task in which two-year-old children when faced with one known object 'a banana' and an unknown object 'whisk', on the command 'Show me the fendle', always pointed to the whisk, probably associating the new object with the novel, though nonexistent, word 'fendle'. Children are hypothesised to have solved the task by a step-by-step reasoning process, by eliminating already known words and deciding to refer a new label to the new object, which is a tenet of the Lexical Contrast theory proposed by Eve Clark (2003). Consequently, very young children at least initially exclude synonyms.

This preference to exclude synonyms was also observed in FL learning in a two-year-old child who acquired some foreign words earlier than those in her mother tongue, Polish, most probably on the grounds of ease of articulation (Rokita, 2007). The cited examples concern acquiring the L2 English words 'apple', 'truck', 'bus' earlier than L1 Polish equivalents: 'jabłko', 'ciężarówka', 'autobus'. The L1 words were either longer to articulate or contained a cluster of glide vowel, bilabial – liquid – vowel syllables, and thus were more difficult to pronounce.

Although one-word utterances have the function of whole sentences (called *holophrases*), children gradually learn to combine acquired words into longer sequences, that is, two-word and then multi-word sentences, which signifies the acquisition of syntax. Language production is usually measured by the number of morphemes being combined (the measure of the so-called Mean Length of Utterances). Since babies first acquire bare stems and free morphemes, the stages they pass through are described by the length of these utterances and are referred to as one-word, two-word, multi-word and sentence stages. The more complex the utterances, the more sentential meanings they can express, such as negation (e.g. 'Bed no' – meaning 'I do not want to go to bed'), reoccurrence ('More milk'), lack/disappearance of something ('Milk gone') or drawing attention to something ('Hi, Daddy'). These are later followed by other meanings such as describing someone's or their own activity, modifying an object or indicating possession.

Toddlers also use the bootstrapping strategy to discover rules for word order and the function of words in a sentence, hence referred to as syntactic bootstrapping. Children have been found to show preference for dividing longer utterances into clauses rather than random chunks. It is the exaggerated prosody in child-directed speech that allows children to identify clause and phrase boundaries, and distinguish, for example, a noun phrase or a verb phrase. Pauses between words and prolonged last syllables serve as important prosodic cues which allow children to observe phrase units within a clause (Christophe *et al.*, 1994; Gerken *et al.*, 1994; Hirsh-Pasek *et al.*, 1987; Kemler Nelson *et al.*, 1989). Christophe and Dupoux (1996) hypothesise that, thanks to the distinction of stressed and unstressed syllables, children are able to distinguish between content and function words. Additionally, by their second birthday children use function words to determine the syntactic category of unknown content words (nouns vs. verbs) and deduce their probable meaning (object vs. action) (Christophe & Dupoux, 1996).

Furthermore, phonologically salient morphemes are observed, firstly inflectional ones, which allow the creation of novel forms of acquired words. Brown (1973) established a typical Order of Morpheme Acquisition in the English language, showing that the *–ing* morpheme is the first acquired due to its saliency. When other inflectional morphemes are acquired, such as the *–ed* ending for the past tense, the evidence of applying this rule is observed in the incorrect forms produced by children, such as *goed and *buyed, the phenomenon described as overregularisation.

Derivational morphemes are acquired later; however, their acquisition depends on their saliency and frequency in a given language. For example, in Polish the derivational morphemes referring to diminutives are acquired as the first type of morphemes due to their frequency in child-directed speech (Haman, 2003).

Rules for ordering words in a sentence are also discovered systematically. The evidence for this process can be observed in the developmental stages that babies go through when learning to formulate questions and negations. In the case of the former, children first ask a question just by raising intonation and only later use inversion or an auxiliary verb (do/did). The acquisition of question words such as *who, what, where* comes last and is determined by the understanding of the concept. For this reason, question pronouns such as *why, how, when*, which require understanding of temporal and causal relations, are acquired last (DeVilliers, 1985). Negations, in turn, are first constructed by insertion of the word 'no' and only later by using auxiliaries. Understanding the underlying rules of syntax, as reflected in word order and assigning grammatical functions to words, or by adding inflectional and derivational morphemes, manifests itself in linguistic creativity, such as creation of novel sentences or even words, called neologisms, which takes place around the age of 4;0 (Gleason & Ratner, 1993) and signals the development of MA.

1.2 Children's Ways of Learning

The aforementioned stages of linguistic development of a child indicate that babies and very young children are active learners in the process of discovering language rules from the input that they receive. This is the tenet of the cognitive view of learning, which shows that a baby is an active individual attempting to discover knowledge by themselves, by trial and error, by referring to their experiences and finding common features between objects and events, by referring them to the existing mental schemata or broadening them, or even inventing new ones.

The cognitive propensities of children in self-learning were first described by a renowned Swiss psychologist, Jean Piaget, who demonstrated that child development proceeds in stages, coinciding with particular age thresholds. Although he did not directly refer to language development, he described what a child can do cognitively at a particular age, and for this reason it is worth recalling these stages which coincide with the pre-primary age. At the first *sensori-motor stage* (up to 2;0), toddlers have poor mental representations of reality; their knowledge about the environment is gathered from the physical operation of objects. At this stage, children do not have a concept of *object permanence* developed as yet, which means that when an object is removed from their sight, they immediately lose interest in it. Nor do they have a concept of Self, which means the children do not see themselves as separate from the environment, which is evident in child egocentrism, that is, looking at the environment only from their own perspective (Schaffer, 2004).

The child's perception of its own separate identity starts to develop in the next, *preconceptual*, stage (age two to seven), when children start to think symbolically. This is evident in their liking for *pretend play*, which denotes a distinction between fantasy and reality, whereas using objects for other than their ordinary purpose shows reliance on their mental representations. Connected with this is the feature called *animism*, whereby children ascribe animate features to inanimate objects. At this stage, children have not developed the concept of reversibility, and so they are not able to reverse the sequence of events in complex clauses (especially denoting cause and effect) and narratives or learn calculations. This manifests itself in producing illogical sentences such as 'I didn't have a nap, so this can't be afternoon yet' or 'This man fell off the bike because he broke his hand' (Schaffer, 2004: 196).

Such erroneous examples show that very young children are already capable of discovering meanings of words for themselves and that they are not 'empty containers' to be filled with knowledge. Instead, they learn by interacting with their environment, by manipulating objects and concepts with a view to discovering their potential. In the reasoning process, they mainly use two major learning processes: *assimilation*, which denotes acquiring knowledge by means of already existent mental structures called schemata, and *accommodation*, which denotes modification of existent mental structures to acquire new knowledge (Piaget, 1926/2012; Wood, 1998).

Caregivers' presence and involvement in child communicative development is vital for two major reasons. Firstly, an adult serves as a source of language input and a model of language use. Secondly, they act as a Significant Other, with the help of whom the child's communicative development can proceed faster. As the sociocultural theory posits, by attuning to the child's current linguistic ability, that is, his Zone of Proximal Development (ZPD), the adult can prompt the child to exceed their linguistic limits and produce novel linguistic forms (Vygotsky, 1985). This is usually done in joint parent-child activities, such as meal routines, play or shared book reading. By asking questions, asking for clarification about an object or a fact, checking facts and so on, the adult builds 'scaffolding', the term introduced by Jerome Bruner (1983), to reach higher communicative levels (Pinter, 2011).

1.3 How First Language Development Impacts Early Foreign Language Learning

The survey of communicative development discussed above is to serve as a backdrop to the discussion of how very young children can learn a FL as opposed to an L2. The distinction between L2s and FLs is based on the concept of varied exposure: an L2 is frequently available in the environment (e.g. in multilingual societies or families) and can be picked up implicitly, while contact with a FL is restricted in terms of time (e.g. a few times a week) and space (usually in the formal classroom).

When it comes to the acquisition of an L2 in the natural environment, be it simultaneously (from birth or below the age of 3;0, before L1 acquisition is complete) or successively (after the age of 3;0), the process of bilingual language acquisition resembles to a large extent L1 acquisition, that is, the child goes through the same stages and uses similar strategies to discover meanings of words and language rules from context (Ervin-Tripp, 1974). Additionally, Łuniewska et al. (2022) found that when it comes to the acquisition of early words, which are also highly frequent and highly conceivable, there is no difference in the rate of acquisition between monolingual and bilingual children. The disparities begin to form when it comes to lexicon, which is acquired later, is of lower frequency and consists of more abstract words. In relation to these words, an advantage can be observed in monolingual children, which is probably due to the fact that bilinguals have fewer opportunities to associate word labels with concepts which are less frequent and/or more difficult to pronounce in the input language.

The major characteristic of the bilingual acquisition process is code-mixing, which can already take place at the two-word stage (Deuchar & Quay, 2000). The reason for this phenomenon is the fact that children initially develop concepts onto which they assign words, that is, those words which they hear most frequently in the environment. Code-mixing is a temporary phenomenon. With time and exposure to language, children learn to distinguish between the two lexicons and grammatical systems, and use one language consistently: that which is dominant in a particular context or required when communicating with a particular speaker, for example, in line with 'one parent, one language' strategy (Döpke, 1992).

Can FL learning at a very early age resemble the natural process of L2 acquisition? It seems any similarities between the processes of L1 and FL acquisition are only restricted to the early stages and concern early lexicon (Rokita, 2007) and receptive knowledge of grammar

(Prošić-Santovac, 2017; Sun *et al.*, 2016) due to the relatively small size of the FL lexicon and low amount of meaningful input which would allow the acquisition of syntactic rules in the minority language. Since FL instruction to very young learners is very often limited to one to two hours per week, unsurprisingly any learning outcome will be minimal. For example, Rokita (2007) found that in a two-year-long programme of low intensity tuition (one hour per week) the most advanced of the children studied, aged 2;6 at the beginning of the study, managed to learn around 200 words both receptively and productively. However, the child's production was hardly ever spontaneous and in most cases denoted elicited response to a cue. Language production manifested itself in the repetition of words after other interlocutors, in object labelling and occasional code-switching, which, in turn, consisted in adding L1 inflectional and grammatical morphemes to L2 words or the insertion of L2 words into L1 utterances. Such code-mixing, that is, the insertion of L2 morphemes into L1 utterances, unlike in naturalistic bilinguals, signified a metalinguistic function, as it was used in order to show off language ability and indicated the acquisition of rules for the L1 morphology, rather than of the target language (Rokita, 2006). The children did not attempt to produce their own sentences. These observations show that it is difficult for very young instructed learners, if not impossible, to move from the one/two-word stages to the multi-word/sentence stages in a FL. The children are not able to derive syntactic rules from the input available from a formal course with a restricted number of contact hours. This observation can be further confirmed in other studies, in which syntactic knowledge is at best acquired receptively. For example, Unsworth *et al.* (2015: 539) in the Dutch context found that 'children with more than 60 min per week acquire as much English in 2 years' time as young monolingual English-speaking children do in approximately 5 months', suggesting that the process is very slow. In addition, after the first measurement of children's performance, which manifested itself mainly in receptive vocabulary and grammar, they observed that there was a significant improvement in the second year. This suggests that children's lexical knowledge accelerates after a certain minimal amount of lexis has been acquired, when the children get older and when they develop MA of the similarities between words in Dutch and English, arguing that similarity in language typology can be a factor that facilitates language development. Furthermore, in the Zagreb 1975 project on early language learning (ages six to nine) Vilke (1976b) found that within a year, study children were observed to commit L1 interference errors which were different from those indicated by Dulay and Burt (1973) in the 'natural order hypothesis', and which led the author to conclude that 'acquiring a second language and learning a foreign language are different processes, and it may be dangerous to confuse the two' (Vilke, 1976b: 101).

Another study (Sopata, 2009), describing the morpho-syntactic acquisition of children aged 2;6–9;1 in a much more intensive content and language integrated learning/immersion type of instruction of L2 German, found that very young children (some of them as young as 2;6) are more likely to acquire morphological and syntactic rules if they are exposed to the L2 below the age of three. After that age, learning the new language resembled more the learning process of adults, that is, it was based on memorisation.

Evidence of the acquisition of L2 syntax by FL learners has been noted in the case of those children who have learnt a FL at home with their parents and who thus have had much more frequent exposure to the language. Learning the FL with a parent may resemble a natural bilingual situation and the establishment of a 'one-parent, one-language' or 'non-native parents' strategy of developing a bilingual child (Romaine, 2000) and thus be more akin to L2 learning.

As a case in point, Scheffler (2015) observed that his own children after 30 months of daily viewing of cartoons, to which they were introduced at the age of 21 months, could produce a variety of sentence patterns, although they still relied on memorised chunks and formulae. The children were able to participate in L2 discourse by responding to L2 questions, sometimes inserting L2 chunks in L1 sentence patterns, but they never asked the questions themselves.

Similarly, Prošić-Santovac (2017) reports on her own daughter's progression with language upon exposure to TV viewing assisted by scaffolded learning of the task. She claims that between the ages 3;4 and 4;10 her daughter's productive vocabulary tripled and amounted to 419 words in 20 different lexical categories concerning the child's surroundings, similar to an L1 lexis. Examples of intra-sentential code-mixing of L2 words into L1 utterances were also noted. Exceptionally, the salient morpheme *–ing*, one of the first to be acquired in the natural order (Brown, 1973; Dulay & Burt, 1973), was also added to the L1 words. Transfer was also evident in the substitution of some L1 phonemes with those from L2. These findings were similar to those found in Rokita (2007) and Scheffler (2015) and indicate that a variety of lexis (mainly concrete nouns) in L2 can be acquired, yet communication in the L2 relies on L1 structure. In terms of syntactic acquisition, Prošić-Santovac (2016) also observed the acquisition of formulaic chunks and cross-linguistic interference where similarity between the two systems occurred (such as gender marking or word order). Yet, in contrast to previous findings, she also noted that when the two language systems differed considerably, no such interference was noted, and the children were able to produce quite long sentences, also using conjunctions, for example, *'Peppa is tidying up the room, but George is not doing anything; Our car is red and our campervan is yellow'* (Prošić-Santovac, 2016: 12). However, the acquisition of negation and questions was found to be more problematic.

These findings show that signs of successful L2 acquisition can only be observed at a very early age, that is, when the acquisition of L1 is not yet complete, when a lot of time is spent with the child's major source of language input in the form of their principal caregivers, for example, parents who are effectively the L2 teacher. It can be hypothesised that children acquire this language due to the close emotional bond with their caregivers.

All these findings suggest that very young children do learn some foreign vocabulary and acquire some L2 phonemes and elements of L2 structure. They are able to participate in the discourse directed at them, although often responding in L1 or in mixed or erroneous L2 forms. How much language the children will acquire (and how correct it will be) will depend on the intensity of instruction and variety of L2 input provided. This suggests that home learning can be more effective than course learning, partly due to the fact that parents can mediate linguistic input (build 'scaffolding' in Bruner's (1983) terms) and adjust it to the individual child's attention (e.g. by drawing attention to objects, asking questions and asking for repetition), and are able to provide more intense and varied exposure, by revising language with the children, engaging with them in pretend play, introducing them to FL cartoons and so on.

Despite relatively small learning outcomes in a FL, it is likely that some other long-term benefits can be attained in the overall children's linguistic competency, as the languages present in the child's mind mutually interact and impact each other in various domains. As the Linguistic Coding Differences hypothesis posits (Sparks, 2022; Sparks et al., 2019), skills acquired in early childhood in the mother tongue have an impact on children's later learning of L2. This assumption concerns mainly phonological awareness in L1, as manifested in discriminating phonetic segments (phonemes, syllables) and in early L1 spelling skills, which correspondingly have an impact on children's later L2 phonological awareness and L2 spelling skills and are useful for emergent literacy and decoding words in both L1 and L2. Furthermore, the transfer of these skills from L1 to learning L2 has been found to be possible many years after the experience of learning L1 (Sparks, 2022).

By the same token, it could be hypothesised that early L2 learning experience can feed back into L1 development, particularly in relation to the development of MA, which can predispose children to learning to read. In a specimen study, Łockiewicz et al. (2018) investigated the impact of early exposure to L2 English on the general phonological abilities of kindergarten children. Using a battery of tests of both non-verbal IQ and phonological awareness in L1, as evident in children's segmenting skills, distinguishing rhyme, alliteration, phonemes and syllable, they found both measures to be important predictors of children's English oral language skills. However, no evidence that L2 learning can impact L1 development was found, and thus the hypothesis of mutual interaction of languages in very early FL learning could not be confirmed. The authors concluded that skills possessed in L1 can enhance oral language learning in an L2 among preschoolers as they have a common linguistic system. The authors also suggested that non-verbal IQ and phonological awareness are abilities related to aptitude and as such may impact very young children's outcomes. Additionally, the authors (Łockiewicz *et al.*, 2018) observed that English language skills and retention of lexical items correlated with age and, in parallel, the length of learning, because it corresponded to the amount of language practice. In other words, the more frequently a certain item has been repeated, the better its retention. Such learning is further evidence of rote memorisation being involved in the process of language learning.

1.3.1 How very young instructed learners learn a foreign language

Language learning can take place both through implicit and explicit processes. Central to this distinction is the interaction of consciousness and attention, which should not be regarded as synonymous (Dörnyei, 2009). Attention is a cognitive process that mediates access to consciousness, in other words, one must pay attention to a certain object before it is registered by consciousness. On recognising their role, *explicit learning* is defined as 'the learner's conscious and deliberate attempt to master some material or solve the problem; requires effort and strategic expertise' (Dörnyei, 2009: 136). It implies intentionality of the learner, who plans and organises their learning; thus it is typical at higher stages of formal learning. *Implicit learning* is an automatic process that assumes no conscious attempt to learn the language, no awareness of learning nor of the result. It is also related to as the '*bottom-up mechanism of learning* through growing sensitivity to certain regularities in the environmental displays' (Dörnyei, 2009: 132). In other words, the learner is not aware of the learning process and does not consciously attend to new linguistic forms, yet that does not mean that attentional resources are not involved. On the contrary, attention has the function of mediating access to the WM by filtering from an abundant number of various stimuli those that are meaningful to the learner.

In the case of very young children, it is commonly believed that learning takes place by implicit processes, that is, incidental acquisition from the input surrounding (d'Ydewalle & Van de Poel, 1999). Yet, in the context of limited language exposure, retention of novel language is enhanced if it is accompanied by explicit instruction (Yeung *et al.*, 2020) which consists in drawing learners' attention to new linguistic forms. Explicit teaching to preschoolers does not mean, however, translation or rote repetition of the same words, but expanding on the language that has been previously introduced in a meaningful context, such as storybooks or physical activity with further deliberate practice (Toumpaniari *et al.*, 2015). Recycling those linguistic forms by teachers draws children's attention to those linguistic forms with the aim of memorisation (Laufer, 2017). Hence, if the teacher aims for certain information to be learnt by their young learners, they have to plan activities that will draw the learner's attention through various sensory channels, will be meaningful to them and will stimulate oral production. Therefore, the same linguistic input should be provided repeatedly but in various contexts. As Yeung *et al.* (2020) found, such explicit teaching enhances children's productive vocabulary, while implicit teaching impacts children's passive knowledge of vocabulary. Rote repetition of the same material, as in cue-response drills, helps to retain phonological representation of a word in the verbal memory (see below), yet is not sufficient for its long-term retention because it is deprived of meaningful context. After prolonged repetitive practice, children stop paying attention to the repetitive input in the same form. It is therefore vital for teachers to remember that revision of vocabulary should not mean rote repetition but recycling in novel contexts.

1.3.2 Factors affecting children's foreign language development

It is a truism to say that child language development, be it first or second, is characterised by huge interindividual variability due to both internal (i.e. biological) and external factors.

While the latter will be discussed in the following chapters, the former concerns the limitations of WM capacity, MA, phonological memory, attentional control, aptitude, non-verbal intelligence (as the children are preliterate), temperament, and so on.

Little research has been conducted on very young learners' individual differences, with the exception of Unsworth *et al.* (2014) and Sun *et al.* (2016, 2018). Yet, these studies emphasise that in early FL learning the role of external factors, such as the amount of exposure to the particular language, is more significant than internal factors. While investigating English language development in a cross-sectional study of two- to five-year-old Chinese preschoolers, Sun *et al.* (2016) traced the development of the child's productive and receptive vocabulary, as well as receptive grammar, and the impact of the following factors: age of starting instruction, non-verbal intelligence and short-term memory, and the total amount of language input, which also included home exposure and maternal proficiency in L2 English. Out of these, the total amount of language exposure, encompassing both formal instruction and home language exposure, appeared to be the most significant factor. This was irrespective of the age of starting instruction, although older children, given a similar amount of input, acquired more language than younger learners, which is consistent with findings in relation to primary learners (e.g. Muñoz, 2008, 2011). Yet, as Unsworth *et al.* (2015) claim, it is not only the input quantity, which should amount to at least 60 minutes per week, but also the input quality, as manifested in teacher language proficiency, that plays a role. The authors found that groups of children who were taught by native, or near-native-like teachers, performed better in a language test, which can be explained by the fact that such teachers are capable of using a wider array of various discourse strategies and therefore can engage child learners in meaningful interactions much more efficiently.

Intraindividual factors are of little interest to researchers, mainly because at pre-primary level, children are still developing their L1 skills. It would also be too limiting to deny a child the right to learn a FL on the grounds of a lack of predispositions. Besides, although there may exist variability in the rate of learning, all children eventually learn to speak their mother tongue. When it comes to a FL, all children who receive instruction acquire some language skills, yet some children learn more at earlier ages than others. For this reason, any assessment of achievement is viewed by many (e.g. Prošić-Santovac & Rixon, 2019) as unjustified, as it may turn out to be too judgemental and inhibiting, and the results are likely to fluctuate over time.

Nevertheless, it is advisable for teachers and parents to know in what ways children may differ and why they do not all achieve similar results when exposed to similar amounts of language input. It seems learners' attention levels are a prerequisite of language intake, as Schmidt's (1990) Noticing hypothesis posits.

Attention facilitates access to WM where linguistic input can be further processed before it is stored in the long-term memory. WM is defined as 'those mechanisms or processes that are involved in the control, regulation, and active maintenance of task-relevant information in the service of complex cognition' (Miyake & Shah, 1999: 450). According to Jia *et al.* (2018) WM plays a crucial role in goal-directed behaviours, requiring the retention and manipulation of information to ensure successful task execution.

It is argued that WM consists of three subcomponents, that is, *phonological loop* (also referred to as the verbal WM), which is responsible for maintaining a new phonological representation for a period of time long enough to build permanent phonological representations; *visuospatial sketchpad*, responsible for visual–spatial signals; and the *central executive*, which involves the attentional control system (Baddeley & Hitch, 1974). In the year 2000, another component called 'episodic buffer' was distinguished, which was regarded as 'a temporary storage system that modulates and integrates different sensory information' (Baddeley, 2000). Thus, WM is a cognitive mechanism that allows the commitment to memory of information that we are currently processing, and it is particularly relevant in complex cognitive operations requiring performance of several operations simultaneously. In FL learning, two components particularly play a role: the phonological loop and the central executive, 'where the former is a temporary verbal-acoustic storage system, whereas the latter is a system responsible for attentional control of WM' (Biedroń & Veliz Campos, 2021: 47). This means that the linguistic input must be first attended to before it is further processed at the central executive stage. Processing means auditory reoccurrence of the same input and/or its rehearsal in order to retain it and store within long-term memory.

WM capacity matures with age as it is connected with the growing maturity of those areas of the brain which are responsible for it, that is, the fronto-parietal brain regions, including the prefrontal, cingulate and parietal cortices. Ageing affects WM as it is also connected with expressing and controlling emotions, and hormones, which 'affect the performance of WM at the "neurobiological level"' (Jia *et al.*, 2018). It is thus evident that WM in very young children is still developing, which is what limits their learning ability. WM capacity denotes how many items of new information (figures, morphemes, words, etc.) can be processed at one time and recalled after a single exposure. Cowan (1997) reports that on average a two-year-old child can hold two items and a three-year-old child can hold as many as three elements. A seven-year-old child can hold in their memory as many as five items. These figures denote how many new lexical items the child is capable of processing at a single time (e.g. during a lesson) and how many should be presented. It is only through multiple revision and reappearance of the items in the linguistic input that they become automatised and stored within long-term memory. In the case of child learners, chunking language into larger wholes in collocations (e.g. 'jump high', 'catch that fly'), formulas and routines is a teaching strategy that can facilitate the increase of WM capacity with older preschoolers (aged 5;0 and above) (Cowan, 1997).

WM has recently come into focus as one of the *executive functions* responsible for cognitive processing. The executive functions as identified by Miyake *et al.* (2000) are: '(1) focusing attention on relevant information while inhibiting irrelevant information, (2) scheduling processes, including switching attention between tasks, (3) planning, (4) updating and checking working memory contents and (5) coding representation in working memory' (Campfield, 2021: 18). From this definition it can be clearly seen that these skills are responsible for the child's self-regulation and so enhance the child's cognitive and socioemotional (because of self-regulation) learning. Thus executive functions have been found to account for school readiness as well as later schooling success, and are regarded as a more valid predictor for school achievement than intelligence (Ardila, 1999). Consequently, those children who have deficits in executive functions are recommended to undergo training to enhance these skills, as they may impact on the child's later well-being (OECD, 2020).

There has been sufficient empirical data (e.g. Tao *et al.*, 2011) confirming that early bilingualism (both simultaneous and sequential) enhances executive functions due to the necessity of constantly paying attention and switching between languages in communication. However, no such impact can be observed in preschool children if the contact with an L2 is limited to approximately 60 minutes per week (Campfield, 2021). As an illustration of this argument, Goriot et al. (2018) conducted a study in which child learners of English as a second language were tested on such measures of executive functions as switching attention, inhibition and WM in three age groups, the youngest of which were four- to five-year-olds. The researchers found that the ratio of acquired English to L1 (Dutch) vocabulary was related to switching, but not to measures of inhibition or WM. Thus, the authors concluded that interlingual switching ability is related to lexical size in L2, which, in turn, is an outcome of exposure to that language. This finding was interpreted as what matters in very early instruction is the amount of overall input received and not the mastery of executive functions.

Conversely, Kapa and Colombo (2014) found that WM, and attentional shifting in particular, was a good predictor of learning vocabulary in an artificial language in both preschool children and adults. They conducted an experimental study in which they asked child participants to identify the meaning and repeat 12 nouns in a picture book. After two additional training sessions, in which the vocabulary was reinforced and elicited through videos, the children's lexical knowledge of an artificial language was tested by means of six different receptive and productive vocabulary and sentence tests, including a grammaticality judgement test. The results showed that those children who performed well in the WM test performed better on the lexical test as well. This finding suggests that a high level of executive functions such as WM enhances language learning capacities. Furthermore, in view of the training sessions that the children underwent, it was also found that the relationship between language learning and the development of executive functions can be reciprocal, that is, the very experience of language learning can enhance executive functions skills, particularly in the early stages of language acquisition, while learning the lexicon. The authors concluded with a recommendation for including training on executive functions in early language learning programmes.

Similar benefits of early FL learning on executive functions were observed by Purić et al. (2017) among Serbian 2nd graders. The study compared the level of executive functions by reference to the amount of language exposure. One group of children was immersed in a FL for five hours a day, while the other only for one and a half hours a day. The results showed that those children who were immersed in an L2 more intensively also showed higher levels of executive functions. Similarly to Kapa and Colombo (2014), this finding led the researchers (Purić et al., 2017) to conclude that early intensive exposure to an L2 can lead to an improvement in executive function skills. Although the study was conducted on lower primary children, it seems similar findings could be expected in pre-primary children, which is yet another argument for teaching FLs to very young learners. Instructional FL learning at an early age can be a cognitively enriching experience, enhancing overall cognitive processing and so helping children to prepare for successful formal learning at school.

These findings indicate that WM/executive functions being a predictor of success in language learning can by modern definitions be regarded as a component of aptitude (Biedroń & Veliz Campos, 2021; Wen, 2016, 2019). Language aptitude so far has been scarcely investigated among very young learners, largely due to the fact that the L1 (mainly syntactic and pragmatic use) is still being developed. Thus, studies on aptitude that have been published have so far focused on lower primary children (e.g. Kiss, 2009; Kiss & Nikolov, 2005; Lambelet & Berthele, 2019). Their findings, however, do not provide a unanimous answer to how language aptitude in young learners should be conceptualised.

An attempt to measure FL aptitude among very young learners as a composite of various cognitive skills was conducted by Alexiou (2009). While realising the fact that conducting aptitude tests on such young learners may be deterministic and thus exclusive (of instruction), the author supported the idea that many of the skills can be modifiable, especially in early years before a certain stage of maturity is achieved. The cognitive skills on which the children were tested were presented in a game-like format, which the authors found to correlate to language learning as manifested in receptive and productive vocabulary tests. The cognitive skills tested were as follows: *short-term memory* (testing rote learning in Kim's game), *associative memory* (capacity to memorise associated pairs, e.g. picture–word cards), *semantic integration* (testing recall, recognition of old and identification of new items, serving to increase memory storage capacity), *visual perception* (analytic ability in the spot-the-difference task), *spatial ability* (testing analysis by synthesis in a jigsaw task), *inductive ability* and *reasoning ability*.

Alexiou (2009: 58) concluded that cognitive abilities 'relate to certain task types. Memory, semantic integration, visual perception skills are related to visual task types. Spatial and reasoning skills relate to kinesthetic task types while phonetic skills fall into auditory task types'. These skills were tested on techniques typically used in a FL class. Varied levels of child performance in the tasks indicate that children have varied cognitive predispositions towards learning a language in general, which calls for more varied language practice and more support for some children than for others.

Researchers investigating aptitude debate whether this cognitive trait is modifiable (Biedroń & Veliz Campoz, 2021). A key feature that would account for the dynamic nature of aptitude would be previous language learning experience, which has been found to improve scores of the testees on the MLAT (Modern Language Aptitude) tests (e.g. Grigorenko *et al.*, 2000). Also, the findings of Sparks and Ganschaw (1993) and Sparks *et al.* (1997), showing that instruction improves not only FL skills in the long run but also performance in L1, could support this view of modifiability.

Whether aptitude is a trainable feature seems to depend on its conceptualisation. Biedroń & Véliz Campos (2021) say that when aptitude was associated mainly with working memory, it was regarded as trainable by, for example, e.g. a specialised computer program (such as EEG Biofeedback). Yet, they criticise this approach saying that such WM training leads to automatisation of certain routines and not necessarily an improvement in WM capacity, that is, it 'has produced short-time effects not transferrable to real life activities' (Biedroń & Veliz Campos, 2021: 48). Other researchers point to a closer relationship between aptitude and intelligence (Lambelet & Berthele, 2019; Li, 2015). In that case, it must be recognised that intelligence is heritable and largely unchangeable throughout an individual's lifetime, which would mean it is highly unlikely that aptitude could be modifiable.

One other trait that determines to what extent different children will benefit from the same quantity and quality of input is the child's *temperament*. Monitoring four three-year-olds' participation in a FL class, Sun *et al.* (2014) observed that depending on the child's mood and how adaptable to the new situation they were, the children showed different levels of non-verbal responsiveness to class activities. Non-verbal participation in classroom tasks in turn predetermined verbal production, which for highly responsive children took place earlier than for those who were less responsive. Although this was only a small case study, it draws attention to the importance of child personality traits that should be examined under closer scrutiny as they mediate very young learners' preparedness to participate in formal instruction.

1.3.2.1 Metalinguistic awareness

MA 'may be defined as an individual's ability to focus attention on language as an object in and of itself, to reflect upon language, and to evaluate it' (Schönpflug, 2001: 1171). It may be further subdivided into such components as: phonological awareness, word awareness, syntactic awareness and pragmatic awareness. Children start to develop MA at around the age of 4;0 (Ratner & Gleason, 1993), which is when they transform their implicit knowledge of a previously acquired language into its more explicit representation. They are then able to reflect on and analyse the structure and form of language, which boosts their lexical and then syntactic productivity. The development of MA in preschool preliterate children, particularly phonological awareness, vocabulary size and word recognition, is a prerequisite of acquiring literacy in the mother tongue (Alexiou, 2019). Yet, it must be recognised that MA in such young children does not manifest in an ability to *talk* about language rules *explicitly*, which is developed through school instruction in lower primary school (Roehr-Brackin & Tellier, 2019), but is visible indirectly through their ability to discriminate between similar-sounding words (phonological awareness), yet differing in single phonemes and also in two languages, the ability to manipulate language forms in order to create novel word forms (neologisms), or detecting syntactic errors in grammaticality judgement tasks.

Phonological awareness, which is the first subcomponent acquired, denotes the ability to discriminate between different sounds of language, understanding phonotactic rules for the sequencing of phonemes in a particular language, which in turn helps children to recognise and retrieve from memory plausible lexical items quickly. For this reason phonological awareness is usually deliberately developed in instruction by asking children to spell words or divide words into syllables, by tapping/clapping the rhythm, by drawing children's attention to alliteration and rhyme. Recognising single phonemes facilitates the development of the link between them and the corresponding graphemes. Understanding phonotactic regularities also prepares children to observe orthographic regularities (Gathercole *et al.*, 1991).

Naturalistic bilingual children are believed to have developed enhanced MA when compared with monolinguals in certain domains. Some advantage has been found in respect of word (lexical) awareness (e.g. Altman *et al.*, 2018; Ben-Zeev, 1977; Cummins, 1978; Yelland *et al.*, 1993) and grammatical awareness (Galambos & Goldin-Meadow, 1990; Galambos & Hakuta, 1988), but less so in reference to phonological awareness (Bialystok *et al.*, 2003). While early research on phonological awareness in bilinguals seemed to show such an advantage (e.g. Campbell & Sais, 1995), later research explicated further on possible factors impacting such results.

On measuring kindergarten and lower primary children's phonological awareness, Bialystok *et al.* (2003) showed that the two groups of learners did not differ significantly on any kind of phonological awareness tasks, such as phoneme discrimination, phoneme substitution or phonemic segmentation. Some differences were shown in the phonemic segmentation task, which were attributed to general cognitive functioning of the participants rather than bilingualism *per se*. Additionally, they argued that there may be some advantage for children learning L2 English reading if they know a language of similar sound-symbol correspondence of spelling (like Spanish) over Chinese-English bilinguals, since phonological awareness is a prerequisite to reading. However, they attributed this advantage also to the language of instruction. In summary, in respect of phonological awareness the relationship between its development and bilingualism is not straightforward. Bialystok *et al.* (2003) concluded that it is likely that any advantage of bilinguals may be attributed to their general cognitive functioning (and thus related to aptitude or verbal WM/executive function (Bialystok, 2001) or may be *language specific* (i.e. depend on the constellation of languages in a bilingual), or may depend on the task type in measuring phonological awareness as well as language used in the testing. By contrast, in the Chinese context, Yeung *et al.* (2013) found a beneficial effect of instruction on phonological awareness, focusing on teaching phoneme discrimination, which is particularly important for Chinese learners, speaking a non-alphabetic language. Such an approach may be more useful for future learning to read in L2, rather than a whole word approach, particularly in those contexts where there is a dissimilarity between the writing systems of L1 and L2.

In the case of naturalistic bilingual children, a clear relationship has been established between the amount of exposure to each of the languages and the size of vocabulary in each of the languages (Pearson *et al.*, 1997), which, in turn, impacts different abilities in MA (Altman *et al.*, 2018). However, in a study by Altman *et al.* (2018), it was found that it is the MA developed in the dominant (heritage) language that facilitates the acquisition of lexicon in both languages. The authors concluded that a lack of difference between bilingual and monolingual learners in lexical awareness, tested by fast mapping tasks, manifested in using a similar strategy of fast mapping for expanding lexicon in each of the languages in a bilingual individual. Additionally, they argued that acquisition of a concept in the dominant language facilitates the acquisition of a novel word label in the L2. This was explained by the possibility of acquiring lexis through fast mapping and undermined Clark's (2003) Lexical Contrast theory. As the authors argued, 'having a label for an object in one language does not interfere with acquiring a new label in the other' (Altman *et al.*, 2018: 13). This means that the principle of mutual exclusivity (Clark, 2003), which impedes the acquisition of a synonymous word for the same referent, seems to work only within one language and does not apply when learning an L2.

However, no similarity between monolingual and bilingual learners has been found in respect of morphological awareness, which has been found to be more strongly developed in monolinguals (Altman *et al.*, 2018). This suggests that a certain critical mass of language must be acquired prior to morphological acquisition. In the aforementioned study the languages differed in derivational morphology (in this case Russian having a concatenative morphology, while Hebrew did not). These findings show that there is a reciprocal relationship between language dominance, vocabulary size and lexical awareness.

Little research has been done on the relationship between exposure levels and the development of MA in an instructional setting. The available evidence usually concerns lower primary children, which can be explained by the fact that firstly, in order to develop MA, a certain critical amount of exposure (in terms of cumulative number of hours) must be provided, and secondly, MA is being developed until the age of eight to nine and is impacted by explicit instruction (Roehr-Brackin & Tellier, 2019). However, some studies conducted in relation to lower primary children confirm there is a link between MA and selected aspects of FL learning. For example, Campfield and Murphy (2014, 2017) draw attention to the saliency of prosody in helping L2 learners to discover language rules from linguistic input. In a 12-week intervention study they systematically exposed eight-year-old learners to either a FL rhythmically salient text, nursery rhyme or prose, using prosodic cues, such as pauses and lengthening the final stressed syllable before a pause, but did not teach the language of the texts explicitly. After the intervention, it was found in an elicited imitation that children in the treatment group, exposed to rhythmic nursery rhymes, performed better than children exposed to prose or to no rhythmic text and also acquired some lexis without explicit teaching (Campfield & Murphy, 2017). Rhythmic input used in, for example, storytelling has also been found to facilitate word order acquisition in preschool children (Campfield & Murphy, 2014; Hillyard, 2015), except for function words, which can be explained by the fact that they are unstressed in continuous speech. These findings may corroborate the hypothesis that prosody can act as a bootstrapping strategy in learning the syntax of a FL in the same way as in learning L1, and call for explicit accentuation of meaningful language forms in instruction which could aid learners in their discrimination from context and memorisation. In other words, classroom teacher talk should resemble exaggerated caregiver speech.

Another study on phonological awareness by Marecka *et al.* (2018) focused on how children learn new words in the initial stages by first isolating a set of phonological segments from the stream of speech and how the representation of the new word is retained in the phonological short-term memory. In this process, two mechanisms are involved: universal speech segmentation, which is a general facility used for all languages, and phonological mapping, which is language specific. These mechanisms are relevant also for long-term storage of a novel word, for, in order to be encoded, first there must be an accurate phonological representation of the word in the short-term memory. In order to verify which mechanisms are used by young learners of L2 English, 44 children aged nine underwent a series of metalinguistic tasks both in their L1 (Polish) and L2 (English). The findings indicated that language learning to a large extent depends on the size of vocabulary (proficiency) in that language. If the size of the L2 vocabulary is small, then universal speech segmentation plays a role. Only later, in the course of learning, do children acquire phonotactic patterns typical of an L2 and start to use the mechanism of phonological mapping. The authors concluded that, particularly in early stages of word learning, phonological short-term memory plays a role as it enables the holding in the memory of a few lexical representations. In later language learning, Marecka *et al.* (2018) argued, success depends on non-verbal intelligence as well as efficacy of long-term memory encoding. These findings suggest that phonological awareness is also developed in the course of language training.

To recapitulate, an overview of the process of language acquisition, as well as of research on cognitive factors playing a role in the process, leads us to form the following observations and conclusions about the child's biosystem:

Firstly, very young learners develop a FL very slowly, which is connected with the low amount of exposure provided to them. FL development therefore manifests itself mainly in receptive knowledge of lexis and some grammatical patterns. Productive language use is limited to single words and formulaic chunks. Preschool learners are not capable of creative language use in a FL as they have not acquired a sufficient amount of language to derive the morphological and syntactic rules. Their MA which would enhance the process is constrained, both biologically (mainly develops through explicit school instruction) and environmentally (i.e. determined by the amount of language acquired, and this in turn depends on the amount of language input). In addition, children below the age of 3;0 make even slower progress in a FL as they have not acquired concepts in L1 onto which to label novel L2 words.

Secondly, attention, WM capacity and aptitude seem to tap into similar cognitive factors, which also develop with age. Thus they constrain how much children can take in from the available input. These are intraindividual differences between children that account for the varying rate of their FL development. Other features, such as temperament and intelligence, need further investigation.

Thirdly, FL learning, irrespective of the type of language learnt, can be an enriching experience in itself, helping to develop executive functions and MA, all of which are useful in formal school learning. Yet, any outcomes in these areas also depend on the amount of FL input. Figure 1.1 demonstrates the abovementioned interdependencies.

Bearing in mind the aforementioned biological limitations, it is doubtful whether the very young learner can show agency in learning a FL on their own. For one thing, the child is still developing their mother tongue, and, since this language typically dominates in their environment, the child feels much more motivated to learn that language which enables them to communicate with their major caregivers and later preschool peers. Consequently, a very young child's agentic behaviour can be observed mostly in reference to the mother tongue. Furthermore, learning a FL, to which children have very little exposure, resembles learning another skill in an explicit way which takes place through repetition, through trial and error for which cognitive abilities are utilised, such as WM, metalinguistic development, and these are still developing,

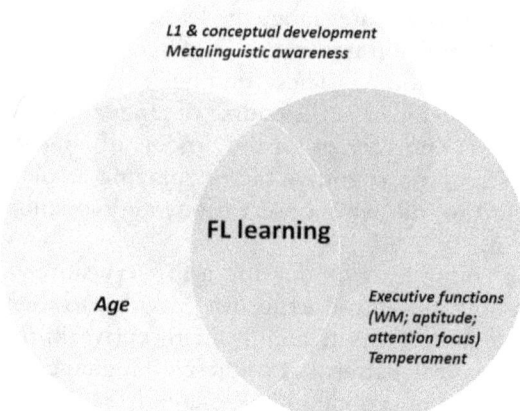

Figure 1.1 Biological, cognitive and linguistic prerequisites of very early FL learning

which is what limits the child's capacity to learn. As demonstrated above, in the case of very young learners, there may be external factors and agents (teachers, parents) present in the child's ecosystem that may play a more significant role in child FL development, which is the scope of the chapters to follow.

Summary

The goal of this chapter was to present the very young child's capacity to learn a FL taking into account their L1 and cognitive development, which is what constitutes the child's biosystem within the Bronfenbrenner model of human development. Firstly, the stages of development of the mother tongue are outlined, with emphasis on possible strategies used by babies in phonological, lexical and syntactic processing, which are later related to the associationist and cognitive theories of learning. Then, possible similarities and interaction of the L1 and L2/FL learning process are discussed, as well as possible outcomes of the latter as evidenced in research. Finally, attention is drawn to intraindividual differences between children, highlighting the significance of attention, WM and aptitude, which coincide with executive functions. MA is also discussed as yet another factor in development and thus decelerating language learning. The chapter finishes with the conclusion that child agency in low-input situations is unlikely to manifest, thus it has to be sought among other agents of the educational ecology.

2 Microsystem: The Educational Institution

This chapter looks at the educational institution in which foreign language (FL) learning takes place (nursery, kindergarten, afternoon classes, etc.). It starts with discussing its role in shaping children's motivation and attitude to FL learning, which are largely impacted by the quality of instruction offered, as characterised by its organisation (frequency and length of classes, size of the group), setting (decor), applied age-appropriate teaching methodology and, last but not least, teacher competences. With reference to the latter two, their efficacy and impact on learners' FL attainment are presented in the light of available research data. Finally, the notions of teacher and child agency are addressed, pointing to the saliency of teacher agency over that of children in low-input situations.

2.1 Children's Attitude to and Motivation for FL Learning

As discussed in Chapter 1, very young children's biological propensities and limited amount of FL input do not predispose them to high FL achievement. Given the popularity of pre-primary FL teaching, other benefits of early instruction must be recognised. These are affective goals, that is, developing children's positive attitudes to FL learning and motivation for further lifelong FL learning (Edelenbos *et al.*, 2006; European Commission, 2011). Both attitudes and motivation are affective variables which impact educational outcomes of FL learners in later school years (Tragant, 2006). Nikolov (1999) found that the motivation of young FL learners is mainly intrinsic, that is, it comes from the enjoyment of classroom activities and differs from that of adolescent learners, for whom external motives play a more significant role. Thus, positive early FL experiences are crucial for shaping very young learners' positive attitudes as these, in turn, impact the development of their intrinsic motivation.

In relation to a project introducing English and German to kindergartens in Slovenia, Brumen (2011) asked 120 children (aged 4;0–6;0) an open-ended question about which FL activities the children enjoyed the most. The children indicated playful activities, movement, social interaction with peers and the teacher, art and routine activities as the most enjoyable. They did not perceive FL classes to be onerous but rather a natural part of their learning, satisfying their inner curiosity and search for novelty. Additionally, the children indicated movement as an important aspect of FL learning. Thus, total physical response (TPR) songs, games (Asher, 1969) and drama should be a part of every FL teaching programme for very young learners. Furthermore, the children were positively motivated, gaining confidence in using the FL, for example when responding to the teacher, which suggests that productive language activities should be used alongside receptive activities. As a result of using such playful methodology, in the study nearly 97% of children responded positively to the question of whether they liked learning a FL. However, they also indicated that they did not like it when the activities lasted too long and they were forced to do the same activity persistently, when the pace was too fast or when discipline problems arose.

Similar conclusions were reached by Wu (2003), who studied five-year-old children learning English in a Hong Kong kindergarten. He found that it is 'a predictable learning environment, moderately challenging tasks, necessary instructional support, and formative evaluation that play the largest role and boost children's perception of competence' (2003: 515). The children's perception of competency, as well as of autonomy, were identified as other intrinsically motivational factors.

From studies of primary school learners' motivation, we learn that the earlier one starts to learn a FL the more likely it is that the individual will develop positive attitudes towards FL learning (Cenoz, 2004; Mihaljević Djigunović, 1993; Nikolov, 1999; Vilke, 1976a, 1976b). This is typically explained by the fact that the playful methodology used in FL teaching makes the learners enjoy language lessons more than other subjects. It is also noted that while initially children's motivation is impacted by that of their parents and the teacher (Ahn & West, 2018; Choi et al., 2020; Jin et al., 2016), with time children are able to develop motivation of their own. As shown in the results of the Zagreb Project 1991 (Mihaljević Djigunović, 1993/2015), this preference was maintained among nine-year-olds three years after starting to learn a FL, despite the shift towards more serious studying. Furthermore, Mihaljević Djigunović (1993/2015: 211) observed that as far as the starting age is concerned, 'the majority of young learners thought age 7 was optimal, but an increasing number of them opted for the pre-school period too', which could be influenced by positive memories of the learning experience. As regards long-term effects of an early start on children's motivation, fluctuations in motivation were observed which were attributed to teacher competencies (Nikolov, 1999) and changing teaching conditions, such as the size of the group and frequency of classes (Jagatić, 1993; Mihaljević Djigunović, 2009). Additionally, children's motivation was found to be dependent on their idiosyncratic learning abilities, such as hyperactivity, attentional ability and shyness, thus resulting in varied levels of achievement and self-concept (Mihaljević Djigunović, 2015).

In a Korean setting, motivation was found to be influenced by anxiety. Kiaer *et al.* (2021) discovered that those children who are enrolled in highly intensive FL programmes where there is insistence on an 'English-only policy' are more anxious than children who are enrolled in less intensive and less ambitious programmes. This finding further supports the view that in teaching very young learners, age-appropriate methodology and allowing children's use of their mother tongue are indispensable for building positive experiences and attitudes to very early FL learning.

Affective goals of FL learning are also mentioned in key policy documents (European Commission, 2011; cf. Ch. 5) as well as reports surveying earlier research findings (Blondin, 1998; Edelenbos *et al.*, 2006). The report prepared by Blondin *et al.* (1998) highlighted the relevance of the amount of exposure, the size of the learning group, the duration of learning and teacher competencies to learning outcomes and motivation. The subsequent report developed by Edelenbos *et al.* (2006: 13) identified key principles that should underlie instructional programmes, among which the most relevant for pre-primary learners seem to be the following:

- Key learner characteristics contributing to L2 proficiency are *motivation and aptitude*; the latter can develop progressively through primary school especially in areas of metalinguistic awareness and sound sensitivity
- Initial motivation is mainly intrinsic, derived from enjoyment and fun in classroom activities
- Children should be given both positive and corrective feedback on their language production to help them refine it further.
- Recognising the value of spontaneous play, as it allows children to attend to form and meaning,
- It should be recognised that children develop FLL at an individual rate, progressing through a series of non-linear stages.
- Recognising the onset of metalinguistic knowledge, which can be utilised e.g. through narrating stories, listening tasks.
- Language-related outcomes are related to the model of curriculum adopted (i.e. intensity of instruction).

In conclusion, positive attitudes and the arousal of intrinsic motivation in young and very young children can be attained only if the children have access to high-quality instruction, that is, instruction that provides rich linguistic input yet is adjusted to the learners' language level. At the same time, using age-appropriate methodology, that is, that takes into account the children's linguistic and cognitive capacities and socioemotional needs, is advocated. For these reasons, any form of assessment should promote learning in the form of constructive feedback, appreciation and reward (Prošić-Santovac & Rixon, 2019). The teacher's role as the provider of linguistic input through appropriate child-oriented methodology comes to the fore. Thus, the following sections focus on research findings confirming these assumptions with a view to characterising quality pre-primary FL education.

2.2 Defining Quality in Very Early FL Instruction

In the case of very early teaching of FLs, the educational institution plays a major role in providing language input, as it is in the FL classroom where new linguistic forms are presented and reinforced. Thus, the efficacy of instruction depends on its quality. Crabbe (2003: 10) states that 'quality can be sought both in the product—the achievement of specific objectives—and in the process—the availability and use of learning opportunities'. From an ecological perspective, van Lier (2010) claims that quality of teaching/learning and standards of teaching, although related, are not the same. In recent years, quality education seems to be a major concern of policymakers and funding institutions who associate quality with accountability and thus are mainly interested in measuring learning outcomes. As van Lier (2010: 4) argues:

> perceived success of an educational system is based on the quality of the standardized test. (...) such a standards > accountability > testing system largely bypasses the all-important notion of the quality of the educational experience, of learning opportunities, and the wellbeing of the learners.

While quality measurement based on standardisation seems to be pervasive in a lot of European schools, pre-primary FL teaching is less standardised, partly because it lies outside policy regulations in many settings (cf. Chapter 5) as it is often organised by private institutions, that is, private kindergartens and afternoon courses, which devise their own curricula and materials and train their own teachers. Besides, providers are not accountable to any authority other than parents as clients. In addition, it can be argued that due to the cognitive limitations of very young learners and dynamics of their linguistic competence, development of any standardised high-stakes measurement of language learning outcomes would be unjustified. For these reasons, when evaluating the quality of early FL instruction one should focus primarily on the process of teaching and the extent to which it provides opportunities for language intake (Gass, 2018) as well as the extent to which it caters for the child's overall socioemotional growth (OECD, 2020). In respect of the former goal, one should take into account the quantity of teaching hours (and thus the amount of exposure), the organisation of the teaching process (which includes the size of the groups) and the qualifications of teachers, as well as the curriculum and methodology used. Variability in these aspects may account for the external differences in instruction offered. In other words, children learning a FL at pre-primary level do not necessarily benefit equally from very early instruction. In respect of the latter, one should take into account the methodology of FL teaching and evaluate to what extent it appeals to children's socioemotional needs.

2.3 Organisation of Instruction, Institution Type and Curriculum

Very early FL instruction can take place either in kindergarten or in early school years, for example in Spain, the United Kingdom and the Netherlands where compulsory schooling begins at the age of 4–5 (Eurydice, 2023). Alternatively, or additionally, FL instruction may also take place in the form of private courses attended by very young learners, often in the company of their caregivers. The market for institutions offering private instruction is booming worldwide.

Both forms of instruction, that is, private and state, may vary in respect of the amount of contact hours offered. According to Edelenbos *et al.* (2006), language courses for young and very young learners can vary from one hour per week to daily contact with the language, as in the bilingual/immersion type of education. Since, in many contexts, contact with the FL is limited to the classroom, the quantity of contact hours can be of primary importance in predicting language learning outcomes. Unsworth *et al.* (2015) are of the opinion that children who have exposure to a language for more than 60 minutes per week achieve significantly higher results in tests of receptive vocabulary and grammar after two years of instruction than children who have less than 60 minutes of contact with the language. It must, however, be emphasised that these results relate to reception; productive knowledge is less predictable.

The differences in the amount and quality of FL contact depend to a large extent on whether the institution is *state-run* or *private*, on whether a FL is a component of the compulsory curriculum or voluntary. It can also depend on the form of employment of the FL teacher, who can be either a language specialist who visits the kindergarten a few times a week for language lessons (also called an itinerant teacher, cf. Mourão, 2021) or a generalist teacher who, in addition to teaching general child education courses, switches into a FL for a class or for set periods of the day.

Private and state-run institutions may also differ in terms of teacher employment. Often in non-compulsory, that is, fee-paying kindergarten instruction, lessons are taught by an itinerant language specialist with formal language qualifications (cf. Mourão, 2021). In that case, visits by the language specialist are generally limited to a few hours a week, which constitutes too little exposure if the language is to be effectively acquired through this contact. By contrast, in state-run kindergartens, it is often a generalist early childhood education and care (ECEC) teacher with additional language qualifications who conducts FL lessons (Mourão, 2021).

This variability in teacher qualifications results in varied policies regarding FL use in the classroom. Scheffler and Domińska (2018) found that in the Polish context in state kindergartens, code-switching into the children's mother tongue is used much more often and is more accepted by teachers, parents and children themselves as child well-being is placed at the forefront, which would otherwise be threatened if they were forced to use a FL. By contrast, private institutions were found to be much stricter in adherence to the target-language-only policy as they prioritised FL achievement as proof of effectiveness to parents as clients.

Very early FL instruction may also take place in additionally paid afternoon courses, which claim to follow an innovative method but, in reality, consist of a mixture of well-known techniques for teaching young and very young learners (see below). Enrolling a child in such a course aims to imitate the 'one language, one environment' strategy (Romaine, 2000) whereby the children will associate language use with a particular time and space, and thus attending a FL course can constitute an emotionally engaging language adventure, associated with fun and aimed at developing intrinsic motivation.

Another difference between private and public institutions boils down to the size of the group: fee-paying courses usually entail smaller groups which can be between 5 and 10/12 children, whereas in the state setting the classes can comprise the whole childcare group, which may exceed 15 children in one language class (Johnstone et al., 2006). Needless to say, a larger group size limits language learning opportunities by restricting the methodology that can be used and due to class management difficulties, not to mention problems in maintaining the attention of all the children.

Furthermore, private kindergartens may also differ in a more diverse language offering. Driven by parental demand and competition in the neoliberal market, institutions aim to offer more languages and an earlier start; therefore, apart from English, they also offer instruction in other FLs of potential utility, such as Spanish, French, German or even Chinese, thus fostering in children the development of plurilingualism (Rokita-Jaśkow, 2013a).

Finally, a private institution may prioritise FL learning in its mission statement, as a result of which nearly all activities, interior design and cultural events (e.g. theatrical shows, song festivals) may relate to the target FL, as its goal is to instil bilingual identity. This is typical of bilingual/immersion-type kindergartens where contact with a FL is provided daily and permeates different activities of the general ECEC curriculum.

Bilingual kindergartens are an exceptional type of educational institution in which instruction is held in two languages, most of the day in the official language of the country and in the target language at selected times. They adopt content and language integrated learning (CLIL) methodology which is 'an educational approach where curricular content is taught through the medium of a FL' (Dalton-Puffer, 2011: 183) and thus 'offers more flexible and real opportunities for language learning' (Otto & Cortina-Pérez, 2023: 1). Such instruction is most commonly offered in the most prestigious language of global communication and use, that is, English, for example in Serbia (Prošić-Santovac & Radović, 2018b), Spain (Fleta, 2018, 2019; Otto & Cortina Perez, 2023), Germany (Kersten *et al.*, 2010), South Korea (Song, 2011), Poland (Loranc-Paszylk, 2019) but occasionally also in other languages of historical significance locally, such as German in Poland (Bielicka, 2017; Olpińska-Szkiełko, 2013; Sopata, 2009), Italian in Turkey (Carbonara, 2019), Russian in Finland (Protassova, 2018), Catalan (Arnau, 2000; Urmeneta & Unamuno, 2008) or Basque (Barnes, 2008) in Spain or Gaelic Irish in Ireland (Hickey & Cainín, 2001).

Bilingual kindergartens are usually private enterprises which provide daily target language exposure. While they are obliged to follow the compulsory ECEC curriculum in the dominant (societal) language of the children, the organisation of FL teaching depends on the head of the institution and can vary extensively from 10–15-minute 'language showers' at different points during the daily routine to whole subject/content-oriented lessons (Ruiz De Zairobe, 2023). Thus, a FL can occasionally be introduced by a generalist teacher. Another solution is that a FL specialist teacher steps in for selected periods of the kindergarten day, pretending to only be able to speak the target language and thus prompting children to attempt communication in the FL. The organisation of the instruction in such kindergartens aims to imitate the well-known bilingual strategy of 'one parent, one language'. For a long time, following this approach was regarded as beneficial as it deterred children from code-switching and forced the children to speak the minority language (Genesee, 1989). However, more recently, adherence to this principle and the avoidance of code-switching have been questioned (Prošić-Santovac & Radović, 2018b; Scheffler & Domińska, 2018). In a Serbian bilingual kindergarten, Prošić-Santovac and Radović (2018b) observed that the teachers promoted language separation, that is, speaking the target language only during the FL class, while the children opted to use their first language (L1) while communicating with the second language (L2) teacher, which was interpreted as signaling their agency in acquiring bilingual competence. The authors concluded that adhering to the 'one teacher, one language' policy is too stressful for children who would prefer to be allowed to speak their language and code-mix when addressing their teachers, even though this solution may lead to problems in mastering linguistic accuracy and fluency (Prošić-Santovac & Radović, 2018b). This finding indicates that allowing code-mixing/code-switching in the FL class is gaining in popularity and is applied depending on the goals of the curriculum. If the goal of early FL teaching is the overall child's development, code-mixing, on the part of the children, not the teachers, should be allowed. If the goal of very early teaching of a FL is mainly the efficacy of linguistic development, which is particularly aimed for in low-input situations, children are more strongly encouraged to attempt FL production. As Loranc-Paszylk (2019) found in her study of parental motives for enrolling their children in bilingual/CLIL-type instruction, parents do so because of expectations of high-quality instruction and, consequently, facilitation of attainment of bilingual proficiency. Finally, attending such intensive instruction is voluntary, so the child or their parent may withdraw from it if emotional difficulties arise.

Early bilingual education is difficult to implement successfully as there are many obstacles that impede quality assurance in such instruction. These are, first of all, the shortage of linguistically qualified teachers and second, difficulties in mastering the curriculum contents, particularly at primary level. Other obstacles include the high cost of employing native-speaking or near native-like teachers and consequently high tuition fees, as early bilingual education is generally a private enterprise (Loranc-Paszylk, 2019).

As hinted above, private institutions devise their own curriculum in which they usually attempt to provide as much FL input as possible. However, depending on the temperamental and cognitive predispositions of children, not all of them can successfully participate in such classes. Being surrounded by an unknown language may be too stressful for some of them. If pre-primary FL learning is intended to be inclusive, as language policy dictates (European Commission, 2011; cf. Chapter 5), thus encompassing all children, then the focus of early FL experience should be the child's overall development, which includes cognitive, affective and, to some extent, linguistic goals. Rather than aiming for native-like mastery of the target language, FL teachers should cater for the children's well-being and their general cognitive and socioemotional growth. Thus, socioemotional learning is the approach advocated in general ECEC learning (CASEL, 2013; Durlak et al., 2011; OECD, 2020; cf. Chapter 5), including FL learning (Mortimore, 2023), which manifests in using age-appropriate methodology. Additionally, well-qualified teachers who are motivated and willing to work with pre-primary learners should be employed.

2.4 Methodology

The methodology used in early education programmes is a key variable that impacts outcomes (Nikolov & Lugossy, 2021) as well as the quality of the teaching-learning process. The effectiveness of early FL teaching consists in the application of age-appropriate methodology, which caters for children's psychoeducational needs and abilities (Garton & Copland, 2019; Jalkanen, 2009).

2.4.1 Main principles and techniques

The methodology of teaching a FL to very young learners is similar to that in general ECEC education and is rooted in cognitive constructivist and social constructivist theories of learning (Schaffer, 2004; Waite-Stupiansky, 2022). Cognitive constructivist theory, derived from the discoveries of the Swiss psychologist Jean Piaget (1926, 1953), posits that a child has natural curiosity and a willingness to learn and is able to arrive at an understanding of new phenomena on their own if they are involved holistically in the learning activity, that is, has interest and intrinsic motivation to learn about the new subjects and phenomena. In the case of social constructivist theory (Bruner, 1983; Vygotsky, 1985), it is assumed that the child is able to learn things that are beyond their current level only if they are assisted by the Significant Other, an adult who is able to build scaffolding between the child's current knowledge and expected achievement (Pinter, 2011). 'Socio-emotional learning' is another term that is used in reference to the goals of ECEC pedagogy, including language pedagogy, which emphasises that the goal of early education is not only cognitive or linguistic growth but also children's social and emotional growth, that is, teaching them to cooperate with others, understand and manage their emotions (Akmal *et al.*, 2021; CASEL, 2013; Durlak *et al.*, 2011; Mortimore, 2023).

In order to fulfil these goals in early language learning, first of all the development of intrinsic motivation towards learning the FL should be stimulated. The teaching methodology and learning environment should then be directed towards this goal. Incidental/implicit language learning takes place when the children are so engrossed in a learning activity that they do not pay attention to the linguistic form. Nevertheless, they still acquire the FL input, especially if the words/phrases are repeated, are easy in form and their meaning is easily derived from context. Incidental learning closely resembles early stage L1 acquisition in that respect.

For these reasons, techniques regarded as engaging, intrinsically motivating, meaningful for the child and age-appropriate are based on play as a natural child learning activity and are aimed at arousing curiosity. These techniques are mostly teacher-led, as the teacher is the main provider of the FL input, and comprise the following: visual presentation of new lexis, TPR games, chants, rhymes and songs, routines, storytelling, storybook reading, arts and craft activities and drama, in addition to preparation for literacy and CLIL-type tasks which allow language to be embedded in meaningful content themes, such as science, mathematics and history, as well as by means of technology (Garton & Copland, 2019; Mourão & Ellis, 2020; Mortimore, 2023). There is a proliferation of methodological guidelines for using games, songs and stories as a means of contextualising vocabulary and developing phonological awareness in a FL, the efficiency of which has been empirically proven and will be briefly outlined below.

Language teaching of new forms typically starts with the presentation, reinforcement of meaning and pronunciation of new linguistic forms by means of visuals (flashcards, pictures), objects and gestures or movement. Research has shown that preschool children are able to quickly acquire the phonetic representation of a word and associate it with its meaning even if it is presented ostensively and in reference to the visual context (Esteve-Gibert & Muñoz, 2021). This finding proves children's ability to map new meaning upon even a single exposure. In other studies (Toumpaniari et al., 2015; Padial-Ruz et al., 2019) new word presentation was found to contribute to long-term retention when it was associated with gestures and physical movement, which only confirms the usefulness of the TPR methodology and its appeal to children's kinesthetic style of learning.

Naturally, the newly acquired words need to be reinforced and recycled if they are to be stored in the long-term memory, which is typically done through games, songs, rhymes and stories, as well as drama, in which the newly presented language reappears, often building scaffolding for the incidental acquisition of other lexis from context. Griva and Sivropoulou (2009) showed that new lexis should be presented and recycled in stages: first children should be taught the meaning of new lexis by means of pictures assisted by teacher-detailed questions (e.g. *Who, What, Where?*). Controlled situational role-play should then follow, which helps children to reinforce formulaic phrases and stimulates oral production, finishing with game-like assessment. This approach resulted in a considerable growth of lexis over a semester of such intervention (Griva & Sivropoulou, 2009). In a more recent study, Milosavljevic and Reynolds (2024) showed that vocabulary can be as efficiently retained by means of craft activities as by means of drills.

The effectiveness of reading aloud from storybooks for the development of general text comprehension as well as implicit learning of selected vocabulary and formulaic chunks has been well documented in a variety of contexts and in reference to various languages (McElwee, 2015; Mourão, 2015; Yeung et al., 2016). Due to the multimodal context of the stories in storybooks, which contain not only text (often in varied graphic form) but also pictures, moving elements (as in pop-up books) and kinaesthetic elements (when children respond to the text, imitating some gestures, sounds, etc.), understanding and acquisition of new language is facilitated. Similar to parent-child joint reading in L1, the teacher can read the storybook in a FL to children. By pointing at relevant pictures that illustrate the meaning of novel FL words, by imitating characters' voices and by emphasising and repeating key words, the teacher not only engages the children in listening to the story but also builds scaffolding that facilitates children's comprehension of the text. By listening to the same storybook on separate occasions the children start gradually to participate in the storytelling by joining in, for example repeating key words, labelling pointed elements in illustrations, finishing suspended lines of the text, such as a rhyme, and imitating voices (especially of onomatopoeic words) and gestures. After a few storytelling sessions the children can remember whole lines of the text (Rokita-Jaśkow, 2014). In another study, Hillyard (2015: 286) observed that it is not necessarily the rhyme but 'the repetitive phrases and the rhythm involved in the telling of the stories [that] invited the children to interact spontaneously, producing the language in a safe context, due to the predictability of the expected utterance'. Thanks to these features of language, the children are able to acquire not only single words but also grammatical frames (such as adjective + noun). Needless to say, exposure to printed words also prepares children to develop literacy in a FL as they learn to associate a phonetic representation of a word with its visual form. This can be particularly important for children learning a language which has deep orthography, such as English, that is, whose alphabetic system deviates from clear one phoneme–one grapheme correspondence. In the early stages of developing literacy, children will need to memorise whole words rather than phoneme-grapheme correspondence rules. Additionally, the typical rhyming and rhythmic text of many storybooks helps children to develop phonological awareness, that is, distinguish sounds, syllables and words from a stream of continuous speech, which is yet another way of preparing for literacy. Additionally, reading aloud will be vital preparation for learning English for those children whose mother tongue does not use Latin alphabetic literacy, such as Chinese (Ng, 2013) or Arabic (Ghosn, 2022), as reading aloud exposes the children to different graphemes and encourages association with the corresponding sounds.

Mourão (2015) argues for the necessity of repeated storytelling with very young learners, even in low-exposure contexts. By analysis of videoed lesson excerpts she found that children respond to the text both physically and verbally in their mother tongue and in the FL, which proves their engagement with the story and analytical response to the text, manifested in 'analysis of narrative meaning, analysis of illustrations, analysis of story language, analysis of book as object, analysis of relationship between fiction and reality and analysis of (linguistic) code' (Mourão, 2015: 69). Out of this, the analysis of illustrations, consisting in labelling objects and naming actions, and analysis of narratives, such as describing the plot and predicting incoming events, were the most common. The latter were mainly conducted in the children's mother tongue while the former prompted the children to use FL words. Code-mixing was a common yet acceptable feature of children's discourse about the picture books which did not cause a misunderstanding but rather demonstrated engagement with the text, further proven in the children's willingness to analyse the linguistic codes and enquire about the equivalents of FL words in their L1 and vice versa and/or voluntary translation of peer utterances while talking about the book, often in response to a prompt from the teacher.

Using the children's mother tongue while introducing picture books appears to be both acceptable and indispensable in following Cameron's claim (2001: 36), 'meaning must come first'. Yet storytelling allows child learners to both 'observe and participate in the discourse' (Cameron, 2001: 36). Paralinguistic features, such as prosody and rhythm (Campfield & Murphy, 2017), can enable children to single out words from continuous speech and facilitate the development of phonological awareness. These findings show that children are able to comprehend and participate in discourse about an authentic text which was primarily written for native English-speaking children. Using such texts can therefore contribute to the children's acquisition of FL words and phrases and the growth of the child's overall plurilingual competence. It may also be hypothesised that text comprehension takes place at the conceptual level and therefore its manifestations appear either in L1 or L2/FL.

Storytelling has also become a widely used technique in teaching other languages into which well-known English picture books have been translated, for example German. Iluk and Jakosz (2017) tested the impact of storybooks on the general development of receptive skills. Through pre-test and post-test study analysis they observed that the children had no problem in understanding longer utterances, combining even up to 12 words, and that recognition abilities diminished only by approximately 20% after a three-month interval when no instruction was delivered. These findings confirm that storybooks used to teach any FL constitute a powerful didactic tool, as they enhance overall understanding of sentences as well as implicit vocabulary learning.

Other studies aimed to compare the effectiveness of storybook reading with other techniques in vocabulary retention. For example, songs alone were found to be useful for text comprehension only, although associated with play and enjoyment and not effective in stimulating language production (Coyle & Gomez Gracia, 2014). This may be due to the fact that songs are usually presented in a TPR manner, that is, using gesture to illustrate the meaning of the song lines, but it may be difficult for children to single out whole words/chunks from a continuous and melodious stream of speech. In the study conducted among preschoolers between 2;0 and 3;0 in a Spanish context, Albaladejo *et al.* (2018) found that stories were more meaningful to children and enhanced their target receptive vocabulary acquisition to a greater extent than songs. They also analysed the children's behaviour while listening to the stories and songs and noticed that paying attention while listening played a role. Surprisingly, while listening to the songs the children focused more on imitating gestures than listening to the song's lyrics. Therefore, storytelling was hypothesised to be more effective as the storybook readers are better able to hold children's attention by modulating their voice, rhythmical reading, suspending voice and other non-verbal strategies.

These results stand in contrast to those obtained by Leśniewska and Pichette (2014) who investigated the lexical acquisition of 57 French words from four stories and four songs in a four-week period by learners as young as 35–54 months, that is, as soon as they acquired their mother tongue. The authors did not find any difference in the recall of words in respect of the input source, that is, songs versus stories. However, they observed that the results depended on the number of encounters with a word during the course as well as its features. It was easier to recall words which denoted animate objects and those which reappeared in the course more frequently. This finding suggests that the key features impacting word retention are the amount of exposure (the number of encounters) and the multimodality of a word meaning, which allows children to associate the words' form and meaning with movement.

2.4.2 Role-playing and communicative tasks

Children have a natural capacity for engaging in pretend play, also called symbolic play, that is, imitating situations from their surroundings (e.g. routines at dinner tables, imitating a parent) and/or a favourite storybook or TV series. They willingly act out selected scenes pretending to be characters from a film or a book. The scenes evoke vivid images in children and reflect their willingness to follow in their heroes' footsteps. Imitation of either a character from a scene or an adult is a way of learning (language) behaviour. For this reason, a controlled role-pay/drama activity or performative play is advocated as a natural follow-up activity to any storybook reading. The children are not only engaged in play but also utilise movement to show comprehension and can attempt oral FL production by using memorised words, chunks and formulae (Coyle *et al*., 2018; Faitaki & Murphy, 2023; Winston, 2022). This seems to be the best technique to stimulate very young learners' oral production as in low-input situations they will hardly ever initiate their own FL production, not to mention create novel utterances. At pre-primary level it must be an adult who initiates the pretend play/drama activity in a FL by establishing the L2 context. They may use puppets or other branded toys for this purpose to establish an authentic FL environment (Prošić-Santovac, 2017), following the 'one language, one environment' rule. The adult (the teacher or the parent) using the puppet may involve the child in the conversation using a number of discursive techniques such as elicitation, call for repetition and comprehension checks. It depends on the discursive skills (and FL proficiency) of the teacher how much the child will be involved in the performance. Little research has been done on the effectiveness of theatre/drama in preschool; however, the preliminary data obtained by Faitaki and Murphy (2023) in a four-week intervention study of learners of English as an additional language allows us to speculate that preschoolers benefit from theatre socially, emotionally and linguistically. The study pointed to increased integration and participation of the children involved, enhanced interest of other stakeholders, such as parents, teachers and theatre instructors, as well as linguistic achievements which 'had greater lexical variation and syntactic complexity' (Faitaki & Murphy, 2023: 246). It can only be speculated that, at least to a smaller degree, similar attainments could be achieved by FL learners who could memorise some language chunks and simple sentence patterns by rote repetition.

2.4.3 Intercultural activities

Considering that the primary objective of current pre-primary FL curricula in European settings is to raise intercultural awareness (cf. Chapter 5), it is crucial to understand how this can be achieved. Raising the intercultural awareness of pre-primary children means raising the young children's awareness of the existence of other languages and cultures, which in consequence should result in them developing interest, curiosity and positive attitudes towards those cultures, which may be yet another means of enhancing intrinsic motivation and encouraging the pursuit of lifelong language learning. It is also a prerequisite of developing future intercultural and communicative language competence. In his definition of intercultural competence, Byram (2008) claims this is a construct consisting of five elements: attitudes of curiosity and openness, knowledge of products and practices in a learner's and a foreign interlocutor's countries, skills of interpreting and relating documents and facts from another culture to a native culture and their critical evaluation, skills of discovering new knowledge about a culture and an ability to utilise it in the situation at hand (Byram, 2008). It is vital to understand that intercultural competence is aimed at supporting an individual's plurilingual competence, which means one will be able to mediate between the home and foreign culture and critically evaluate the products of other cultures.

Tools that can be advocated as means of raising the intercultural awareness of pre-primary FL learners include picture books, intercultural projects and the learner's language portfolio. While there is no empirical data supporting their efficiency, it seems their impact on the development of intercultural competence can be ascertained only in the long term. Nevertheless, raising intercultural interest can undoubtedly enhance children's positive attitudes to the FL and culture and thus enhance their intrinsic FL motivation.

Authentic picture books instantiate authentic texts for very young learners whose understanding is dependent on both the text and the pictures (cf. Section 2.4.1 above). Covering a myriad of topics, they also present insights into other cultures and thus are suitable for stimulating discussion of intercultural topics, such as diversity and inclusion. The illustrations often present children from diverse ethnic backgrounds, thus serving as a springboard for interpretation and teaching the message of the book. Various authors have suggested different books as being suitable for raising intercultural awareness in pre-primary learners, for example *Head, Shoulders, Knees, and Toes ...* by Annie Kubler (2003; in Mourão, 2015) and *Handa's Surprise* by Eileen Browne (2014; in Fernández-Fernández & López-Fuentes, 2023). Other suitable books and accompanying materials have been recommended as an outcome of the ICEPELL project (Icepell Consortium, 2022).

ECEC teachers may also formulate an intercultural project with another similar institution using the eTwinning platform. Endorsed by the European Commission, the platform supports collaboration and the exchange of ideas, experiences and artefacts between educational institutions, often by means of technology, at all educational levels, including pre-primary (Akdemir, 2017). For example, children can collect artefacts connected with their home culture and language and send them sequentially to other kindergartens taking part in the project. On receiving the culture kit from another institution, the ECEC teacher can organise a presentation and talk with the children about what the objects mean, how they are used in the given culture and how they compare with the home culture.

Another idea is to ask children to keep a portfolio of their work and progress and of their plurilingual and intercultural encounters. An example of such a portfolio is the Polish version of the European language portfolio for children aged 3;0–6;0 (Pamuła *et al.*, 2007) which follows the guidelines of other types of portfolios published by the European Centre for Modern Languages in Graz, the aim of which is to foster learners' self-awareness and reflection on learning progress as well as raise awareness of other languages present in the child's surroundings (Becker, 2015). It typically consists of the Language Passport, the Language Biography and the Dossier. The version prepared for pre-primary learners (Pamuła *et al.*, 2007) is designed in a child-friendly manner. The children obtain the caterpillar prop (standing for language passport), which can be expanded (i.e. made longer) as the children assess their progression with FL skills after each kindergarten year. Additionally, the children are encouraged to take notes (i.e. draw or paste tickets, postcards, photos, etc.) of their intercultural encounters (meetings with foreigners, travelling abroad, etc.) in a special notebook, that is, a dossier. They can be filled out by children at table time in kindergarten after some meaningful intercultural encounters, for example, guests visiting, or with parental assistance at home. The portfolio can also be used as an alternative form of assessment of the child's progress (Becker, 2015).

2.4.4 Technology in the very young classroom

Educational technology occupies a prominent place in education, including the pre-primary classroom, which can be equipped with, for example, interactive whiteboards, via which child L2 learners can be exposed to various internet content, such as electronic books, films, song recordings accompanied by TPR movements and visuals. Technology also encourages learner engagement and interaction by appealing to many senses at the same time, such as sight, hearing, touch and movement.

Likewise, the same content could be accessible to children for home use, for example on tablets and smartphones, thus potentially increasing the amount of contact with the language. Additionally, various educational apps can be installed, such as DuolingoKids® or EAN Digital Games App (Alexiou, 2023), which present and practise new vocabulary in a multimodal manner or enable children to watch and listen to captioned stories. An additional motivating boost that technology offers is the gamification aspect, that is, rewarding children with stars, points and so on for correct answers when practising vocabulary.

This multimodal feature of screen media can be particularly appealing to very young learners, especially in that they are considered to be digital natives, that is, many of them have been exposed to such media from a very early age, if not from birth. However, does multimodality and apparent engagement contribute to the retention of the new linguistic material? Early research in this area (cf. Alexiou & Vitoulis, 2014) showed promising results of using interactive websites on productive and receptive vocabulary retention, provided that they are used in the presence of a supportive teacher. The research also pointed to an advantage in girls and younger learners (four-year-olds as opposed to six-year-olds) in the productive mastery of new lexis, which may indicate that digital natives may treat learning by means of interactive media in the same way as learning by means of realia and other authentic materials. Similarly, Gohar (2017), in a quasi-experimental study, showed that interactive ebooks can be more efficient in terms of developing children's print awareness, phonological awareness, text comprehension and discovery of word meaning when compared with traditional books. By contrast, Butler (2022), in her review of available research in line with Mayer's (2001) *Cognitive Theory of Multimedia Learning*, argues firstly that the multimodality of the media and FL input place too much of a cognitive strain on the children who have to process too much input at the same time. It is explained that pre-primary learners may not be able to grasp new meanings in a FL from multimedia because their attention is caught by something else, that is, the multimodal effects such as sound and flashing colours. Secondly, Butler (2022) argues that if the linguistic input is presented totally by the multimodal input, without teacher mediation, it is difficult for the children to associate new words and phrases with new labels. It is even more unlikely for children below the age of two/three, who have not yet fully acquired their mother tongue and therefore have not developed required concepts onto which to map new word labels.

A further potential advantage of the use of technology is noted when it is used in the company of parents (e.g. Prošić-Santovac, 2017; Scheffler & Domińska, 2018) who are able to scaffold new meanings for their children and in fact use a range of discourse strategies to do so and to elaborate on the content (e.g. through pretend play). For the same reason, Butler (2022) recommends using media technology at home only in the presence of parents who act as language mediators to their children. She also pointed to social robots which can decode children's emotions to be capable of interacting like parents, which can be a more promising technological device for language teaching than screen media that merely offer passive exposure to content. It seems therefore that an interactive element provides an advantage in some tools (cf. Alexiou & Vitoulis, 2014; Gohar, 2017). For the same reason, solitary use of learning apps is more often recommended for maintaining heritage language, that is, children who have already mastered their mother tongue orally and wish to become acquainted with literacy in that language (Little, 2019). Currently, digital stories can also be used for the same purpose. Children can watch an animated series with story words being highlighted concurrently. The children can watch the series alone, can repeat the highlighted words and so acquire some lexis from context. The potential of acquiring vocabulary from captioned videos has been sufficiently documented (Pattemore & Muñoz, 2020; Scheffler et al., 2021) as the children recycle the same words and sentences embedded in stories during repeated viewing sessions until they finally internalise them.

For this reason, Korosidou and Griva (2021) argue that digital stories can act in the same way as traditional storybooks, that is, children can be engaged in story reading by being asked questions about items on the page, asked to turn the digital page and so on. In a project conducted in Greek kindergartens the teachers first exposed learners to self-prepared stories oriented at teaching one of a selected thematic vocabulary range. This vocabulary was further reinforced in the main stage of the project by various tasks reinforcing target vocabulary, such as digital memory games, digital puzzles, online painting and even educational robots. The researchers found the course effective because the children showed gains in receptive vocabulary knowledge and the learners had generally positive attitudes to the English classes conducted by means of the technological devices. However, it is not known how many words from the input were actually acquired, how long they were retained and if they were recognised when also presented in other contexts (e.g. in traditional pictures) as well as how the results would compare to a similar intervention but by means of traditional tools. It has to be recognised that this instruction was a short yet costly project. An open question remains whether children would benefit from similar tools at later stages of learning and if they were transferred to more traditional teaching. The fact that children are engaged by the multimodality of the media is not surprising. However, it is not certain whether the multimodality overshadowed the linguistic aspects as any gains were reported only in reference to receptive knowledge, which seems a low return given the financial input placed in the technological devices.

2.5 The Teacher

The teacher appears to be the most significant element of the FL teaching–learning process, as Crabbe (2003: 15) highlighted: 'the quality of the instruction offered in the majority of institutions is dependent solely on the training and experience of the teachers they employ, rather than on a managed procedure for defining and monitoring that quality'. In pre-primary FL education the role of the teacher is even more prominent, as they are the major provider of linguistic input and all the lesson activities are teacher-led. It is thanks to a close emotional bond between the teacher and learners that the latter are willing to attend and to engage in classes.

If the teacher is a key factor that motivates learners towards language learning, it can be concluded that it is not so much learner agency but teacher agency that plays a role in ultimate learner attainment and motivation. Teacher agency in ecological approaches is defined as 'a "quality" of the engagement of actors with temporal-relational contexts-for-action, not a quality of the actors themselves' (Priestley *et al.*, 2015: 3). In early language learning, teacher agency can manifest in teacher attitudes towards young learners, willingness to teach them, careful lesson planning and support given to children throughout learning. Agency can be connected with personality characteristics of a teacher but more so it is also related to the formal qualifications obtained in the course of teacher education programmes and the status of the very young learner teacher in the light of language education policy.

Due to the unprecedented growth in demand for early FL education globally, a shortage of well-qualified teachers can be noted (Alstad, 2020; Černa, 2015; Zein & Garton, 2019). As a result, there has been an ongoing debate regarding who makes the best language teacher of very young learners; is it a language specialist, possessing FL skills at C1/C2 level, which allow them to communicate freely in a FL, or an ECEC specialist, also referred to as a generalist teacher, with knowledge and practical skills in how to work with very young children and respond to their psychoemotional needs? Different countries have resorted to different solutions. In many European countries, such as Poland (Rokita-Jaśkow & Pamuła-Behrens, 2019), Portugal (Mourão & Ferreirinha, 2016) and Italy (Langé & Lopriore, 2014), initially very early language teaching has been conducted by the language specialist entering the kindergarten group for a few hours a week and thus called an itinerant teacher. As regards Asia, in some countries, such as China, Taiwan and Vietnam, the governments decided on a language specialist while in others, such as Indonesia, Japan, Korea and Thailand, they opted for a generalist teacher (Butler, 2015a). Additionally, non-local teachers (i.e. from abroad) are recruited in Japan, Korea and Thailand, which include both native and non-native speakers, to satisfy the demand for language teachers (Butler, 2015a).

In view of the above data, it is clear that the most frequent dilemma is to choose between the language specialist and the generalist ECEC teacher. There is no doubt that no matter what their formal qualifications are, their competences should go beyond the ability to 'sing a few songs and know a couple of words' (Nguyen, 2019), which is an opinion held by many lay people of the required skillset and results in little legitimacy for the profession of teaching young and very young learners of FLs. Instead, teachers within the profession require possession of the following competences (Goullier *et al.*, 2015; Rokita-Jaśkow & Pamuła-Behrens, 2019):

- linguistic skills that allow them to communicate in that language freely, present new linguistic material in an appealing manner, have knowledge of the target language culture as well as possess intercultural competence and sensitivity. The teacher should also be familiar with the processes of L1 and L2 acquisition and should know the methodology of supporting the latter;
- knowledge and skills of working with very young children, that is, psychopedagogical skills, so that they can cater for children's overall growth and socioemotional learning by providing meaningful and enjoyable language experience. Additionally, they should have collaboration skills that will facilitate their cooperation with other teachers as well as parents;
- knowledge of FL didactics, so that they are prepared to conduct lessons appropriate to the particular age and maturational capacity of learners. They should be familiar with available materials as well as products (e.g. films, software, etc.) that can potentially be used in the very young learners' classroom.

Clearly, the linguistic aims can be best achieved if the teacher can speak the target language fluently and with high proficiency, which allows them to speak freely in the target language, easily recasting children's L1 utterances in L2. For this reason, in the opinion of many individuals, including pre-service ECEC teachers, native speaker teachers or language specialist teachers are believed to be the best teachers in pre-primary FL education. In this respect Waddington (2021) found in the Spanish context that a native English-speaking teacher (NEST) sounds more authentic and can provide a better pronunciation model. This belief is, however, commonly held also in other contexts where, by starting FL learning early, attainment of FL proficiency is falsely expected.

A language specialist can speak the target language freely and is able to set up an authentic bilingual situation, imitating the 'one person, one language' principle, known from studies on childhood bilingualism (Romaine, 2000), which in the instructed setting has been adapted as 'one teacher, one language' strategy (Schwartz, 2018). It helps children to associate FL use with a particular person and potentially can prompt very young learners to use the FL when addressing the teacher and consequently stimulate the child's FL development. Yet, this solution can only be used in highly intensive courses, which aim to imitate naturalistic acquisition in second, as opposed to foreign, language learning contexts.

A generalist teacher is employed in the ECEC institution and delivers the general ECEC curriculum, occasionally switching to FL activities. The advantage of the generalist teacher lies in the fact that they are with the children most of the time, know them well and usually have created an affectionate bond with them. If the child recalls a FL phrase at any time outside class, the generalist teacher may react to it by, for example, elaborating on the child's production (Prošić-Santovac, 2017) or stimulating FL play (cf. Mourão, 2015). However, too often the generalist teacher may not have a fluent command of a FL, which may reflect in the quality of language input provided. Even though the language competences of many young ECEC teachers in Europe have improved greatly over the last decade, as they have had FLs in the course of their education as part of their compulsory curriculum, the idea of lifelong learning of languages, not only by language learners but also by language teachers, is not familiar to all teachers. As a result:

> it appears to underpin and perpetuate a deficit view of the non-specialist teacher which excludes them from what should be a collaborative practice (teaching in the early years), and can also have a debilitating effect on their own language learning processes, by reinforcing the assumption that some people are 'just good at languages' while others are not. (Waddington, 2021: 14)

Yet, the language specialist, often a graduate of a university's language department and expected to have command of the language at B2/C1 level (European Commission, 2011), may not have a vocation to work with young learners. Mourão (2021) argues that collaboration between the language specialist, even if they are an itinerant teacher, and the generalist teacher is plausible and the best solution. Yet, as she remarks, such collaboration requires the support of the institution, for example, through in-service training. She pinpoints key elements of such successful collaboration, that is, 'communication between professionals, mutual trust, common goals, and joint responsibility for outcomes and decision-making' (Mourão, 2021: 456), and concludes that it should be mainly the ECEC teachers that take up the proactive role in initiating the collaboration with itinerant teachers. Of a different opinion is Ng (2015) working in Hong Kong, where she found collaboration between the itinerant NEST, in this case a language specialist, and the kindergarten teacher difficult, which may show that collaboration may not be plausible in all settings for cultural, but also organisational, reasons. For example, Luo (2007) noted that the major obstacle on the part of non-native speaking teachers was their low proficiency in the language and resistance to trying out new pedagogical solutions, such as communicative teaching, while on the part of NESTs it was a lack of pedagogical content knowledge and unfamiliarity with and lack of adjustment to local cultural rules.

It is worth mentioning that teaching a FL to pre-primary learners is a novel phenomenon in many contexts. Thus, it can be guided by many false beliefs and expectations rooted in teachers' own language learning experience, the observation of how children learn either an L1 or L2 in naturalistic contexts or even the observation of how primary and even upper-primary learners learn, without thorough consideration (Mourão & Ferreinha, 2016). A common misconception of ECEC teachers that is overwhelmingly held by in-service and pre-service teachers in various contexts such as Poland (Rokita-Jaśkow, 2016), Slovenia (Fojkar & Skubic, 2017) and Macau (Reynolds et al., 2021) is that very young children learn languages fast and with ease, and that the goal of very early teaching of FLs is to achieve native-like fluency in the future. However, they also admitted that the pedagogy that should be used while teaching pre-primary learners should include play and fun activities and focus mainly on the development of vocabulary, listening and speaking. These findings indicate that ECEC teachers, or teachers to be, are more knowledgeable of how to work with very young children; yet as Reynolds et al. (2021) conclude, their training to teach a FL should involve the rudiments of second language acquisition (SLA) in instructed contexts as well as the enhancement of FL skills, because ECEC teachers express concern that they will not be able to cope with teaching the content in a FL and will not master native-like pronunciation (Reynolds et al., 2021; Waddington, 2021).

These findings are in line with recommendations of the European Commission (2011) which state that the best teacher of very young learners is the teacher who knows the specificity of working with such young learners and thus can meet their psychoemotional needs as well as being motivated to work with very young learners. For this reason, the generalist ECEC teacher, with at least upper-intermediate level (B2) of FL competence, is recommended to be adequate, which finds support in research (e.g. Cortina Perez & Andugar, 2021; Reynolds et al., 2021). In those countries in which early FL learning has become a policy, ECEC teachers are trained during their graduate and postgraduate courses to teach FL, for example in Poland (Rokita-Jaśkow & Pamuła-Behrens,

2019), Cyprus (Karoulla-Vrikki & Vrikki, 2014) and Spain (Cortina-Perez & Andugar, 2021). The language education component includes principles of teaching English to young learners (TEYL) methodology as well as improvement of FL skills so that future ECEC teachers reach at least B2 level in a FL according to the Common European Framework of Reference for Languages scale.

Considering also the fact that a FL, most often English, has been a part of the compulsory school curriculum and tested in school-leaving exams for over two decades (European Commission, 2011), many young people today who aspire to become ECEC teachers already possess sufficient language knowledge (approx. at B2 level) which allows them to communicate freely and teach the language. What they need is to build confidence in their language abilities through adequate training, which will also familiarise them with TEYL methodology. This should be a component of graduate and postgraduate ECEC teacher preparation programmes.

2.5.1 Quality of teacher language

The teacher is the main source of input in the language classroom. However, their role is not only to speak to children as passive recipients but also to prompt them to produce language. It is through interaction that language presented in the input can be further clarified, made comprehensible and thus acquired. Subsequently, it is through the child's overt linguistic production that we can observe how much language they have acquired, as posited by Gass (2018), the interaction hypothesis of Gass and Mackey (2007) and the output hypothesis of Swain (1985). The view of teachers mediating between the sources of input and learners' output within the classroom ecology also coincides with van Lier's (2004) ecological theory as it looks at 'the multilayered nature of interaction and language use, in all their complexity and as a network of interdependencies among all the elements in the setting' (van Lier, 2004: 3).

With the goal of facilitating language acquisition in mind, the teacher should use a range of discursive strategies that promote the engagement of children in classroom discourse, which should be authentic and contextualised. For this reason, it is not enough to rely on presenting and drilling single words as is sometimes wrongly assumed by non-expert teachers (Černa, 2015). Unsworth et al. (2014) found that there is a significant difference between teachers' language proficiency and children's learning outcomes, most probably attuning to the quality of language input provided. In their study conducted among four-year-old Dutch learners, the authors found that children who were taught by a native speaker after two years of instruction performed significantly better than children who were taught by non-native speakers with language proficiency at A2/B1 level. This finding suggests that language teacher proficiency is an important factor influencing child FL learning outcomes. Possessing a high level of language competence, the teacher can use appropriate discourse strategies that engage very young learners in L2 discourse (Fleta, 2018; Schwartz, 2023). Teacher discourse strategies enable the scaffolding of language learning tasks, to echo the works of Bruner (1983) and Vygotsky (1985). The use of such strategies is vital for children to both observe and participate in discourse (Cameron, 2001). Likewise, discourse has to be teacher-led as pre-primary children are not capable of planning their own speech in L1, not to mention in a FL. Fleta (2018) enumerates the following strategies that could be used by teachers in discursive practices directed at young and very young learners:

> teachers' positive feedback to foster language and content comprehension (questions, elicitation, metalinguistic feedback, expansion, cognates); teachers' corrective feedback (recast, explicit correction, clarification requests); and children's spontaneous productive strategies (repetition, language mixing, formulaic expressions). (Fleta, 2018: 299)

In her empirical study (Fleta, 2018) conducted in a Spanish bilingual kindergarten which consisted in recorded observation of over 30 English as a foreign language (EFL) lessons of a fairly intensive language course, she found evidence that the children were 'progressing through a series of developmental stages comparable to the stages found in English L1 acquisition' (Fleta, 2018: 296). She attributed these results not only to the high amount of exposure to the FL but also to the fact that despite speaking solely in the target language, the teachers used discourse strategies so skilfully that the children were able to derive meanings from context and also initiate FL production, which was evident in single word and formulaic production as well as in code-mixing/translanguaging in the emerging bilinguals.

In the same vein, Schwartz (2023) claims that the teacher should use such strategies that allow the creation of language conducive contexts, defined 'as contexts rich in multisensory activities with a wide array of semiotic resources and diverse teacher-child and peer interactions, encouraging the child's engagement in the novel language learning' (Schwartz, 2023: 6). Although mainly directed at L2 learners, the didactic strategies she proposes could also be of value in the FL classroom. They consist in facilitating comprehension of unknown language and fostering the child's language production and denote the following: ritual repetitions, elicitation, associative mediators, gestures and body enactment and teacher-mediated sociodramatic play. Additionally, Schwartz (2023) distinguishes management strategies that relate to establishing and maintaining discipline in class and to supporting peer language learning and encouraging parental engagement.

Repetition seems to be the most basic strategy that allows the engagement of very young learners in the class and familiarisation with classroom rules 'in terms of turn-taking procedures, topical choices, and learning strategies' (Roh & Lee, 2018: 121) even if they are complete beginners to a FL. In a study conducted in two Korean kindergartens, Roh and Lee (2018) demonstrated the usefulness of repetition strategy, not as reinforcement of the target language (English) input but as a way of engaging children in classroom discourse when the teacher is a native speaker. This example shows that it is possible to speak only the target language even to very young beginner learners provided the teacher uses appropriate discourse strategies, in that case repetition. Repetition of actions and language allowed the establishment of routines from which three other pedagogical actions emerged: 'eliciting synchronized student response, having students recognize and practice target language items, and pursuing particular answers' (Roh & Lee, 2018: 135).

Effective engagement of children in classroom discourse determines its effectiveness and defines the quality of instruction. The more the teacher speaks in the target language, using varied language to talk about class activities and appropriate strategies to scaffold new meanings to children, the richer the FL production of the children. This observation has been evidenced in a number of empirical studies.

Weitz *et al.* (2010) conducted a project in bilingual kindergartens in Germany, Belgium, Sweden and England comprising 20 FL teachers and 400 learners. As one of the tasks they devised an input Quality Observation scheme which allowed the evaluation of the quality of teacher talk. Close scrutiny of its components allowed the observation of which aspects of teacher language can pertain to quality. Both quantitative and qualitative aspects have been taken into account. As regards the quantitative aspect, they distinguished low-inference categories 'which do not require any judgement and comprise general information, such as (...) categorisation of situation and activity or the duration and the overall focus of the activity' (Weitz *et al.*, 2010: 11) and high-inference categories, 'which require more judgement and interpretation on the part of the observer' (Weitz *et al.*, 2010: 11). High-reference categories in reference to *quantity* inquired about the *amount of L2 input* offered (as measured by reference to time or a number of turns), absence/use of L1 or translation. In reference to the *quality* of input, it is vital to observe whether the teacher adapts their speech to the level of the children (e.g. by slowing the rate of speech, using high pitch for emphasis, etc.), uses varied vocabulary and complex structures, introduces routines for the same type of activities or demonstrates verbal reactions to children's talk, explicit focus on form (e.g. explanation, correction), facilitating comprehension (by using body language, contextualising language with pictures, realia, self-paraphrasing, comprehension checks), encouraging children's output and giving implicit feedback. The scale also included an item on children's attentive listening which shows engagement. In their study, Weitz et al. (2010) used an observation scheme in order to find answers to such important questions as, for example, whether there is any link between the teachers' input quality and children's progress in lexical and grammatical production over a period of 12 months. Additionally, they aimed to check whether there are any differences between teachers' language in various institutions. The results showed that there were significant differences between the quality of teacher input and receptive knowledge of grammar, indicating that 'rich sentence structures are indispensable for the development of morpho-syntactic knowledge, receptive word learning and the development of the mental lexicon (in terms of breadth)' (Weitz et al., 2010: 37). However, no such correlation was observed in reference to the receptive knowledge of lexis. The intensity of the course, that is, the amount of input, did not impact the preschoolers' achievement either. The authors concluded that 'new vocabulary can become accessible to learners also with a qualitatively less beneficial input' (Weitz et al., 2010: 37) relying on high frequency, that is, frequent repetition and clear context for deriving meaning. They also admitted that productive lexical use, which usually requires connecting with other words and morphosyntactic knowledge, is also related to richness of input. These findings are very revealing and support the commonly held belief that language input has an impact on language acquisition. The authors (Weitz et al., 2010), however, acknowledged that other variables, such as children's age or prior experience of language learning, were not taken into account.

The interrelationship between teacher input quality and learners' FL achievement has been verified in a few studies, albeit on lower primary children. In the Croatian setting, Erk and Pavičić Takač (2021) investigated the impact of teacher language input over young learners' (aged 6;5–7;5 at the beginning of the study) first two years of their FL learning. What they found was, firstly, a significant variability in the amount of teacher use of the target language, which impacted the children's listening comprehension abilities and accounted for 6% to 11% of variance on listening tasks. Students who performed best on listening comprehension tasks had received the largest amount of teacher input. Additionally, the authors observed that 'high amounts of teacher target language input at the very beginning of the FL learning have a snowballing effect on later development' (Erk & Pavicić Takać, 2021: 17), that is, continued throughout the whole period of the study. This observation runs against the popular belief that the teacher should not speak a FL to beginner learners. Similarly, Wilden and Porsch (2020), in a survey conducted among primary school EFL teachers in Germany, found there was a correlation between teacher language proficiency as confirmed by their formal qualifications and the reported amount of a FL used in teaching young learners. This finding denotes that higher proficiency in a FL gives teachers more confidence to use it in class and perhaps better competency to use varied discourse strategies, which is an argument in favour of employing language specialists.

There has been an ongoing debate whether in the FL classroom, and especially in the very young learners' classroom, only the target language or mixed languages (translanguaging) should be allowed (Mifsud & Vela, 2020; Prošić-Santovac & Radović, 2018b). Mifsud and Vela (2020) point out that very young children's L1s may not be fully established. Therefore, when introducing a FL, a clear separation of the two languages is recommended. If learning a FL is the goal, then keeping the two languages, that is, an L1 and a FL, separate should be a norm.

From an ecological perspective (van Lier, 2004) this dilemma seems to be a choice between the issues of quality and equity. Prioritising quality means that one should aim to provide the best learning opportunities. Intensive FL courses and the teacher speaking solely a FL constitute means towards this goal. It is notable that the aforementioned studies on the reciprocal relationship of teacher language and child FL production were conducted mainly in bilingual kindergartens, that is, institutions of relatively high FL intensity which are usually private, costly and thus elitist.

On the other hand, if one aims for equitable and inclusive FL education, very early FL education should be democratic, that is, encompassing all children. From this perspective, one should take into account individual children's varied cognitive predispositions as well as their socioeconomic and, in increasingly culturally diverse kindergarten classes, their linguistic background. In those settings where FL instruction is part of a compulsory ECEC curriculum usually only a limited amount of contact with a target language can be provided. Therefore, in such low-exposure environments, insistence on the target use only in class may be too stressful for many children. On these grounds, and also with a view to showing respect to children's rights to use their first languages in ECEC instruction, translanguaging on the part of both teachers and learners is a promoted solution (Kirsch & Mortini, 2023). This means the teacher can insert children's own language in the FL speech when addressing them in order to make them feel at ease. By the same token, children can use their own language while responding to the teacher, retelling a story or enquiring about new information, which the FL teacher should be able to recast in the FL. In this way, children's comprehension, and thus their well-being, is prioritised. Several empirical studies also show that allowing children to use their own language in a FL class does not deter them from making progress in the target FL language, which was found particularly in monolingual settings such as Colombia (Guevara & Ordoñez, 2012), Poland (Scheffler & Domińska, 2018) and South Korea (Song, 2011).

2.6 The Role of Peers in FL Instruction

It goes without saying that language serves communication. It is the desire to play with other children that motivates children to undertake cognitive effort to utilise available linguistic resources to establish communication with peers (Washington-Nortey et al., 2020). In other words, it is children's own agency in establishing relationships with other members of the community that boosts their language development (Schwartz, 2018). In return, the L2 peers, in responding, often provide corrective feedback on language produced, stimulating further language production in minority language users. Interaction with peers is therefore a vital source of language learning in naturalistic *second* language settings.

This process is, however, not possible in a classroom where all learners share the same mother tongue, in which the communicative desire and need disappears. For this reason, teaching activities in the FL classroom are mainly teacher-led and it is the teacher who has to stimulate children's interest in the lesson and learners' FL production.

However, as a means of boosting child FL learners' agency, Mourão (2014, 2018; Robinson et al., 2015) proposed an innovative concept of children's English language areas (ELAs), also known as English corners. Based on the Montessorri® method (American Montessorri Society, 2019), ELAs are spaces in the ECEC classrooms where copies of FL learning materials (e.g. flashcards, game boards and game cards, puppets, storybooks, etc.) can be left by the teacher for later child-initiated use and play, especially during the time dedicated to free play.

Robinson et al. (2015), using ELAs in kindergartens in South Korea and Portugal, empirically found that children used the resources left by the teacher and replicated teacher-led activities, such as playing favourite flashcard games, labelling pictures on display in English, singing a song stimulated and recalled upon seeing a storybook as a cue, playing with puppets and even pretending to 'read' the books. Usually, one of the children took the role of the teacher while others acted as pupils. Furthermore, children were observed to go beyond single word production and use pre-fabricated chunks known from stories and drama activities. In another study, Waddington et al. (2018), in a Spanish setting working with four-year-olds, observed that children voluntarily participated in the ELA activities and even if they were silent they carefully observed other children playing. This finding was interpreted as observation, being a socialisation strategy, giving slower children additional time and opportunity for language acquisition. Waddington et al. (2018) also observed that there is a clear correlation between the frequency of activities used in class (such as songs and routines) and their replication in free play, which suggests that the activities undertaken in ELAs were those that were well memorised in EFL class. All these findings show that ELAs can 'provide a happy place in the classroom which is attractive to a range of children and which is also conducive to learning' (Robinson *et al.*, 2015: 23). Children use the FL productively and to some extent for communicative purposes. To this end, ELAs seem to be the only technique promoting spontaneous FL use among preschoolers and therefore are worth promoting in other educational settings.

Similarly, repetition and imitation as social learning strategies were identified by Vičević Ivanović *et al.* (2021) among very young Croatian learners of French, German and Italian by means of the projection technique. The children were asked how they would help their plush toy to say particular words and structures in the L2 (e.g. 'How would you help the elephant to learn to say "der Apfel"?'). The findings revealed that by using the toy as a learner the children demonstrated a number of teaching strategies which imitated class teacher techniques. They were memory-based strategies such as repeating after a model and listening to the interlocutor as well as informal strategies like showing and naming objects. The frequency of these strategies varied with the intensity of the participants' exposure to the FL; children with more intensive exposure tended to use informal strategies such as learning through songs and rhymes as well as social strategies like contact with a native speaker. Interestingly, some formal strategies such as learning by drawing or writing words were not linked to the intensity of L2 exposure.

2.7 Teacher Agency

From the above overview of teaching methodology in an instructional setting (mainly the kindergarten) it can be observed that the teacher, as an embodiment of linguistic, didactic and pedagogical competencies, is the key element guaranteeing effectiveness of FL teaching. Their role is not only to provide FL input but also to arouse interest in the language that is totally foreign to them and generally rather absent in their surroundings. The only way to achieve this is to motivate very young learners intrinsically by setting up such learning tasks and an environment that will appeal to children's natural curiosity and eagerness to play. Furthermore, the teacher's role is to enhance children's participation in the educational discourse by asking questions and provoking learners' response in a FL. Quality early FL teaching requires quality FL teachers. From this account, it is self-evident that teachers' agency, understood to be their readiness to act and implement quality methodology in their practice, here to introduce a FL to very young children, is of crucial importance. It matters much more than children's agency. Children's agency is subsidiary to that of the teacher. This means that children's agency will materialise only after the teacher has enacted playful FL methodology, which is evident in their initiatives to engage in pretend play in ELAs. This communicative practice, however, consists much more in imitation and repetition, rather than creative language use.

Child FL agency differs considerably from the agency exercised in a naturalistic setting, where the children are motivated to acquire L2 as a means of socialisation with peers and the wider community of L2 speakers (Schwartz & Deeb, 2018). As emphasised by Çekaite (2020: 5), 'peer cultures involve common cultural activities such as play, verbal genres, as well as the use of material artefacts as shared affordances for engagement'. Thanks to participation in such peer groups, children learn the rules for participation and collaboration in the given school (kindergarten) culture. Additionally, through interaction with peers, they obtain much more and varied L2 input than solely from the teacher and also corrective feedback on their own L2 production. Thus, interaction with peers contributes to their development of communicative competence in the target language.

Summary

This chapter looks at the very young learner's FL microsystem, that is, the place where FL instruction takes place. Specifically, as a focal point of this description, it focuses on the notions of variability and quality of FL teaching in different types of institutions: public versus private. It is argued that quality is evident in the process of teaching, as manifested by the enactment of teacher competences and methodology used. In respect of the former, differences between language specialists and generalist teachers are presented in reference to the possibility of using diverse discourse skills. In reference to the latter, efficiency of various teaching techniques, notably songs, stories, technology and English language areas, are discussed. The chapter concludes by emphasising the supremacy of teacher agency over very young FL learners' agency.

3 Mesosystem: Family Environment

This chapter aims to characterise the proximal and distal characteristics of the young learner's family as the child's mesosystem. By the former, I consider socioemotional ties within the family, which result from mutual interactions catering for the whole child's growth as well as overall parenting style. The proximal features resonate in the amount of parental involvement in child FL education at home as well as in communicating and cooperating with the educational institution. They also relate to parental aspirations in reference to future child FL achievement, as parents may treat very early FL learning as an investment or a form of symbolic capital. Regarding distal variables, the family's socioeconomic status is mainly addressed as mediated by the parental level of education and FL proficiency, as these variables enable access to educational resources, quality instruction and opportunities for intercultural encounters. The chapter concludes that parental agency in early FL education is of high importance for inspiring and motivating the child to participate in FL instruction, for providing opportunities and resources, for liaising with the educational institution and, last but not least, for acting as role models for language use.

3.1 Parental Involvement in Child FL Education

Undoubtedly, all children exhibiting typical development acquire language and learn to communicate. However, the quality of a child's language, as manifested in phonological and structural accuracy, lexical size and structural complexity, largely depends on the quality of language input provided in the family environment in which the child grows up, as it is from caregivers' speech, that is, language directed to the child, that the child learns to distinguish language phonemes, associates word labels to meanings, acquires rules for forming sentences and finally learns the pragmatics of language use (cf. Chapter 1). This interrelationship between parental language input and a child's language output seems relevant not only in relation to first language (L1) acquisition but also to second (L2) and foreign language (FL) development, although to a minor degree and less directly. In the latter case, parents may not necessarily speak the FL to the child, yet if they wish to optimise language learning outcomes they need to provide opportunities for FL exposure out of school, that is, in the home/family environment. The family constitutes the first microsystem in which the child grows and flourishes in the early years before going to early childhood education and care (ECEC). However, in reference to FL learning, it should be considered as a mesosystem, as FL is mainly taught in a formal setting, which can additionally be supported in the family environment.

Parental involvement is defined as 'the allocation of resources by the parent of the child in a given domain' (Grolnick & Slowiaczek, 1994: 238). It is associated with a responsive parenting style 'that provides positive affection and high levels of warmth and is responsive in ways that are contingently linked to a young child's signals' (Kagan, 1999). Forms of *parental involvement* that currently guide policymakers and school authorities in establishing home-school relations have been elaborated by Epstein (1996) and constitute the following: *parenting, communicating* (between school and family), *learning at home, volunteering* (assisting with school activities), *decision-making* (involvement in parental committees, etc.) and *collaboration with the community*.

The value of parental involvement in child education has been highlighted in a vast amount of general educational research suggesting that it can positively impact child achievement in school (Crosnoe *et al.*, 2010; Duncan *et al.*, 2007; Grolnick, 2016; Grolnick & Marbell, 2009). Specifically, children from stable families with established predictive daily routines and ongoing communication between family members developed better self-regulation skills, planning and other executive functions, all relevant to schooling (Cortés Pascual, 2019). Additionally, children who were engaged in home literacy practices developed more positive attitudes towards reading, which had a beneficial impact on their reading development in the early school years (Dickinson & Tabors, 1991; Park, 2008). These findings unanimously show that the early years of a child's life are critical as preparation for later academic success and that variability in child school outcomes is strongly related to variability in home practices and family orientation.

Parental involvement in early FL education seems to follow the same principles because very young instructed FL learners do not yet have agency in that respect. Parents decide to enrol their children into some form of FL instruction motivated by their ideologies, experiences and aspirations. It is the parents who revise and reinforce classroom material with their children or who provide additional language exposure opportunities. Finally, involved parents attach importance to receiving regular information about their child's progress, which is demonstrated through liaison with the educational institution.

Interestingly, parental attitudes to learning a FL and parental involvement have been found to be significant factors influencing young learners' attitudes to learning a FL, usually English, in a variety of settings, such as selected European countries (Enever, 2011), Indonesia (Wati, 2016), Iran (Hosseinpour, 2015), China (Butler, 2015b; Jin *et al.*, 2016) Turkey (Kalaycı & Öz, 2018). Studies unanimously show that parents who have a positive attitude to English support their children both directly and indirectly in learning a FL, by helping them with assignments, memorising vocabulary, providing learning media such as English books, vocabulary pictures, English cartoons, films and puzzles and asking teachers to explain any topics in their children's textbooks that they do not understand. This has a positive impact on children's attitudes to learning English in pre-primary and early school years as well as on their levels of achievement. Yet, depending on cultural and linguistic factors, forms of involvement may differ. For example, in Hong Kong, Forey *et al.* (2016) found that it is not typical for parents to spend as much time reading to their children compared with Western parents, and even training in read-aloud FL books did not enhance parental involvement in that respect.

In sociolinguistic research, parents' engagement and practices fostering L2 use and development have been referred to as *family language policy* (FLP) (King & Fogle, 2006; King *et al.*, 2008; Spolsky, 2004). Its conceptualisation denotes *parental beliefs* about the role of languages, *parental practices* concerning current language use in the family as well as *management strategies*, which denote long-term strategies concerning the mastery and use of languages.

Regardless of the framework or terminology used, parents should be actively involved in their child's FL education as it may also lay the foundations for early schooling and later life achievement in a FL. Parental involvement in that respect will most likely affect *learning at home* activities, *parenting* and *communicating*, in line with Epstein's (1996) framework. Learning at home, to a large extent, depends on the emotional bonds within the family, as children will be willing to engage in home FL activities only if they feel loved, respected and cared for. Only under these conditions will they treat home language learning tasks as valuable play time spent with a beloved parent. The children are unlikely to participate in such activities if they perceive them as yet another chore, a demanding task to complete. Joint parent-child attention on language-related activities seems to be a precondition of fostering a child's FL development.

3.1.1 Learning at home

Learning at home in a FL can include joint literacy activities, joint viewing, joint playing and so on with a view to revising course content and providing additional sources of FL exposure. It is essential that, similar to the caregiver's speech in child L1 development, parents use appropriate discourse strategies that involve the children in the activity (language about the activity), simplify incoming input and prompt the children to engage in linguistic production, even if it is imperfect and limited (Fogle, 2012; Pinter, 2016). Learning at home can complement institutional instruction or denote deliberately establishing a bilingual home, for example, following the 'non-native parents' or 'time strategy' (Murphy, 2014; Romaine, 2000). Non-native parents address their children in a language that is not their mother tongue or allocate regular time for FL activities, for example for reading/TV viewing, as a part of their routine and a way of upbringing, which reflects a specific family language policy (King & Fogle, 2006; Seo, 2023).

Home literacy activities are the most common and influential type of activities promoting child language development, be it L1 or L2. The benefits of adults reading to children in respect of L1 development have been well established. They concern both the expansion of vocabulary and the development of phonological awareness, as shown in rhyme detection or phonological deletion, print recognition, and letter naming speed abilities, which later contribute to the development of the child's literacy (Hood *et al.*, 2008; Weigel *et al.*, 2006). In line with the Linguistic Coding Differences hypothesis (Sparks 2022; Sparks *et al.*, 2019), it can be speculated that by way of transferring strategies, similar benefits could also be expected from reading to children in a FL.

Mourão (2015) argues that reading aloud from storybooks should not only be carried out during formal instruction but can equally be used to engage children at home. Similar to reading in the child's mother tongue, reading in a FL not only arouses the child's interest in the text and its multimodal features but also enables the acquisition of L2 words. However, for this process to take place, careful scaffolding of the text meaning must be done by the parent (Blewitt *et al.*, 2009), which consists of asking for object labelling in the pictures, emphasising and calling for repetition of key words, asking questions about the predicted sequence of events and so on. Since children usually enjoy being read the same book repeatedly, on subsequent reading they can additionally be asked to complete lines of the text, especially when it is rhyming and repetitive. As a result of repeated reading children are likely to memorise some frequently appearing lexis and phrases, also in a FL, as Hunnekens and Xu (2010) observed. In their study, parents of two children read books to their children in their mother tongue (Spanish) and then the same book in the foreign language (English) for 20 minutes five times a week over seven weeks. This procedure proved beneficial for the children's emergent literacy in their L1 and the frequency and length of L2 utterances. Moreover, thanks to acquired lexis, the children gained confidence in using and initiating play in formal FL instruction, indicating that some learning transfer from L1 onto L2 must have occurred. Similarly, Rokita-Jaśkow (2014) in a study of reading aloud in a FL to two siblings found that the children aged 2;6 and 4;10 acquired from storybooks approximately 50% and 80% of keywords tested, respectively, with the older child acquiring more. It was also found that 'word recall was the best (nearly 90%) in the case of phrase cues, i.e. when the child is asked to finish off the lines of the text' (Rokita-Jaśkow, 2014: 214), which was interpreted as both the impact of mechanical memory and transfer-appropriate processing, that is, phrase recall was easily accessible because it was tested in the same context as it was encoded. No evidence was found, however, whether the children could use the lexis acquired from book reading spontaneously in novel communicative contexts.

Another extensively researched home-learning activity that includes parental scaffolding of L2 meaning is viewing TV, usually cartoons. In L1 studies, ample evidence has been found that watching television can constitute a valuable source of language input, provided the language of the TV programme is simplified and the content made educational so that it corresponds to the child's interest and is not perceived as an unintelligible gabble. Much research on the educational benefits of TV viewing has attributed progress in the acquisition of an L2 to educational programmes, such as *Sesame Street* (Rice et al., 1990), *Blue's Clues* (Johnson et al., 1996), *Dora the Explorer* (Gifford et al., 2000) and *Sesame English* (Bernstein, 1999). Some more recent studies have indicated that children can also benefit in language learning from cartoons mainly intended for entertainment, provided they are accompanied by parental mediation or complemented with role play of cartoon scenes. Such joint parent-child FL viewing activities were the object of a study by Prošić-Santovac (2017). She observed her own daughter's FL development between ages 3;4 and 4;10 upon regular daily viewing of the *Peppa Pig* cartoon series and noted that by the end of the study her child had learnt 300 new words actively, without explicit instruction, within 20 different semantic fields. Moreover, the child acquired some sentence patterns although with some interference errors where differences between structures in the child's L1 (Serbian) and English appeared. Linguistic gains were also observed regarding pronunciation, where the child imitated the cartoon character rather than the parents. Moreover, the child appeared to initiate communication in the FL even though no bilingual strategy, such as 'one parent – one language', was adopted. The findings from the study (Prošić-Santovac, 2017) seem to show that it is not necessary to avoid code-switching and separate the languages so that the child associates their use with a particular person/place. It must be mentioned, however, that the viewing was not passive but led to a series of play and game activities, often with the help of branded toys and games (e.g. role play, board games, colouring tasks, jigsaw tasks, etc.) performed with the parent, who was a linguist herself. It seems that maternal mediation and viewing helped the child to achieve considerable progress and aroused the child's intrinsic motivation to learn the language.

In another study, Scheffler (2015) used the same *Peppa Pig* series for daily viewing by his own very young children aged 21 months at the onset of the study over a period of 2;6 years. He observed that the children seemed to go through the same stages as children acquiring an L2 successively in naturally bilingual situations, namely *the silent period*, which lasted for approximately six months, *imitation* of words and word play, *object labelling*, interaction and commenting on events. After two years of exposure, the author noted that the children went beyond one-word level and developed sentential constructions consisting of formulaic phrases and intrasentential mixing into L1. The author concluded that in comparison to other studies of organised instruction (e.g. Rokita, 2007) the children's 'spontaneous output was much more abundant, and second, some of the utterances may be partly analyzed formulas' (Scheffler, 2015: 12). This result was attributed to the meaningful language input provided in the series and the fact that it was easy for the children to transfer the viewed scenes to their daily situations. Following on from that, it was hypothesised that 'television may contribute [to FL learning] provided that children observe situations in which they can make attempts at understanding other peoples' communicative intentions' (Scheffler, 2015: 12). This study shows that some incidental vocabulary and syntax acquisition is possible from viewing TV, even if the parent does not mediate it, provided there is much exposure to TV in a FL (daily) and the children are very young, that is, still in the process of acquiring their mother tongue.

As yet another type of activity suitable for home FL learning, Xia and Gao (2022) indicate mobile-assisted language learning (MALL) as smartphones are used commonly by younger and younger children in China, the United States and probably in other contexts as well due to their 'convenience, immediacy, portability, and sensitivity' (Xia & Gao, 2022: 6). In a study conducted in the Chinese context among L2 parents of children aged below 6;0, they (Xia & Gao, 2022) examined how the educational app, Newstar, which was freely available to kindergarten children and consisted of 'stories and songs aligned with learning content in class, vocabulary, sentence reading, English songs related to the unit topics, and homework tasks given by the teacher' (Xia & Gao, 2022: 7), can be utilised in home language practice. Parental involvement was observed in selecting the app and activities to do, allocating time for the use of the app and assisting children with language tasks and scaffolding meaning when necessary. Parents were found to be involved through reading sentences and stories, doing vocabulary tasks but not singing songs as they perceived them to be too difficult for their children to comprehend. Additionally, the in-built pronunciation function of the app was found to compensate for inadequate parental proficiency in English. These findings show that MALL and the use of educational apps have a promising future in enhancing FL contact and learning in monolingual settings. However, at the same time, it is highlighted that parents play an essential role in developing children's media literacy, which includes self-regulation in their use.

Reported studies were conducted by parents who, as applied linguists, were also knowledgeable about child psychology and pedagogy and therefore were able to guide their children to a tangible learning achievement. While the effectiveness of such parental teaching extends the limits of what the very young child can learn in an instructed course, similar results should not be expected among all preschool children having FL exposure mainly within formal instruction and who cannot count on parental support.

3.1.2 Parenting

Parenting style is the second element of Epstein's model of parental involvement. It is defined as 'normal variations in parents' attempts to control and socialize their children' (Baumrind, 1991, in Darling, 1999: 2) and manifests itself in parental ideologies expressed both covertly and overtly that can subsequently modify parental practices. It could also encompass parental management within the FLP framework (King & Fogle, 2008). Parenting style can affect children's well-being and outcomes in respect of autonomy, motivation for learning, behavioural control and maturity. Different types of parenting styles can be distinguished and are categorised using concepts such as demandingness and responsiveness. The former refers to the parental expectation of a child's behavioural control and maturity whereas responsiveness pertains to parents' emotional sensitivity. The most common parenting styles that are distinguished are *authoritative, authoritarian, permissive* and *neglectful*, which differ in the amount of parental control and emotional sensitivity exhibited. Of these styles, an authoritative parenting style, characterised by setting high demands, guidance, discipline, emotional availability and respectfulness for the child and his emotions, is indicated to have the best effect on children's self-control, maturity, self-confidence and consequently learning achievement (Sanvictores *et al.*, 2022). The relevancy of parenting styles to children's FL achievement lies firstly in the fact that depending on parental aspirations and beliefs about good upbringing, parents may hold different expectations, or none, towards their children's FL achievement, and secondly, a responsive authoritarian style may signify more direct parental involvement in language practices leading to the realisation of learning goals.

Bringing up a child in either partial or full bilingualism can become a parenting strategy and manifestation of family language policy. As King and Fogle (2006) posit, in specific settings bilingual parenting can be regarded as 'good parenting' as it can equip children with skills for future educational and vocational success. Consequently, 'the visions of the child's future are the aspired goals' (Rokita-Jaśkow, 2015a: 461). King and Fogle (2006) observe that the notion of 'good parenting' and consequently family language policies nowadays are shaped less by culture-specific 'notions of what makes a "good" or "bad" parent, mother or father' but more by the market, which sets popular trends to follow and provides tools for their realisation. In respect of FL learning, this refers to the dramatic increase in the production of CDs, videos, flash cards and books aimed at babies or toddlers and marketed at parents who want their children to acquire an L2 as well as the proliferation of parenting guidebooks and the blogosphere (Bello-Rodzeń, 2016). This trend seems to be globally pervasive, making child bilingualism less elitist and yet putting pressure on many parents and their children to start learning a FL very early, thus creating a unique educational project out of child rearing which recognises child achievement as proof of good parenting.

In postmodern times, parents consider very early FL learning as a form of investment in their child's future (Carmel, 2022; Rokita-Jaśkow, 2015a) in the form of linguistic capital (Bourdieu, 1991; Bourdieu & Passeron, 2000) upon which other forms of capital, such as social, cultural and financial, can accumulate. Plurilingual competence, and knowledge of lingua franca English in particular, is recognised as a form of habitus (Bourdieu, 1991; Kramsch, 2020), a tool for social mobility and financial success in the globalised world, particularly by parents who do not have high FL competence themselves and who thus ascribe their failure to the lack of it. They therefore often see a very early start in a FL as a possible means of securing higher social status for their children and the realisation of their own unfulfilled aspirations.

Parental aspirations to teach their children English from a very early age are particularly strong in monolingual educational settings, such as Poland, China and South Korea, where there is little access to the language outside school, a high value is placed on education and the country's economy has abruptly opened to the global market (cf. Chapter 5). Curdt-Christiansen and Wang (2018) argue that FLP is embedded in macro-policy, the broader sociopolitical and cultural context which prioritises certain linguistic varieties over others. They provide an example of China, where among a multitude of local languages and dialects two languages are particularly promoted in the educational system, that is, Putonghua and English, which directs parental agency to endorse the development of the same languages in their children, particularly in middle-class families living in the city. Since education is highly valued, parents are additionally driven by the desire to meet the demands of the educational system. Parental agency was noted, first of all, in providing exposure to the English language at pre-primary level, that is, prior to obligatory instruction, through the employment of English language tutors, sending children to English-learning centres and providing them with books, cartoons and mobile apps. All of these activities indicated strong management strategies in family language planning and orientation towards multilingualism. Additionally, Curdt-Christiansen and Wang (2018: 16) argued that by demonstrating agency in promoting English, parents subscribe to 'the reproduction of language hierarchy' because parental beliefs 'become fuel that forms or strengthens an ideology which perpetuates language functions and values in a given society' (Curdt-Christiansen & Wang, 2018: 16).

The aspirations of parents of preschool children in respect of FL achievement have been the focus of a study conducted in Poland by Rokita-Jaśkow (2013a). It is notable that in this country after the fall of the Iron Curtain in 1989 and the opening of borders to the West, many opportunities for social advancement in newly opened branches of international companies were open to those who knew FLs, and consequently exponential career advancement was possible. Thus, it is not surprising that in this context many parents saw similar opportunities for social advancement for their children thanks to FL knowledge. The study (Rokita-Jaśkow, 2013a) identified that the major motive for enrolling children into very early formal instruction was the recognition of the worldwide popularity of English and its usefulness to future career prospects, as well as perceived child superiority over adults in FL learning. Also the 'earlier [one starts FL learning], the better' was the most commonly held belief, followed by the expectation of achieving native-like competency in the future. As for the future use of FLs, the parents indicated career opportunities and travel. Thus it can be concluded that the desired identity for their children was the 'bilingual and bicultural' (Byram, 2008) or an 'international' identity (Yashima, 2002).

The FL learning situation in South Korea is similarly competitive (cf. Chapters 5 and 6) and parental involvement is deemed necessary to provide an advantage to their children. In this respect it has been found (Kiaer et al., 2021; Lee et al., 2021) that many Korean parents, and especially mothers, ascribe their parenting style to external factors such as competition and comparison to others. While some Korean mothers reported that they realised that pressure on preschool children to learn English instead of playing did them no good, they admitted that they felt they had no choice if they did not want to be left behind as mothers who were not good enough. Neither did their children have a choice as they had no one to play with as all the other children were attending classes.

Parental attitudes and views on FL learning impact children's attitudes towards learning a FL (Butler, 2015b; Jin *et al.*, 2016). Choi *et al.* (2019) investigated Korean mothers' motivations and the corresponding impact on their preschool children's (aged 3–5) interest in English. The results showed that where mothers demonstrated strong integrative motivation for English culture, this impacted positively, enhancing their level of involvement in FL learning activities with their children in the home, such as reading books, singing songs, doing finger-play or chanting, using the internet and communicating in English. They spent more time on FL play with their children and in consequence boosted their children's interest in the FL. However, if the mother's motivation for her child's FL learning was mainly instrumental, she was less likely to provide for additional language learning activities at home. Interestingly, no relationship was found between the mother's integrative motivation and the child's interest when the child was sent to private lessons and the mother was not involved in additional home language practice. This finding shows that FL education in preschool years is mainly motivated intrinsically and that formal education may not sufficiently provide for its development, whereas the home environment, in which there is a close emotional bond between parents and children, can do so.

These findings imply that in order to raise the child's interest in the FL, mothers have to instil in their children an additive bilingual identity. This is a strategy that some parents, assuming 'non-native parents' bilingual development (Murphy, 2014; Romaine, 2000), attempt to achieve (King & Fogle, 2006; Rokita-Jaśkow, 2010; Szramek-Karcz, 2016). Such an approach is nowadays morally and ethically questioned as prioritising Anglophone culture over local culture and, especially when one does not have direct access to it, can have other detrimental effects on a child's identity, sense of belonging, learning literacy and future socioemotional development (Curdt-Christiansen, 2016; Lee *et al.*, 2021). This issue poses an ethical dilemma as it promotes a move away from the use of the mother tongue. Through linguistic practices, parents, and mothers as main caregivers in particular, pass on to the child the family's social, cultural and linguistic capital (Rokita-Jaśkow, 2015b), the system of values and traditions that they ascribe to, and which they would like their child to adopt, in this way shaping their child's identity. As Curdt-Christiansen (2016: 706) argues, 'conflicting ideologies within families arise from the parents'/caregivers' different concerns about their children's identity, education and survival in a competitive society'. For this reason, it is now generally recommended that rather than aiming for the new target language identity, parents should aim for a bi-cultural identity. Consequently, during home FL learning activities, code-switching and translanguaging should be the norm where the whole linguistic repertoire of the child is used without derision of the mother tongue.

On transition to elementary school, when FL is learnt more formally, the role of parental involvement undergoes change and impact. Fan and Chen (2001), in their meta-analysis of the available studies, noted that in the case of school-aged learners, parental involvement understood as homework assistance does not impact learning results as much as parental aspirations and expectations in reference to the child's future achievement, as measured through global educational achievement rather than scores from particular subjects. While it would be an overstatement to refer this conclusion directly to pre-primary learners, it does provide an argument for further consideration. It is possible that parental aspirations which are evident since early childhood may reflect parenting style and general outlook on the child's upbringing, and in this sense may impact child education in the long run, including FL education. However, one should be cautious with long-term predictions, as parental aspirations are also modified depending on the child's ability and school achievement. One explanation for this fact is that low-achieving children may be more likely to ask parents for assistance. Alternatively, higher-achieving students are more independent and autonomous learners and thus can achieve more when they take responsibility for learning on their own (Fan & Chen, 2001; Wilder, 2014).

3.1.3 Partnerships with educational institutions

Ongoing teacher-parent communication appears to be necessary for the child's overall growth in respect of education in ECEC and primary schools. This seems also to be relevant to FL education. As a result, parents not only remain informed of what material is being introduced in formal FL instruction but may also provide reinforcement and practice of the material, which consequently provides increased exposure to the language and provides the child with greater confidence in language use. However, not all parents know how to provide for language practice nor how to create a cognitively stimulating and authentic language-conducive FL environment. Therefore, they need teacher guidance on how to introduce language-related activities (Rokita-Jaśkow, 2019).

Few studies demonstrate the possibilities of kindergarten-home collaboration, probably because in many contexts such instruction is often conducted as an extramural activity and often by itinerant teachers who feel less attached to the educational institution and are less available to parents. More opportunities for communicating can be conducted in a FL afternoon course conducted by the FL instructor, often in the company of parents. This may explain why delegating FL instruction totally to the institution may turn out to be less fruitful for child achievement, especially if the instruction is scarce and the parent has no knowledge of the material taught and to be practised. Communicating with the FL teacher about the child's progress has been found to be the most frequent type of parental involvement with an institution (Rokita-Jaśkow, 2019).

Since not all parents are prepared to assist their children in FL learning, they need to be informed of its benefits and how to do it. Based on Epstein's framework of parental involvement, an innovative programme of creating partnerships between kindergarten and parents has been offered by Korosidou et al. (2021) in a Greek kindergarten where in a programme called 'PIECE' (Parental Involvement for Engagement, Cooperation and Empowerment) they aimed to enhance teacher–parent–child collaboration in their children's English language learning by means of multimodal activities. Based on parents' needs analysis, the researchers offered the following support to parents:

- to enhance parenting, they offered educational software and online resources;
- to enhance communicating, two-way parent-teacher exchange of information on the child's progress was established via interactive journals and reports;
- to enhance partnership, parents were involved in school events, often in the role of leaders;
- to enhance volunteering, parental presence was valued by the teachers; and
- to enhance learning at home, parents were given a digital storytelling game to play for their children at home.

The effectiveness of the programme was measured after its completion by means of parental surveys, focus group discussions and the teacher journal. The findings showed that the programme met parental expectations and that home literacy practices in a FL became more frequent. Both parents and teachers reported that 'guidance, support and material provided to parents concerning some "recipes" for enhancing their children's learning was recorded as being of particular importance for children's progress' (Korosidou et al., 2021: 118). It was also found that contrary to the apprehension that parents may not be willing to become involved in collaboration with the institution, cooperation turned out to be fruitful and enhanced levels of engagement among parents who were not proficient in the FL in the support of the initial stages of their children's FL learning. Yet, it must be acknowledged that solid engagement and preparation of teachers is a prerequisite for successful collaboration with parents.

An international 'Bilfam' project (Pirchio et al., 2014) is yet another example of successful collaboration between educational institutions and parents in Romania, Slovakia and Italy. Its aim was to promote FL learning in the family by means of the narrative format, the programme based on storybook reading and related activities, such as songs, drama and play. Parents involved in the project chose a FL to teach their children and were assisted in this endeavour with guidance, training and materials such as ebooks, puppets, speaking Voki Avatar, Dinobooks, Bilfam video, H&L board game, video-conference and Dino quiz and access to the Bilfam website with downloadable materials. The data obtained after eight months of project duration, through parental survey as well as analysis of blog posts, showed that parents developed positive attitudes towards teaching their children a FL and were willing to engage in it even if they were non-proficient in the FL, on condition that they were provided appropriate materials.

The necessity of teacher-parent collaboration turns out to be of particular importance in times of crisis when the continuity of teaching may be threatened as, for example, during kindergarten closures due to the COVID-19 pandemic (Giannakopoulou, 2021). The author presents an example of successful collaboration with parents in respect of FL learning which consisted in teacher instruction and parental engagement in child learning by working on the material provided by the teacher, organised around a theme of one storybook handled over a week. Each day the teacher presented different material online, for example reading a storybook aloud, while the parents were expected to assist the children during the online sessions which were both teacher-led and conducted in groups. At times, the parents were found talking to the teacher instead of the child, who may have been too shy, as well as performing selected activities such as colouring and then conducting 'show and tell' tasks in which the children were supposed to talk about their pictures. The collaboration, although enforced by an emergency, made parents more confident that they can conduct language learning activities with their children, even if they are not proficient in the FL.

Parents seem to be more involved with the educational institution at primary level, where the learning results of the child may matter more for future child achievement. For example, in the Turkish context (Kalaycı & Öz, 2018) parents perceived their involvement as a factor that can make a difference to the children's achievement and reported to maintain regular contact with their children's teacher by, for example, consulting the teacher when the child struggled with homework or thanking the teacher for what they had done for the child to show appreciation, trying to follow the teacher's teaching strategies at home and so on. The involvement also consisted in keeping a close eye on the child's learning, supporting in times of failure or frustration and providing help with Turkish equivalents of English words when needed. Assistance, rather than explicit teaching, is therefore an example of involvement in relation to lower primary school children. The older the children become, the less parents seem to be involved in both child learning and collaboration with the institution.

3.2 Factors Affecting Parental Involvement

From the aforementioned studies it seems there are three significant factors that could be distinguished as impacting parental, and maternal in particular, involvement, namely their *FL proficiency* (often an indicator of their overall educational level), their *attitudes* to FL learning (Choi et al., 2019), as manifested in ideologies/beliefs and aspirations (Carmel, 2022; Kiaer et al., 2021; Lee et al., 2021; Rokita-Jaśkow, 2015a), and their *socioeconomic status* (SES).

In most societies it is mainly mothers who predominantly take care of their very young children's development, spending most of their time with them. Mothers, as main caregivers, are therefore major sources of linguistic input for their children's speech development. Likewise, mothers speaking a FL fluently can address their children in a FL equally easily, thus supplying additional exposure to a FL as well as easily being able to engage their children in FL play and conversations. In order to acquire a FL, children need both to observe and participate in FL discourse (Cameron, 2001). An illustration of this argument can be found in a study by Unsworth et al. (2019) conducted on Dutch preschoolers aged 2;0–3;0. Acquiring Dutch and another language showed that quality of linguistic input, understood as 'the extent to which parents undertook language and literacy activities with their children (input richness)' (Unsworth et al., 2019: 1204), as provided by highly proficient mothers, was the most salient factor in facilitating child L2 development and that it was more relevant than the amount of exposure provided or the nativeness of the parent. In other words, native-speaking parents did not necessarily provide a higher quality of L2 input than proficient non-native parents.

For this reason, the maternal level of FL proficiency seems to be of utmost importance in facilitating maternal involvement in their children's FL learning. This factor may also coincide with a higher level of education as especially in dominantly monolingual societies a FL is mainly acquired through formal education. This, in turn, may be indicative of positive attitudes to the FL, as it requires a lot of stamina and hard work to attain high proficiency in a FL in low-input situations.

Parental FL proficiency has been found to correlate with the level of parental involvement and children's learning outcomes at primary and pre-primary levels in diverse contexts. For example, Unsworth et al. (2014) found that mothers' FL proficiency (English) was a factor that predicted children's performance in productive vocabulary tests. In a different setting, Lindgren and Muñoz (2013), conducting a study in seven European countries within the ELLIE project (Enever, 2011), found that parental proficiency in the FL (English) and its use in their professional work was a strong predictor of the learner's performance in FL listening and reading, mainly due to the fact that parents were able to provide opportunities for language practice both at home (by engaging in FL interactions with the child, playing films and music in the FL or using the internet) and by providing opportunities to use the FL abroad.

Similarly, in reference to pre-primary children, Rokita-Jaśkow (2019) found that parental levels of FL knowledge can determine the type of activities used at home. Parents with lower levels of English proficiency were more likely to use repetitive techniques aimed at rote learning of class material, whereas parents who had a fluent command of English were more likely to engage in authentic communicative activities which demanded fluent language use such as pretend play. They were also more inventive as regards types of home tasks, offered their wider array, and used scaffolding in their FL discourse directed at children. Similar mediatory practice of parents was noted in the studies of Prošić-Santovac (2017) and Scheffler (2015), who were linguists themselves conducting research with their own children. These findings suggest that high-quality FL input, as manifested in discourse strategies and communicative tasks/games, can only be provided by parents proficient in a FL. It must be noted that parental involvement in a FL, similar to the bilingual development of very young children, is most successful with parents who are proficient in the FL themselves.

Similar results were found in a Singaporean context, where English is an official language of education, by Sun and Ng (2021) who noted that preschool children's early English reading skills were related to the quality of teacher-child interactions at school as well as the quantity and quality of maternal involvement at home, which consisted in reading books to children and correlated to the mothers' level of education. By contrast, in a study conducted among very young Chinese learners of English, Sun *et al.* (2015) observed that mothers, even though they possessed a bachelor's degree level of education, estimated their FL proficiency as rather low and for this reason were unwilling to speak to their children in a FL. They were concerned they would instil in their children wrong pronunciation models. Nevertheless, the mothers' levels of proficiency were found to correlate with children's FL productive vocabulary levels. Input quality was measured as the additional amount of media exposure at home and proved to be a significant predictor of productive and receptive vocabulary and receptive grammar. This finding suggests that even less-proficient parents can have an impact on their children's FL achievement by providing additional sources of FL input, such as books, cartoons, Tablet games and apps and smart-pen readers, and supervising their frequent use in order to maintain the child's interest and motivation. Media use at home as an additional FL input was particularly predictive of the development of receptive grammar for which large quantities of varied input are necessary. However, the authors also emphasised that advice to parents as to the selection of appropriate level materials and ways of working with them should also be provided.

Maternal involvement in their children's FL learning is strongly emphasised and expected in South Korea, where *Mommy-English*, that is, providing exposure to the FL through mother-directed speech, is gaining in popularity and supported by parental guidebooks, lectures and so on (Choi *et al.*, 2019), even with mothers non-proficient in English. To this aim there is a prolific educational market supplying tools which will enable FL teaching at home. Choi *et al.* (2019) investigated their impact in reference to parental variables such as level of education and financial capital (SES). They found a statistically significant relationship between both the mother's level of education and age and the frequency of using educational media, such as books, CDs and DVDs. Additionally, fathers were found to be equally supportive and their level of education similarly correlated to the amount of media use, which was interpreted as typical male interest in media entertainments. Internet and smartphone usage were not mentioned as the children were too young (below 3;0) to be exposed to them according to the parents. Furthermore, it was found that parents living in the suburbs used media more frequently than parents living in the city. This fact was interpreted as being due to less accessibility to instruction in the suburbs than in metropolitan areas and thus a desire to compensate for less classroom contact through greater use of media. Additionally, the researchers found no correlation between financial capital and media use, which led the authors to conclude that it did not matter how much money the family possessed but how much they were willing to invest in the FL education of their children. In the Korean context, it was found that families were willing to spend a substantial amount of money to guarantee their children good English learning opportunities. A similar trend has been observed by Jin *et al.* (2016) in China. Through a large survey study they found that parents gave their children a lot of financial as well as emotional support so that they could learn a FL. Yet, regional differences were observed between a large city, Shanghai, and a peripheral town, Mudanijang. In the former environment, parents were more willing to enrol their children in extracurricular activities, whereas in the latter they relied more on home learning.

All these findings show that if there is little opportunity for FL exposure in the community, media exposure can constitute a supplementary means of contact with a target language. Yet, in order to access the relevant media, the family must have sufficient financial resources. This is where the family SES can play a role as a mediating factor in access to educational resources, such as media, learning materials and services (Butler *et al.*, 2018). Parents of higher SES can first of all afford private FL tutoring or extracurricular classes as in Korea (Park & Abelmann, 2004) or private ECEC education (Rokita-Jaśkow, 2013a) where children are offered more languages than just English, and at an earlier age. Additionally, a FL teacher may be employed on a regular basis, thus providing the children with more frequent contact with the language. It is also assumed that there is closer supervision of the quality of teaching by a private kindergarten headteacher (Rokita-Jaśkow, 2013a) who is accountable to parents as clients.

Higher SES parents typically possess higher levels of education which enable them to find better-paid occupations. A higher level of education, may, but it does not have to (cf. Butler & Le, 2018; Sun et al., 2015), correspond to a high level of FL proficiency although FL knowledge is an indispensable competency in a knowledge-based society based on meritocracy. Also higher SES parents may live in bigger cities, thus having better access to quality FL instruction. Location, however, is not a determining factor, as higher-SES parents may also live in the suburbs and may compensate for a lack of available instruction through home learning and the purchase of educational resources (Rokita-Jaśkow, 2013b).

The SES of the family, and particularly that of mothers as the main caregivers in the early years, has been found to have an effect on the development of the L1 (Hoff, 2006; Hoff & Laursen, 2019). Depending on the status of the family, mothers have been observed to use different conversational styles towards their children, which in turn transferred to the linguistic output of their children. For example, mothers from lower-SES families tended to use more directives, while middle- and upper-class mothers tended to talk to their children more expressively. As a result, the preschool children of the latter have developed wider vocabularies and produce syntactically more complex sentences (Huttenlocher et al., 2002). Furthermore, this effect is particularly relevant in reference to *first-born children* (Fenson et al., 1994) who are an only child in their early years, as the language addressed to them is usually the same as language directed towards adults. Also, in reference to first-born children, mothers can dedicate more *time* to their children's upbringing. It follows that mothers can be more actively involved in their children's home FL learning by playing, reading and so on with their children if they have more time available.

The SES of parents may also be a factor in how parents formulate aspirations in relation to their children's achievement. As Rokita-Jaśkow (2015a) found, lower-SES parents were more determined to become involved in child FL education and practices, which put pressure on the children. Parental involvement consisted of rote revision of class material. The parents perceived FL proficiency as being key to social mobility, securing better life prospects and higher social position, whereas higher-SES parents, who were also proficient in the FL and thus possessed appropriate linguistic capital, were more relaxed about their children achieving this goal as a FL was already a part of their home routine and their children were socialised to it from an early age from hearing it in their surroundings (cf. Rokita-Jaśkow, 2015b). Thus, they trusted that through plurilingual practices their children would gradually develop plurilingual competence. They also realised that other factors, such as networking, would also play a role in their children's success, rather than merely command of the FL.

Similarly in a Korean setting Choi *et al.* (2020) found that the family's SES correlated with maternal educational level and their beliefs about the necessity to start teaching English as a FL in kindergarten as well as their supportive practices at home. In other words those mothers provided more varied learning at home activities which resulted in positive children's attitudes to learning English while lower-SES mothers put more pressure on children, generating children's anxiety and negative attitudes to learning English.

To sum up, from a poststructuralist perspective, SES can be interpreted as a 'set of social practices and questions of access and agency, of privilege and power' (Butler, 2018: 2) and as such constitutes an important component of identity. Middle-class parents seeking to secure their children a similar SES to themselves treat FL learning as an important investment and are willing to allocate a substantial amount of financial, cultural and linguistic capital towards that goal.

3.3 Parental Agency

Parental agency seems to play a crucial role in the decision regarding the choice of language(s) that are promoted and handed down in the family. Curdt-Christiansen and Wang (2018: 2) define parental agency 'as the capacity of parents to make decisions about what measures should be implemented to promote or discourage the use and practice of particular languages based on their understanding of the functions and perceived values of the languages'. Parental agency has been observed to manifest itself in the provision of resources and language learning activities and in the implicit socialisation into language, which is evident through parents' own literacy practices and language modelling and verbalised ideologies about the necessity of learning a FL.

As regards very early FL education, it is self-evident that the learners have very limited contact with the language, ranging from one hour per week to a few hours per day (in the case of bilingual/immersion-type kindergartens). Therefore any learning outcomes will be limited, corresponding to the amount of input obtained by the child in each of the languages (Pearson *et al.*, 1997). Furthermore, if the amount of exposure to an L2 is less than 25% of total exposure time to all languages available, the acquisition of the L2 is likely to be minimal. One possible way to increase the amount of exposure to the FL is through additional contact with language provided at home. Parental involvement, understood as home learning, communicating with an institution which will instruct parents in appropriate learning strategies and parenting, is aimed at providing additional affordances for child FL learning. Parents need to show agency in this respect by being personally engaged in the very young child's learning process, as delegating FL learning solely to the institution limits FL learning opportunities. Also, it does not give parents an insight into what learning material is being introduced, which inhibits further practice.

Parental agency is also indispensable because in very early formal FL learning, child agency is lacking. This is due to the fact that child learners typically all share the same mother tongue and have no motivation to make a cognitive effort to learn a new code of communication. This lack of child agency has to be compensated for, either by the teacher' agency (in kindergarten) or parental agency at home. Parents can achieve this by engaging in various language-related activities, which will help both to revise classroom material and expand the available input. They can also engage children in FL discourse, that is, by addressing them and prompting responses in a FL. Needless to say, such activities should bear the characteristics of play, as it is only play that can engage the child's attention and interest and motivate them to use the FL. Parents of lower FL proficiency can also show agency by communicating with the institution, which should in turn provide instruction and guidance for parental activities to be conducted at home in a FL.

Summary

This chapter focused on parental involvement as a necessary precondition of FL achievement by a very young child, understood in line with Epstein's (1996) framework as learning at home, parenting and communicating with an institution. Parental involvement is an outcome of an interplay of proximal and distal features of the family environment. It denotes a bilingual parenting style, a form of habitus, in Bourdieu's (1991) terms. The factors that have been recognised to mediate parental involvement are parental (especially maternal) FL proficiency, paternal level of education and the SES of the family. To a minor degree, living location can also play a role. Parents who are less proficient in a FL can be successfully trained in ways of supporting home learning and can be equally involved in the process. Finally, parental agency in the process of very early FL learning is highlighted, which can be manifested by parents of both high and low FL proficiency. Other factors, like SES and living location, play a less determinant role.

4 Exosystem: The Affordances of the Linguistic Landscape

This chapter emphasises the saliency of the linguistic landscape that creates space and possible affordances for acquiring language(s) early, either because of historical factors or because of the current sociopolitical situation of a country, and so indicates the value and status of foreign language (FL) learning. These, in turn, seem to be influenced by two dominant trends, that is, globalisation and the neoliberal economy. The former grants a special status to mainly one language, that is, English, while the latter denotes privatisation of the educational market and competitiveness between individuals. These trends manifest themselves in the semiotics of the linguistic landscape, in media, in the digital world, in the mission of educational institutions and so on, which both arise from and influence the general public's beliefs. This will also manifest in the educational market that arises in response to those beliefs and aspirations and, consequently, the choice of languages offered for instruction.

4.1 Globalisation, Englishisation and Neoliberalism as Drivers of Early FL Education

Individuals learn foreign/second languages for various reasons and in varied conditions. One common way is when they live close to each other and/or come into regular contact with speakers of another language, either because of living in a multilingual society or when engaging in trade or other occupational contacts with outsiders. In such cases, individuals are motivated to learn another language for utilitarian reasons, albeit often they do so implicitly by interacting with those speakers. Typically, members of the minority ethnolinguistic group learn the dominant/official language of the ruling state if they wish to advance on the social mobility ladder through education. These are just a few reasons why many societies and individual speakers are multilingual, to take the example of countries such as Spain or many countries in Africa and Asia, where both indigenous and official languages are spoken as a result of colonial heritage.

Another way of becoming multilingual is *displacement*, that is, relocation. At the end of the 20th century, the landscape changed due to increasing globalisation, manifesting itself in international trade and the transfer of production out of the home country, which, in turn, generated the international transfer of money and goods. The advent of the internet has facilitated these processes, enabling fast communication and financial transfers around the globe. Consequently, these processes have also created many jobs in global corporations which further precipitated increased migration in the search for better employment and life opportunities. Rapidly growing international transport accelerated the process even further.

Notably, communication across the globe and in global institutions has been conducted via English, which has become a global language, a new lingua franca that has permeated all spheres of life, the phenomenon referred to as Englishisation. This status has been ascribed to the English language mainly as an outcome of the global political and economic power of the United States as well as historic colonial/imperialist British policy (Crystal, 2003). As a result of the latter, English is still an official language, in addition to the indigenous language, in many former British colonies. This means that English is spoken worldwide by millions of people as either a first or second language in countries that Kachru (1992) referred to as the Inner Circle (i.e. United States, United Kingdom, Canada, Australia, New Zealand) and in the countries of the Commonwealth, referred to as the Outer Circle. However, what is also notable due to the process of globalisation is the increasing number of English speakers and learners in countries in the so-called Expanding Circle, that is, where English was previously not spoken at all and which were often monolingual. The omnipresence of English in many spheres of daily life in all countries around the globe, as Gorter and Cenoz (2023: 252) point out, is visible 'in the visual scenery of the streets of urban centers, not only in the names of shops, brand names, advertising slogans, and other commercial and private messages, but also in official information directed at tourists and visitors'. They underline that '[t]he proliferation of English itself is a factor that is not only caused by but also helps to strengthen globalization' (Gorter & Cenoz, 2023: 252).

Globalisation has changed the role of nation states to the benefit of supranational organisations and institutions, such as the World Bank, International Monetary Fund and European Union, among others, which have had to open their labour markets. State 'sovereignty is increasingly limited as regards the movement of capital, markets, and information across frontiers' (Williams, 2010: 219). These organisations also set the rules for the new neoliberal economy (as opposed to the industrial), which is characterised by deregulation on the one hand and consumer demand on the other. These principles boost market growth by increasing the competitiveness of services and individuals and increasing consumer expenditure.

Consequently, globalisation has stimulated an increase in demand for highly skilled intellectual labour, which includes a high level of proficiency in English language skills. This new kind of neoliberal economy that has been introduced is also referred to as the 'knowledge economy' (Williams, 2010) in which immaterial labour has an advantage over manual labour, which is easily replaceable and transferable to other parts of the world. Desired skills in postmodern knowledge-based society that guarantee innovation and progression are creativity and education, as '[t]he creation of wealth is held to increasingly involve the generation and exploitation of knowledge' (Williams, 2010: 10). The neoliberal economy has practically done away with traditional class society. With the fall of class society, upward social mobility seems to be possible based on individual competences and merit. Meritocracy thus has become the driving force of human development, which consists in the belief that one can achieve vocational (and consequently financial) success through achievement.

The neoliberal economy also offers limitless opportunities for individual growth. The vast array of options underlines freedom of choice as a new form of personal identity. Additionally, mass media and electronic communication tools create identities to aspire to. One such promoted identity is that of citizen of the world, travelling across borders, working from different parts of the world, which is possible if one deprives oneself of the ties of local identity, that is, association with a nation or an ethnolinguistic community. One can adopt a type of international posture (Yashima, 2002) or a bicultural identity (Byram, 2008) in which cosmopolitan identity absorbs national identity, but in order to function well within it one must possess plurilingual skills and, first and foremost, knowledge of the global language, English.

These phenomena, that is, globalisation, meritocracy, neoliberalism and Englishisation, have laid fertile ground for early (English) language learning, which has become a commodity in this context. This is because the possession of unique yet desirable skills provides an advantage in the competitive occupational market. In times of globalisation, such a role is also attributed to knowledge of other FLs, also referred to as plurilingualism (Byram, 2008; Coste et al., 2009) or linguistic multicompetence (Cook, 1991). Thanks to plurilingual skills, an individual can be more mobile in search of better life prospects and seek employment outside of their own country. In addition, employment opportunities are provided by global organisations, which have opened branches in less-developed countries. These opportunities are discerned by parents aspiring to the middle classes who desire their children to participate in the global economy in the hope that this will lead to upward social mobility. Likewise, middle-class parents desire their children to maintain their middle-class status. This issue has only recently been identified in applied linguistic research (cf. Block, 2014). However, it must be recognised that motivation for language learning is primarily social, denoting aspirations, future visions of one's Self (Dörnyei, 2009; Rokita-Jaśkow, 2015a) and determination to achieve set goals.

Thus, FL competencies can be regarded as a form of symbolic capital (Kramsch, 2020) that is strived for by some and gives privilege and advantage over others. It is a capital that is willingly transferred from one generation to the next (Bourdieu & Passeron, 2000 [1977]; Rokita-Jaśkow, 2015b), it refers to linguistic practices that are distinctive of a social class and is also referred to as linguistic capital. In the past, individual multilingualism, in European policy referred to as plurilingualism (Coste *et al*., 2009), was characteristic of aristocratic circles (Komorowska, 2014) in which code-switching into French or English was a social practice and a means of social exclusion of those who did not possess such skills. Thus it was regarded as a class marker. Nowadays, plurilingualism, notably including the knowledge of lingua franca English, appears to be a competence that allows one to obtain middle-class jobs and is an indispensable skill for progression within the meritocracy.

Privileged individuals are naturally multilingual as they grow up in multilingual environments and acquire their languages relatively quickly. Yet, this opportunity is not available to all and in all settings. In specific dominantly monolingual settings, such as Poland, Hungary, Japan and South Korea, exposure to other languages is severely limited for historical and political reasons. Thus, languages are acquired mainly through formal instruction. Therefore, starting to learn languages earlier may prolong the overall duration of language learning up until the completion of education and entering the job market. Furthermore, ambitious middle-class parents educating their children in the private sector opt for their children to learn not just one FL, but several. Thus, not only 'the earlier, the better', but also 'the more, the better' seems to be the guiding motto for designing the educational path of young children (Rokita-Jaśkow, 2013a). Early FL education is treated as an investment that will reap rewards in the child's future occupational prospects (Rokita-Jaśkow, 2015a).

This trend is typical of societies that have found means of development in education, such as Central Europe (Rokita-Jaśkow, 2013a), where countries of the former 'satellite Soviet hegemony (Poland, Czechoslovakia, Hungary, Romania, Bulgaria) have experienced increasingly neoliberal linguistic, cultural, and economic invasion and dependence' (Olszewska *et al*., 2022: 54), characterised 'on a macro-level by economic privatization, decentralization, political pluralism, mass migration, and social and legal transformation. On the micro level, there has been the formation of civil societies, changing beliefs and identities of communities, a decrease in state support, a growing sense of uncertainty, and transformation of peoples' everyday lives, mentalities, and customs'. (Olszewska *et al.*, 2022: 54)

Similar underpinning ideologies for the so-called 'English fever' or 'English frenzy' have been noted in other countries and described as an awareness of globalisation (Park, 2009), internationalisation in Japan (Kubota, 1998) or a way of 'revitalisation and reintegration of the world systems' in China (Hu & McKay, 2012: 345) and implied limitless vocational opportunities for which meritocracy was vital. As Hu and McKay (2012: 354) observed, in East Asian countries, 'English language education is seen as a public good that can benefit the country and, consequently, its citizenry'.

This interest in very early FL instruction has given a boost to the educational market as is evident in the proliferation of usually private FL learning/teaching institutions, the production of materials (coursebooks, interactive whiteboard/computer software, etc.), the development of assessment tools and finally teacher development courses, dedicated to teaching languages to the very young, and again associated materials, projects, workshops and conferences. Indeed, early language learning has become a real industry.

This trend is evident in countries that are dominantly monolingual or where access to English in the real world has been limited. For example, in South Korea FL teaching essentially takes place in the private sector with an economic value estimated to amount to $15 billion in 2005 (Park, 2009) and constantly increasing. The enterprises include afternoon classes, cram schools (Korean: *hagwon*), English-only teaching methodology, hiring private tutors who are often native English-speaking teachers, learning materials for kids, conversation service and certified testing (Park, 2009). An unprecedented practice is sending young primary school children abroad (Song, 2011) either in the company of one parent or even alone, or to an English-speaking village for those who cannot afford to send the child abroad (Park & Abelmann, 2004). The so-called English villages are campsites to which learners come for a certain period of intensive language training. They are immersion-type settlements where only English is present in the public space, for example on signs, in shops and so on, and only English is used in spoken interaction. The benefits of attending such camps consist of maximised exposure to the target language and lower expenses compared with travel abroad; however, the downsides to this solution include the development of a negative attitude towards the mother tongue, Korean (Park, 2009). In other East Asian countries (Butler, 2015a), such as China or Japan, private FL education, including at kindergarten level, is also growing but not on such a scale as in South Korea.

In Poland, very early teaching of FLs on a private basis has been popular since the 1990s on the same principle as in South Korea, that is, abolishing the dominance of the occupying power, here of the Soviet Union, and opening up to westernisation and neoliberalism. This political breakthrough created fertile ground for setting up private enterprises offering early FL instruction and competing against each other on the grounds that they offer more and better by providing immersion-type instruction, such as bilingual kindergartens. In time, private kindergartens decided to offer more and earlier, that is, introducing not just one but two FLs from a very early age, such as French, Spanish, German or even Chinese (Rokita-Jaśkow, 2013a). The choice of languages usually depended on the availability of teachers who also sought new employment opportunities. Neoliberal trends were also evident in the growth of FL afternoon classes where instruction was held totally in the target language, such as Berlitz® or Helen Doron® international chains of schools. They usually operate on a franchising principle and have patented their teaching solutions such as principles, methodology used and accompanying materials, which can comprise textbooks, learning apps and audio/videos for home use. The variability and wide choice of these aids demonstrate that FL courses have become branded learning packages. Two decades later, such enterprises have also proliferated in home-grown branded school chains such as *Early Stage®*, *Teddie Eddie®* and *Mała Lingua®*. They compete with each other by offering teacher guidelines and the whole package of materials (books, workbooks, flashcards, worksheets, additional book readers, etc.) embedded within story-based, task-based/content and language integrated learning methodology, as well as the use of ICT. This indicates that there is still a niche in the educational market to be filled (Rokita-Jaśkow, 2022).

4.2 Affordances of Linguistic Landscapes

In line with van Lier's (2004) ecological theory and the theory of affordances (Aronin & Singleton, 2012), multilingual society can provide language affordances for the growth of individual multilingualism. Language affordances are 'affordances through the realization of which communication via a language or languages or the acquisition of language or languages is possible' (Aronin & Singleton, 2012: 318). This means that a child growing up in a community where various languages are used in the public space is exposed to them frequently from birth, thanks to which they become accustomed to auditory and visual input in those languages and consequently acquire their rudiments prior to formal instruction. In the case of English, this is clearly much more common in former British colonies where English has retained its status as the language spoken by the elite. In such settings, for example India and Malta, children are exposed to English prior to schooling via signs in public spaces and/or discursive practices (e.g. media and other people speaking). English-medium instruction (EMI) is practised there more commonly than in monolingual countries as there is a tradition of such teaching and good availability of fluent speakers of English. Thus, the linguistic landscape of society can impact the development of a child's multilingualism as it provides opportunities for multilingual encounters before formal instruction. This is how van Lier (2004) describes the role of the exosystem.

The linguistic landscape (henceforth: LL), in its classic definition, denotes 'the visibility and salience of languages on public and commercial signs in a given territory or region' (Landry & Bourhis, 1997: 23) and refers to 'public road signs, advertising billboards, street names, place names, commercial shop signs, and public signs on government buildings' (Landry & Bourhis, 1997: 25). The LL is often used synonymously with or subordinately to the term 'semiotic landscape', which pertains to the perception of written language forms as signs as well as the interaction of language with visual signs and public spaces, thus emphasising their multimodal character (Gorter & Cenoz, 2023). By studying the LL, one can learn which languages are present in a given society and their status and function. For this reason, one can observe how many minority languages strive to become visible in the public space, on the one hand, while noting the pervading omnipresence of the global language, English, on the other. The state typically regulates the presence of particular languages, that is, their promotion or suppression by its policy legislation. Thus, the LL provides information about societal beliefs, ideologies, policy and politics, historical past and future aspirations. Additionally, signs visible in public spaces can serve as a prompt to stimulate discourse which is the scope of geosemiotics (Scollon & Scollon, 2003) and enables 'researchers to fully analyze public discourse not only in terms of linguistic content but also ethnographically in their physical, social, and cultural contexts' (Al Zidjaly, 2014: 3).

The linguistic/semiotic landscape can also become a resource in educational settings in the form of so-called schoolscapes, defined as 'the school-based environment where place and text, both written (graphic) and oral, constitute, reproduce, and transform language ideologies' (Brown, 2012: 82). It constitutes the physical and social setting in which teaching and learning take place and which thus includes signs, symbols, images, textbooks and artifacts inside classrooms, and also in the entrance, foyer, corridors, in a school museum, and the curriculum, as well as spoken languages. (Gorter & Cenoz, 2024: 343)

Consequently, schoolscapes, which refer to the use of multilingual signage in public places, inform attendees about educational aims, attitudes and local policies about languages present in the school premises (Pesch, 2021). Possible functions of schoolscapes are: *informative*, that is, refer to school management (inform of locations of places by signposting), *classroom management* (inform/remind of the class language to be used; tag children's places/belongings, etc.),

Figure 4.1 Visibility of English in the linguistic landscape of Krakow, Poland, as portrayed in the names of kindergartens

teaching about subject or language (by labelling objects in the FL or reminding of valuable phrases in the FL for class communication); and *symbolic*, that is, conveying teaching values (e.g. with slogans) and developing intercultural and language awareness. Other functions include: announcing collective events (e.g. the English theatre, English song festival, etc.), provision of commercial information (e.g. school trips) and decoration (Pesch, 2021).

Clearly, educational institutions, such as kindergartens, can create natural opportunities for children to experience and cherish the multitude of languages present in their surroundings. Finding space for displaying various linguistic signs and cultural artefacts is associated with recognising and acknowledging children's rights to use their mother tongues in the educational institution while at the same time aiming to enable them to acquire the dominant language of the host society. This is a typical solution in multilingual societies like Norway (Christison *et al.*, 2021; Krulatz, 2022) and Luxembourg (Kirsch, 2018; Kirsch & Mortini, 2023). There, the use of children's varied linguistic repertoires is seen not as a threat but as an asset that enriches pedagogical practices on the one hand while fostering children's multilingual development on the other. Children who grow up multilingually are treated with tolerance in relation to linguistic errors. The multilingual lens adopted towards multilingual children acknowledges that each child develops linguistically at a different rate and that multilingual competence is a composite of various languages known to various degrees, usually none of them to the proficiency level of a monolingual speaker. Acknowledging all children's languages also complies with the tenets of ecological theory (van Lier, 2004), which emphasises adopting a critical stance towards the existing monolingual macro-order and calls for equitable and inclusive language pedagogy.

An example of such use of schoolscapes is provided by Pesch (2021) in her study of two kindergartens in Norway and Germany, through which she noted that the visual linguistic environment can serve as an essential learning resource as 'discourses on multilingualism in the semiotic landscapes are negotiated, transformed or contrasted in oral communication practices' (Pesch, 2021: 365). By the same token, schoolscapes are regarded as critical semiotic resources, that is, areas in which different languages are present in visual and written form, such as greetings, flags and country symbols, which show children and their parents the status of various languages in an institution and so can encourage or inhibit multilingual discursive practices. Likewise, the classroom decor can promote multi/plurilingualism and, in consequence, increase children's interest in languages and motivation to learn them. Thus, as Szabo (2015) argues, the discursive analysis of schoolscapes enables an understanding of which language policies are shaped and enacted, whether mono-, pluri- or multilingual.

Additionally, the presence of various languages in the public space denotes that the pedagogy of translanguaging is accepted and fostered in a given environment (cf. Kirsch & Mortini, 2023). García (2009: 45) defined translanguaging as 'multiple discursive practices in which bilinguals engage to make sense of their bilingual worlds' as distinct from code-switching or translation, which presuppose 'languages or codes as separate entities' (Cenoz & Gorter, 2024: 156).

In line with these functions of schoolscapes, kindergartens that are mainly monolingual but aspire to foster plurilingualism among children can utilise target language(s) signage to increase language exposure and implicit acquisition in the target language. Having other languages on display can foster the development of children's language and cultural awareness, which is also conducive to developing communication skills in the FL (Coelho et al., 2018; Lourenço et al., 2018). It can also facilitate the implicit acquisition of written language forms as the children frequently encounter them in their surroundings. The labels on objects in the target words enable the child to associate the oral and written forms of words and recognise them while seeing them outside class, which prepares children for the development of literacy in the FL by global word recognition. Additionally, as Cenoz and Gorter (2024: 334) argue, through schoolscapes children can acquire not only lexicon but also elements of syntax and pragmatics, for example using forms of politeness that are explicitly posted on display. Thus, the LL truly affords the children's multilingual development.

The LL can also inspire educational projects, especially among literate children, through which language awareness can be raised. Roos and Nicholas (2019) provide an example of a project conducted among lower primary school children in the German context. The children were given a worksheet with instructions to observe and photograph instances of English words on various objects both at home and in streetscapes. The children provided not only a wide variety of evidenced examples but also observed that it is not necessary to leave the house to encounter the examples of English (Roos & Nicholas, 2019) as it is standard on toys, clothes, accessories, books, newspapers and food products. The children also commented that English nowadays was not totally foreign to them. English was frequently encountered in such areas of life as sports, fashion or digital media, which is yet another sign of globalisation, and many words were similar to German words. Comments like these show that analysis of LLs contributes to the development of children's language awareness as well as 'the learners' beginning sensitivity to connotational meanings of English' (Roos & Nicholas, 2019: 104), which manifested itself in the perception of English words as 'more cool' and modern than German words and thus preferably used.

While to date, no similar project or study has been noted in reference to pre-primary children, as in investigating the LL some degree of literacy in the target language is required, it is conceivable that paying attention to frequently encountered words in the target language, such as brand names (e.g. Coca Cola, McDonalds, etc.) both in streetscapes and in the home can facilitate global word recognition and in this way can prepare children to acquire literacy in that language. Additionally, analysing the LL can be used as a teaching strategy, that is, learners can be asked to find word labels that they have learnt in class in the outside world and bring the cut-out or photo of them to an English as a foreign language class. Additionally, a translation activity can be conducted in which the children will be made aware of how the names of well-known cartoon characters (e.g. *Peppa Pig, Bob the Builder*) are translated into their languages and consequently what the equivalent words in the two languages are (i.e. *Pig, Builder*). Such a teaching approach may equip children with a strategy for looking at similarities and differences between languages, which develops their metalinguistic awareness for future implicit language acquisition.

4.3 Affordances of Screen Media

One more salient aspect of globalisation is the omnipresence of English not only in the public space but also in the media and digital world, which includes the internet and its various resources, such as films/cartoons and computer and smartphone games, to which access is given to younger and younger children. According to the latest data, internet availability in European households has increased steadily and it is now accessible in over 80% of households. Countries such as the Netherlands, Norway, Finland and Luxembourg have achieved a remarkable 98–99%

internet penetration rate as of the year 2022 (Statista, 2023, https://www.statista.com/statistics/1246141/eu-internet-penetration-rate/). Globally, it is estimated that the internet is used by a population of 5.4 billion as of 2023 and that this represents an increase of 100% on the previous year. This number denotes that 67% of the global population has access to the internet. The highest number of users are in China (1,050 mln), India (692 mln) and the United States (311.3 mln), followed by Indonesia, (212.9 mln), Brazil (181.8 mln), Russia (127.6 mln), Nigeria (122.5 mln), Japan (102.5 mln), Mexico (100.6 mln), the Philippines (85.16 mln), Egypt (80.75) and Vietnam (77.93 mln) (https://www.statista.com/statistics/262966/number-of-internet-users-in-selected-countries).

Apart from the internet, technology accessibility is seen in cartoon-associated branded toys, which may be programmed to use the characters' voices, thus teaching snippets of the target language, such as greetings, counting and so on. Although these products originated in the United States, they are now distributed globally, with both positive and negative impacts. They are beneficial because their widespread popularity increases the amount of informal contact with the English language in the environment and so enables its incidental acquisition. It is also harmful because it reinforces the hegemony of the English language at the cost of other languages (cf. Phillipson, 2003).

As a result, children are exposed to English in many settings before formal instruction and acquire some English vocabulary incidentally, without overt presentation (Kuppens, 2010). Also, learners who start learning an FL in primary school have been found to know English words at the onset of formal courses, which must have originated from prior exposure to language in the media. This typically concerns children aged 10–12 in various European settings where foreign TV programmes are subtitled or captioned rather than dubbed. Supportive evidence for incidental lexical and syntactic acquisition as well as language skill development, such as second language (L2) listening and reading comprehension among primary learners, has been found, for example, in Scandinavia (Puimège et al., 2019; Sylven & Sundqvist), Flanders (De Wilde & Eyckmans, 2017), Spain (Lindgren & Muñoz, 2013; Muñoz and Tragant, 2023), Chile (Avello & Muñoz, 2023) and Croatia (Erk, 2021). While initially TV and music were the primary sources of providing out-of-school audiovisual input (Lindgren & Muñoz, 2013), over the last two decades the possible media has expanded to include computer screens, tablets and smartphones, by means of which learners can have access to various internet content, mainly films and games (Butler, 2018) and story apps (Kolb & Brunsmeier, 2019).

However, depending on the mother tongue spoken, children can benefit from media exposure differently. Implicit FL acquisition has been found to take place with a greater likelihood of success in those settings where there is close proximity between languages, resulting in, for example, a high number of cognates and syntactic similarity. Since English is a Germanic language, evidence of its implicit learning has been most profoundly found in young Swedish and Dutch teenagers compared with their peers in Spain, Italy, Poland and Croatia (Lindgren & Muñoz, 2013) and showed that 'cognate linguistic distance became the strongest predictor followed by exposure and parents' use of FL at work' (Lindgren & Muñoz, 2013: 117) for FL listening and reading.

Learning a new language can be challenging, especially when the language one is trying to learn is from a different language family. Countries where languages spoken are significantly different at phonological, structural and lexical levels, such as Korean, Japanese, Chinese, Hungarian or Slavonic languages, can be particularly challenging for learners. This is also why many learners struggle with mastering English, even if they receive early and long-term instruction. For the same reasons, speakers of those languages can differently use multilingual affordances available to them in their environment.

4.3.1 Viewing

In reference to very young children, the most common sources of extramural English are watching films/cartoons and gaming. As regards films, early 1980s research has focused on whether children can acquire language merely from passive exposure to audiovisual input. It has been found that in the case of young L2 learners, for example minority Spanish speakers in the United States, this was possible if children watched an educational programme, such as *Sesame Street®*, rather than a non-educational programme directed at native-speaking children. The reason for this is that educational programmes scaffold meaning to the child by means of sound and repeated exposure of keywords and phrases, using attention-direction and ostensive (providing definition) cues (Neuman et al., 2019) in the same manner as a parent can do to adjust to the child's current zone of proximal development (ZPD) (Vygotsky, 1985), that is, their current language ability level. This impact of educational media has also been explained by the Dual-Coding theory (Paivio, 1986), which claims that when information is encoded through auditory and visual channels simultaneously, it is better understood and retained for later recall.

A specimen study that illustrates these assumptions was conducted in the US context by Wong and Samudra (2021), who investigated the impact of media viewing on L2 acquisition in pre-primary (aged 0–5) dual language learners, that is, those who are still developing their mother tongue at home, which is different from the dominant language in society, and who need to learn the L2 in preparation for schooling. Educational media can enrich the young child's L2 vocabulary in the early years, influencing learning success at the onset of schooling.

The study comprised 44 dual language learners aged four to five, who watched six episodes of the *Sesame Street®* series. The results of the study showed that 'visual scaffolds help reinforce vocabulary concepts, deepen vocabulary knowledge, and support oral language development in young DLLs' (Wong & Samudra, 2021: 97) only when sounds and images are presented simultaneously, as was found with the use of an eye-tracker. Yet, they also recognised that children could be at different levels of ZPD and therefore differentially benefit from TV viewing. They identified children's L2 proficiency and parents' L2 proficiency/ability to provide L2 exposure at home as key contextual factors that impact the quantity of vocabulary acquisition.

The *Sesame Street®* series is a classic example of an educational series that can support preschool children's language and behavioural development that has lasted over a decade (Fisch *et al.*, 1999). In the European context, a similar impact is ascribed to the *Peppa Pig®* series, which, though designed for native-speaking children, can be equally comprehensible and beneficial for FL learners, mainly due to the scaffolding cues. Although no cross-sectional study is available to support this view, the case study data provided by Prošić-Santovac (2017), Scheffler (2015), Kokla (2016) and Alexiou (2015) confirms the potential of *Peppa Pig®* and other cartoon series for FL/L2 acquisition in respect of lexical, syntactic and communicative development. However, it must be acknowledged that parental assistance and scaffolding the meaning to the child, as well as further reinforcement through play, may be vital for the child's outcomes of viewing the series. The justification for the suitability of the *Peppa Pig* series for pre-primary FL learners was provided by Scheffler *et al.* (2021), who, analysing a corpus of language used in eight episodes, found that the language used in the series corresponds to 80% of the top 2000 most frequent words in the British National Corpus. This finding suggests that the phrases used in the series present authentic use and are frequently repeated in the series and in the real world, enhancing their retention. In reference to this finding, Kokla (2016) found that preschoolers could deduce the meaning of formulaic phrases from merely watching other series. The older the children were, the more phrases were acquired, that is, five-year-olds learnt more than four-year-olds and six-year-olds more than five-year-olds, which suggests that older children, and those more proficient in a FL, benefit more from TV viewing.

On the whole, studies on the possibilities of language acquisition from screen viewing are pretty positive in respect of educational media, which scaffold new meaning, thus allowing the child to comprehend it. Yet, younger children benefit more if parents assist them as language mediators. Older (literate) children can benefit from viewing more independently by using captions/subtitles as additional cues for learning new meanings from visual context. Additionally, as Teng (2023) in his study of Chinese primary school learners found, it may be the phonological working memory (WM) resources that can influence incidental vocabulary acquisition in the beginning stages of FL learning because 'phonological WM is mainly responsible for the temporary recall of acoustic information (i.e. word recognition, speaking fluency, and reading comprehension)'. This finding boils down to the fact that pre-intermediate learners need to store auditory, visual and semantic information in their WM storage at the same time, which may be too heavy a cognitive burden for the developing child, whereas older and more advanced learners have been found to encode auditory information automatically and rely on previous lexical knowledge to a greater extent when acquiring new words from viewing (Montero Perez, 2020).

4.3.2 Gaming

Gaming seems to have similar potential for language acquisition as it becomes a more and more prominent part of the life of many children who can play games on any technological device (such as computers, game consoles, tablets and mobile phones), at any time. Sundqvist (2016) ascribes the popularity of gaming to the following features: games make learners active and critical, they allow learners to participate in activities that would otherwise have negative consequences in the real world, they provide repetitive practice of language that is not boring, they enable gamers to take on new projective identities and they enable the obtaining of explicit information in real time. In the case of young learners, these are mainly the so-called 'serious games', that is, games specifically designed for instructional purposes that can impact language development (Butler, 2018). However, citing Wouters *et al.* (2013), Butler (2018: 309) noted that even serious games work best '(a) when they were supplemented with other instruction such as explicit practice and follow-up discussions, (b) when multiple training sessions were offered, and (c) when learners played games in groups' (Butler, 2018: 309).

Similar to viewing habits, gaming has been observed to be beneficial, for example in the Netherlands, among dual language/bilingual learners, that is, immigrant children who attempt to acquire an L2 in naturalistic contexts (Segers & Verhoeven, 2003). Segers and Verhoeven (2003) also suggest that kindergarten children may need a certain minimum number of encounters during the game to learn a new word, perhaps due to their less-developed memory and information-processing capacities.

One notable study which includes very young children, that is, aged four to five, as well as other age groups, was conducted by Butler *et al.* (2014) with a view to identifying features of serious games that appeal to young learners as well as their impact on FL achievement as measured in the course mock tests and an online standardised test at A1 level in Japan, called *Jido-Eiken*, in which some tasks also followed a similar game format. The results of the study were mixed, that is, not all games seemed to have an impact on the achievement scores. Also, slightly higher results were achieved in the mock test than in the standardised *Jido-Eiken* test, which may indicate that the learning achievement concerned only those words that were frequently practised in the games. These findings identified features of games that are particularly appealing to players and that should be taken into account by game developers, that is, 'optimal cognitive demand (challenge), elements that evoke curiosity (mystery), and elements that give learners control over the outcome and lead to autonomy (control)' (Butler *et al.*, 2014: 273). Furthermore, it was observed that at the age of approximately ten, gender and age differences in the frequency of playing games and their choice are marked, while younger children seemed to remain unbiased to the type of games.

Children become more avid solitary players when they have acquired literacy (and typing) skills, which allow them to read and interact with other players and which may also lower the cognitive load on their working memory as the children rely on previous language knowledge while decoding the meaning of new words. It remains a consistent finding throughout various studies in various contexts globally and concerning children of various ages (Erk, 2021; Jensen, 2017; Kuppens, 2010; Suh *et al.*, 2010; Sylvén & Sundqvist, 2012) that boys are more avid gamers than girls and play more frequently. This fact impacts performance in language proficiency tests, particularly text comprehension and vocabulary scores. The reason for this may be the fact that in comparison to girls who prefer games that simulate the natural environment, such as *The Sims®* (Sylvén & Sundqvist, 2012), boys tend to prefer massively multiplayer online role-playing games (MMORPG) that involve action and communication with other players and that are deeply engaging. Consequently, boys may 'pay more attention to the language of the games they play and couple their gaming with walkthroughs of gameplay on YouTube as well as other clips' (Jensen, 2017: 14), which enhances the amount of FL input they receive. Thus, the potential of gaming is particularly relevant for boys in primary school FL learning.

As regards pre-primary learners, they are more likely to play simple single-player games either online or in offline apps, typically following the drag-and-drop format, which practise vocabulary and simple phrases. This also means that solitary gaming for entertainment purposes is unlikely to impact a very young child's FL acquisition as the mediation of an adult is necessary, facilitating scaffolding of meaning to the child and monitoring the frequency of game use.

However, the presence of English in various types of digital games can constitute an affordance for L2/FL acquisition in the long run as children demonstrate some knowledge of English before they start instruction in that language. A study conducted among 176 3rd-grade Icelandic children aged 8;0 at the onset of formal English instruction (Lefever, 2010) seems to prove this point. The children studied showed a relatively high ability on tests of FL reading and listening, and selected children showed command of conversational skills that allowed them to freely participate in a conversation in English, 'expand on the topic, use fillers, take turns, and backchannel' (Lefever, 2010: 10). Moreover, these were mainly boys who excelled at communication skills, although girls could comprehend the language directed at them. Following these tests, parents of the ten best-performing children were interviewed and admitted that their children had regularly watched films and programmes on TV which were neither subtitled nor dubbed, such as *Cartoon Network* or *Animal Planet*® and also regularly played computer games, such as *FIFA football* or other PlayStation® games. These findings show that pre-primary children do benefit from out-of-school exposure to English, provided that this exposure is massive. It must also be recognised that the benefits may not be immediately apparent at pre-primary age but will become apparent in later school years. This may indicate that the child FL learner needs to internalise the new language and their competency is primarily visible in the receptive skills.

4.4 Agency and the Linguistic Landscape

Krompák (2023: 6) observes that 'the semiotic landscape of the education institution plays an agentive role in the representation of linguistic and cultural diversity'. For this reason, we can also distinguish a non-human type of agency, addressed as agency of space (Krompák, 2023) or agency of landscape (Malinowski, 2008), in reference to the exosystem. In particular, this agency is visible at the intersection of semiotics, discourse practices, and policy within a particular community or educational institution. The LL shows its agency by promoting a particular language variety; it can denote both the appreciation of multilingualism and children's varied languages, as shown in the schoolscapes of institutions in multilingual societies. It can also denote the promotion of the global language, English, which is particularly prevalent in monolingual societies such as South Korea and the digital world, where publishing in English is omnipresent. The landscape can involve individuals in mutual interactions, serving as a tool for pedagogical practice, that is, encouraging translanguaging and trans-semiotising in multilingual schoolscapes or, in the latter case, providing sources of additional FL input for implicit acquisition. Therefore, agency of the LL can be understood as an endorsement of particular language varieties and language practices and as providing affordances for plurilingual growth.

Summary

The LL, both the natural and the digital world, can afford children the opportunity to develop their plurilingual skills irrespective of, or in addition to, formal instruction as it provides sources of linguistic input.

This particularly concerns English, the most widespread language globally. However, not all children can benefit from these opportunities to the same extent. Regarding pre-primary children, incidental language (mainly lexical) acquisition is possible, albeit limited, but mainly if the language input is adjusted to the child's ZPD by repeated exposure and explicit scaffolding of educational media or the mediating parent. The observation coming from relatively short-term studies shows that very young children are less likely to benefit from solitary video viewing or gaming, firstly, due to cognitive limitation of the developing child (particularly working memory), and secondly, because they are usually not allowed by parents to spend a lot of time on such activities.

However, some long-term benefits of frequent exposure to a FL out of school can be observed among primary school children, even before they begin formal FL education, particularly in some European contexts, where there is widespread access to undubbed TV and the internet and where there is relatively close linguistic proximity between the mother tongue and English.

It is therefore not surprising that in many monolingual settings, where such conditions do not exist, the striving for more exposure manifests in the desire for an earlier start in a FL and an increase in the amount of contact with a FL through formal, often extramural and private, instruction.

5 Macrosystem: Early Language Learning Policy and Planning

The decision whether a foreign language (FL) is part of the pre-primary/ early childhood education and care (ECEC) curriculum is made by top-level decision-makers, such as ministries of education, which constitute the educational macrosystem in Bronfenbrenner's (1979) terms. This chapter aims to briefly outline the reasons behind forming early FL learning policies in Europe and beyond and to exemplify the implementation of such policies in a few selected countries. The agency of institutions and individuals in early FL policy implementation is also addressed.

5.1 An Early Start in a FL in European Language-in-Education Policy

In many countries, language policy, as well as language-in-education policy, also referred to as language planning, is introduced as a top-down directive of the state to 'regulate the use, learning, revival, maintenance or revitalization of a particular linguistic variety' and is defined as the 'process of organizing and managing language policies and practices to influence language use and ideologies' (Olszewska, 2022: 54). Consequently, language policy and language-in-education policy impact the status and prestige of a particular language in a given society, which languages are in use in a specific state and which languages are learnt.

As discussed in Chapter 4, globalisation and neoliberalism have particularly favoured one language, that is, English, as a language of global reach, the phenomenon which is also referred to as 'English fever'. It is this language that is of most benefit in the global labour market and is in most demand to be learnt by adults and youngsters alike, particularly in countries that have been predominantly monolingual (such as South Korea, post-Soviet countries; cf. Olszewska *et al.*, 2022) and where the state determines which languages are to be learnt. A global interest in early and very early FL education is one type of response to this demand, rooted in the common, yet unfounded, belief, 'the earlier one starts to learn an FL, the better' (cf. Chapter 6), thus assuming that an earlier start will lead to a better/native-like FL competence in the future.

As a result, early FL policies seem to be an outcome of two major forces: top-down governmental decisions and bottom-up initiatives arising in response to neoliberal trends, that is, both private educational enterprises and parental aspirations (Rokita-Jaśkow, 2013a). According to Spolsky (2004), there are three significant components of language policy: language planning and management, which manifest themselves in the legislature and directions for governing bodies; language ideologies, which are discursive practices pertaining to language(s) that are promoted in the public space; and language practices, that is, events and activities organised to achieve policy goals. Language policy can manifest itself explicitly, for example in official regulations in written form, and implicitly, in linguistic actions such as the promotion or suppression of certain linguistic varieties, as is often the case with ethnic minority languages.

Language policy and language-in-education policy have mainly been the focus of interest of the European Union (EU). The reason for this is that the basic concept behind the creation of the European Union, whose official motto is 'Unity in diversity', is the integration of European countries, which is to be achieved through mutual understanding, social cohesion and democratic citizenship (Council of Europe, 2006). Through its various institutions, such as the Council of Europe, European Commission and European Centre of Modern Languages (ECML), and their documentation, the EU outlines its primary policy directions. On the one hand, it aims to value and promote EU member countries' linguistic and cultural heritage, particularly by promoting, protecting and even revitalising endangered minority languages, such as Breton, Basque and Frisian. On the other hand, it aims to develop the EU market into one of the leading and thus most competitive markets globally. To reach this goal, FL competence of EU citizens is key.

At this point, it must be emphasised that 'plurilingualism' is a term introduced in European documentation to denote knowledge of several FLs by an individual, which also coincides with the linguistic representation of multicompetence (Cook, 1991). At the same time, multilingualism has been referred to as the presence of several languages in a given territory. Both plurilingualism and multilingualism have been endorsed in European language policy (ELP) because all language speakers have equal rights, and to build a knowledge-based European society that is socially cohesive, using and learning all languages should be supported (European Parliament, 2000). This richness of language diversity has also been valued as a counterbalance against the linguistic imperialism of English (Phillipson, 2003). Yet, since over time the perception of the EU has moved towards a representation of globalisation, the English language seems to have taken the lead in popularity when it comes to its use in public spaces and education.

Several measures, policies, actions and educational projects have encouraged plurilingual development in European citizens. Early language learning was supposed to fit in to the process of lifelong language education, the need for which was first voiced in the *European Commission White Paper* (1995), which stated that

> proficiency in several community languages has become a precondition if citizens of the European Union are to benefit from the occupational and personal opportunities open to them in the border-free single market. [...] Languages are also the key to knowing other people. Proficiency in languages helps to build up the feeling of being European with all its cultural wealth and diversity and of understanding between the citizens of Europe. (*European Commission White Paper: Teaching and Learning – Towards the Learning Society*, 1995: 67)

This statement set out the direction of further language education policy as laid out in policy documents, such as Recommendation R (98) 6 of the Committee of Ministers to Member States Concerning Modern Languages (Council of Europe, 1998), which, among others, recommended starting FL learning below the age of 11 as well as lifelong learning of languages, and called on member states to ensure continuity of language teaching across different educational levels. The announcement in the Lisbon Presidency Conclusions (European Parliament, 2000) of the year 2001 as the European Year of Languages, and the henceforth celebration of a European Day of Languages, emphasised the value of language diversity and language learning in European language education policy and planning. This positioning was marked by further policy acts, such as the Barcelona Presidency Conclusions (2002), which called for the introduction of two FLs in EU member countries' educational systems as early as possible. Following these decisions, a policy guidebook (Beacco & Byram, 2003; revised Beacco, 2007) was issued to aid governments in reforming their educational systems. Furthermore, the second interim Action Plan of the European Union for the years 2004 to 2006 focused on the early learning of FLs, emphasising linguistic as well as cognitive and affective benefits, such as awareness and appreciation of one's own and other cultures. As a result, in most EU countries at least one FL has been introduced below the age of 11. Subsequently, the Lifelong Learning Programme (2007–13) was announced, which as stated in article 1, aimed to 'contribute through lifelong learning to the development of the Community as an advanced knowledge-based society, with sustainable economic development, more and better jobs and greater social cohesion, while ensuring good protection of the environment for future generations' (European Commission, 2006: n.p.). These goals were to be attained by endorsing 'interchange, cooperation and mobility' (European Commission, 2006: n.p.) between education systems of EU members at all learning levels from pre-primary to the third age, emphasising the inclusion of all types of learners, that is, of varying socioeconomic background and ability. Thus, pre-primary FL learning conforms to this concept of lifelong learning of languages.

A decade later, another policy guidebook was issued, recommending the introduction of FL learning at the pre-primary level, as the title had it: *Foreign Language Learning at the Pre-Primary Level: Making It Efficient and Sustainable* (European Commission, 2011). In this handbook, the goals of very early foreign language education were restated, pointing to the benefits in the linguistic, affective, social and cognitive domains:

> Opening children's minds to multilingualism and different cultures is a valuable exercise in itself that enhances individual and social development and increases their capacity to empathise with others. ELL activities in pre-primary settings can be an enriching experience and bring considerable benefits. They are instrumental in enhancing competences such as comprehension, expression, communication, and problem-solving, enabling children to interact successfully with peers and adults. They can increase powers of concentration and strengthen self-confidence. As young children also become aware of their own identity and cultural values, ELL can shape the way they develop their attitudes towards other languages and cultures by raising awareness of diversity and of cultural variety, hence fostering understanding and respect. (European Commission, 2011: 7)

The same policy guidebook officially stated that to reduce inequalities in language learning opportunities at the outset of children's educational careers, early FL instruction should become a part of the compulsory ECEC curriculum. This solution would meet the criteria indicated in the handbook, that is, those of *equity, quality, consistency* and *continuity*. If early FL instruction is available to all children in the compulsory curriculum, teaching will become consistent (identical) across different institutions; thus, a similar quality of education will be provided and continuity of learning on progression to the next level could be guaranteed. Furthermore, the guidebook advocated for the support of all stakeholders involved in early FL learning, such as educational authorities, experts and teachers:

> tailored education programmes; suitably qualified and motivated staff; specific support to schools, staff, and families; and monitoring and evaluation. Education networks can also provide guidance and support in relation to quality, as can the involvement of stakeholders. (*The Pre-Primary Policy Handbook*, 2011: 11)

It is notable that the aforementioned primary policy measures sanctioned what was already happening at the grassroots level, that is, widespread teaching of FLs in the private sector or as innovative didactic projects, both at lower primary (Blondin et al., 1998; Edelenbos et al., 2006) and pre-primary levels, which denotes bottom-up motivations for language policy planning. Furthermore, the conclusions drawn from these overviews of good practice in early FL learning and teaching facilitated the formulation of guidelines for the organisation of the education process and counteracted possible negative consequences of early FL education, such as unequal access to good quality instruction (cf. Chapter 4). For example, a report published by Edelenbos et al. (2006) highlighted that it is not vital that early FL courses should be of substantial duration, but rather that they should be intensive and that continuity of FL learning to the next level should be guaranteed. The authors emphasised that it is natural that the child's linguistic development will undergo fluctuations. Yet, they advocated exposure to FL literacy and prompting towards oracy as early as possible alongside age-appropriate methodology, which included play- and technology-based techniques. The goal of these measures, the authors reiterated, was to arouse children's interest in FL learning and develop attitudes of curiosity, openness and tolerance towards speakers of other languages and other cultures, which in the long term would lead to the creation of social cohesion in European society, a sense of belonging to the European community and provide opportunities for mobility in border-free Europe. The authors also concluded that these policy goals can only be achieved if well-educated teachers of FLs are available, which is yet another indication of the necessity of providing Early Years FL teacher education.

As a result of the 2002 Barcelona policy recommendations of gradually introducing FLs into compulsory education and prolonging the overall length of FL study or lowering the age of starting FL instruction, a steady increase in the number of children learning FLs can be ascertained, which in 2020 amounted to 86.1% of all primary school learners. According to the latest report of Eurydice on *Key Data on Teaching Languages at Schools in Europe* (2023), in most European countries a first FL is introduced from the onset of compulsory schooling, which is between the ages of six and eight, roughly corresponding to primary school level. Moreover, in some countries a FL is introduced at pre-primary level to all children. These are countries where either kindergarten attendance is compulsory or a place in a state-subsidised institution is provided (even if the child does not take up the state-subsidised place). These countries comprise the German-speaking parts of Belgium, Luxembourg and Poland, where an FL is taught to three-year-olds; Greece, where FL instruction is provided to four-year-olds; and Cyprus and Malta, where an FL is taught from age five. At age six, usually the onset of primary education, an FL is introduced in Spain, Italy, Austria, Liechtenstein, Albania, Montenegro, North Macedonia and Serbia (Eurydice, 2023). While, in principle, any FL can be taught, in practice it is mostly English as a language of high international status. English is often chosen in response to parental demand, or 'parentocracy', as Enever (2007) referred to it, which denotes yet another motive for policy planning. The youngest children who are obliged to learn a second FL are in Luxembourg, where FL instruction starts at the age of six. Thus, very early start policies were mainly introduced in central and eastern Europe and Latin countries of Southern Europe, where a language of lower reach was spoken. This concerns predominantly monolingual countries (Poland, Greece, Spain) or those which were also often multilingual (Cyprus, Malta), had more than one state official language and where languages other than the language of school instruction are spoken at home (Malta, Cyprus). Poland and Italy are given as examples where the overall period of language learning has been extended the most. Spain is not mentioned in the Eurydice report (2023), yet a FL is often part of the pre-primary curriculum in selected school districts determined by local authorities. Additionally, it has to be mentioned that in Western Europe, in particular, there is an increasing number of children in the ECEC from migrant backgrounds, that is, they speak languages in the home other than the language of school instruction. A specimen country is multilingual Luxembourg, where over 70% of children come from migrant multilingual families (Kirsch, 2018). Thus, attending kindergarten before school enrolment serves an essential function of preparing the children for education in the official language. The introduction of an additional FL at this level may be a challenge to teachers. Thus, language education policies expressed a need to develop plurilingual pedagogies. Countries approach 'early start' policies differently depending on their historical heritage and social mosaic.

It can be observed from the above that European early language education policy and planning followed Kaplan and Baldauf's (2005) framework of successful language-in-education policy planning as it takes into account the following elements: *curriculum policy*, which means a language is introduced in compulsory school curricula; *access policy*, that is, catering for equal learning opportunities for learners of diverse socioeconomic backgrounds; *personnel policy*, that is, ensuring that well-qualified teachers of young learners are provided; *methodology and material policy*, which means that (re)training of teachers (e.g. ECEC) in child-appropriate methodology as well as appropriate materials should be made available; *resources and community policy*, that is, ensuring that financial support for implementation of the policy is guaranteed; and *evaluation policy*, which pertains to the evaluation of the effectiveness of various teaching programmes although, as will be discussed later, this is the most contentious issue in language policy in respect of pre-primary FL learners.

A specimen country that followed these guidelines while introducing compulsory FL instruction in 2015 is Poland (Rokita-Jaśkow & Pamuła-Behrens, 2019). At that time, the starting age of schooling was also lowered from 7;0 to 6;0, obliging parents to enrol their children in one year of preparatory pre-primary instruction while at the same time introducing FL classes for all children, irrespective of the type of institution they attended (private or state). In consequence, all five-year-olds were included in FL education. The goals of early FL learning were specified and were realistically achievable. As stated in the ECEC curriculum, the purposes of early FL learning were:

> Preparing children to use a modern FL by arousing their language awareness and intercultural sensitivity, as well as building positive motivation for FLL in further stages of education, and in the case of children with intellectual disability – developing awareness of the existence of linguistic and cultural diversity. [Author's translation]
>
> (Ministry of Education, 30 May 2014, point. 895. In Rokita-Jaśkow & Pamuła-Behrens, 2019: 18)

Thus, the goals of early FL learning focused mainly on the affective, that is, raising awareness of the existence of other languages and stimulating motivation for future FL learning rather than achieving native-like/bilingual competency. In terms of attaining linguistic goals, the children were expected to:

> understand simple instructions in a modern FL and react to them, participate in simple games, e.g., musical, movement, art, construction, or dramatic character, use words and phrases relevant to a contest or other activities at hand, repeat rhymes and simple poems, sing songs, understand the general sense of oral stories when pictures, props, movement, gesture, and mime accompany them.
>
> (Ministry of Education, 14 Feb. 2014, point. 895. In Rokita-Jaskow & Pamuła-Behrens, 2019: 19)

Apart from legal directives, a provision for the introduction of this policy was stipulated. FL instruction was to be conducted by generalist kindergarten teachers who were required to obtain formal qualifications/certification of FL knowledge at B2 level and a postgraduate course in language teaching methodology, which were to be completed by 2020. It is thus apparent that these changes were modelled on the *Pre-Primary Language Policy Handbook* (2011) and were aimed at regularising the early FL learning process as fully democratic and counteracting inequality, as until that time, even in public institutions, FL learning was taught mainly by itinerant teachers to only those children whose caregivers had paid for such additional instruction.

In addition, there were plans to introduce compulsory pre-primary instruction to all four-year-olds in 2016 and three-year-olds in 2017, but due to a change of ruling party these plans were not realised. Still, it is noteworthy that if all children from the age of three years had been provided with compulsory FL instruction it would have met the criteria of equity, consistency, quality and continuity. With the 2017 reform bringing back the onset of schooling to the age of seven, all six-year-old children must attend one year of preparatory kindergarten instruction, where FL instruction is included. Children can attend kindergarten at lower ages, but it is not compulsory. Similarly, it is up to individual institutions if and to what extent FL instruction is provided for younger children, but it should be available to all (Eurydice, 2023). The 2014 policy stipulated that it cannot be conducted on a fee-paying basis.

What follows from the above is that FLs are included in the compulsory school and kindergarten curriculum due to overt policy, often changeable due to political whims, and not as a result of evidence-based language education research. The introduction of these policies is driven by top-down motivations, such as developing a common European *identity* and *ideology* of creating a knowledge-based society and competitive economy, following the taxonomy of Ager (2001). Bottom-up drivers in formulating early start policies also seem to have been considered. These stem from parental desires to enrol children into very early FL instruction, which denote the integration motive to join the international community and instrumental explanation for social mobility thanks to plurilingual competence and knowledge of English. It is this demand primarily that has boosted the private educational market and confirmed that neoliberal trends permeate education (cf. Chapter 4). All in all, European early FL education policy seems to be the outcome of interplay between both top-down and bottom-up motivations as it is not only imposed by politicians but also arises in response to the aspirations of middle-class parents (Rokita-Jaśkow, 2013a), also referred to as 'parentocracy' (Enever, 2007), whereby policy regulates the private market.

Murphy *et al.* (2016), in their overview of early language teaching in the European ECEC context, refer to several countries where an FL is taught within ECEC and the problems faced in its implementation. In Italy, although not regulated by an official policy, similar to Poland, the FL provision is conducted in the form of lessons or awareness experiences by both generalist and specialist teachers who usually have command of the language of between B1 and B2 levels and some training in teaching English to young learners (TEYL) methodology. As a result of such teaching, parental satisfaction levels are generally positive. In the Czech Republic, a lack of qualified FL teachers was observed as an obstacle to providing FL lessons to all children. Thus, it was estimated that only 5% of kindergartens could provide instruction, relying on itinerant teachers. In Slovakia, a major problem was the lack of continuity in primary education. In Cyprus, the only country where an FL was introduced via political acts in 2010 (Ioannou-Georgiou, 2015), no such problems were reported, as motivated and qualified staff were provided. English has a high status in Cyprus because it used to be a British colony. These observations led Murphy *et al.* (2016: 71) to conclude that 'different contexts encounter different issues and hence the notion of "one size fits all curriculum" is unrealistic'.

5.2 Early Language Learning Policies Outside Europe

European language-in-education policy has been the focus of attention as it often serves as a model for policy formation in other countries globally, the phenomenon referred to as 'policy borrowing' (Enever, 2018). Manifestations of policy borrowing can be traced back to applying the Common European Framework of Reference for Languages (CEFR) (Council of Europe, 2004, 2020) scale to language assessment in education systems; global standardisation of exams, which enables their comparability, as in, for example, the Programme for International Student Assessment (PISA) study (https://www.oecd.org/pisa/aboutpisa/); and accountability for learning outcomes. It is also evident in the promotion of 'an early start' in a FL as a policy in many diverse settings globally, for the time being mainly in primary education. Enever (2018) argues that these decisions are purely political, aimed at winning the votes of parents who wish to secure their offspring the best educational opportunities, as there is no empirical evidence for the necessity of an early start in order to achieve mastery of a FL in adulthood (cf. Pfenninger & Singleton, 2017, 2019 and Chapter 6). The global spread of early start policies is attributed to the governance of global institutions, such as the World Bank, the International Monetary Fund, and pan-continental bodies such as the European Union, which by sponsoring educational reforms of local governments influence the direction of those reforms. In this way, global institutions are *de facto* responsible for policy borrowing (Enever, 2018).

Even though both UNESCO (1999) and the EU (European Commission, 2002) recommended that a diversity of FLs should be available in education, including ECEC, due to globalisation and neoliberal processes it is first and foremost the global language English that is taught as the first FL from very early years, at times even at the expense of local languages. Due to the desire for integration with global society, for which knowledge of English seems to be a gateway to better-paid jobs, teaching and learning English, or even in English (English-medium instruction [EMI]), has found a prominent place in the policies of many non-European countries, sometimes to the disadvantage of local languages. In Asia (Hu & McKay, 2012), where English was already widely used in public spaces due to historical connections with the British Empire, most postcolonial states, except for Malaysia (Ali *et al.*, 2011), continued to prioritise EMI in education over local languages. For example, in India, where many local languages are spoken, there is a traditional convention among the elite of using English due to historically belonging to the

British Empire. This view of English as a language of social mobility still persists. However, it is now more related to globalisation and the availability of jobs through English (Graddol, 2010; Enever, 2020), which results in the compulsory teaching of English in a majority of primary schools from grade 1, the expectation of mastering English by the age of 14 as well as the boom in private primary schools where instruction is carried out *in* English. Likewise, despite the fact that there is no policy introducing compulsory FL learning at the pre-primary level, there are numerous private preschools and extracurricular courses attended by middle-class children. In addition, to give their children a head start in that language, some parents decide to speak to them in that language instead of their heritage language (Shankar & Gunashekar, 2016).

Similar trends in overpromoting English over vernacular languages for the same reasons, that is, desire for international integration, have been observed in other former British colonies, such as Singapore (LoBianco *et al.*, 2021; Lim *et al.*, 2010), Hong Kong (Lau, 2020), Cyprus (Ioannou-Georgiou, 2015) and Malta (Mifsud & Vella, 2020). It seems there is a willingness among both parents and policymakers to exploit the language, which already enjoyed high prestige in society and was present in the public space, to the advantage of their citizens on the global market. Notably, in those settings, English is a second language to most speakers rather than foreign.

Zein (2021: 2), in his overview of early language learning policies, observes that except for Indonesia, nearly all 42 Asian countries such as Bangladesh (Hamid, 2010), China (Qi, 2016), Japan (Ng, 2016), Malaysia (Ali *et al.*, 2011), South Korea (Kang, 2012), Vietnam (Nguyen, 2011) and Turkey (Kirkgöz, 2007) have made foreign language instruction compulsory to primary school children, but not pre-primary yet, with the majority of them aiming to develop proficiency in English. To illustrate the 'English frenzy' at pre-primary level in the Asian context, we shall look at examples of kindergarten FL teaching in Hong Kong and South Korea.

Hong Kong is a former British colony that was returned to the People's Republic of China in 1997 but was granted autonomy for the next 50 years. Its population mainly speaks Cantonese as their mother tongue, yet English is introduced in education from grade 1 of primary school. Officially, the Hong Kong government has tried to promote a bilingual education policy whereby citizens would be proficient in oral English, Cantonese and Putonghua and written Chinese and English (Lau, 2020). Yet practically, it uses a laissez-faire approach, which means that it leaves the decision as to which language to choose as a medium of instruction in the hands of the school head teacher, depending on the teachers and resources available (Lau, 2020). The English language has retained its high status among the Hong Kong population, not only because of its colonial past but also because of the instrumental motive of social mobility. Hong Kong remains an international financial centre where English is the working language of communication. There, university education is also available mainly in English (Lau, 2020).

Kindergarten instruction is mainly conducted in the children's mother tongue, yet practically all kindergartens introduce English through playful activities. In 2006, an amendment to the official *Pre-Primary Curriculum* was added, where the goals of second language learning were stated to 'develop an interest in learning English, listen to and understand simple conversations in everyday life, and sing or recite nursery rhymes and employ simple words' (Curriculum Development Council, 2006: 30, in Lau, 2020: 461). It also specified the principles upon which English should be taught, emphasising communicative methodology based on play and opportunities for authentic interaction and diverting from traditional approaches such as dictation or textbook-based teaching. In 2017, in the Kindergarten Curriculum, it was further extrapolated that foreign language teaching should focus on catering to children's 'interest, attitude and confidence towards English and the development of basic English skills' (Curriculum Development Council, 2017, in Lau, 2020: 462).

As Lau (2020) reports, provision for quality pre-primary instruction lies with the specifically designated Language Fund and Standing Committee on Language Education and Research (SCOLAR), which has supported language learning curricula, teacher preparation and recruitment (particularly of native English-speaking teachers [NESTs]) since the 1980s. Regarding the kindergarten sector, it provided substantial subsidies for the training of kindergarten and primary language teachers abroad. In 2007, the Quality English Language Education at Pre-Primary Level project was introduced by SCOLAR, which provided onsite training of kindergarten teachers and assistance in syllabus planning and embraced 290 kindergartens and 800 teachers. In 2015, another programme, the Scheme on Early Language and Literacy Development in Chinese and English Language of Young Children, was launched. It offered professional support, training and resources to teachers. It is evident that even though English is present in the public space and NESTs are available, the Hong Kong government has provided continuous support to non-native English-speaking teachers (NNESTs), pumping a lot of financial resources into the sector, thus investing in the quality of early bilingual language education. This example of pre-primary FL teaching illustrates 'the powerful role of market forces and the influence of multiple stakeholders in policy formulation and implementation' (Lau, 2020: 467). Once space for English in education was reinstated it also introduced considerable measures to cater for quality teaching. However, as reality shows, most kindergartens offer instruction mainly in Chinese to cater to children's socioemotional needs. Form and quality of early English instruction continue to vary across different institutions (Lau, 2020).

In other countries, such as China, South Korea and Japan (Butler, 2015a; Hu & McKay, 2012) early FL teaching at the pre-primary level takes place mainly in the private sector and is a consequence of policy regulation for higher levels of education. South Korea seems to be a case in point. Even though South Korea is essentially a monolingual country and does not have historical connections with the British Empire like Hong Kong, the Korean government has adopted a firm policy of popularising English use and education to such an extent that it even planned to introduce English as another official language next to Korean. Its goal was to strengthen the economic position of Korean firms in the global market. Working towards this goal, in 1997 the Ministry of Education introduced English as part of the Seventh Curriculum for children from grade 3 of primary school while recommending the use of communicative and task-based methodology. In order to encourage teachers to use it, the government accredited 16 coursebooks to be used. In 2001, the Korean Institute for Curriculum designed one coursebook for each level, only to accept a vast array of commercial titles in 2011. Additionally, enormous sums have been invested in teacher education and recruitment of NESTs (Butler, 2015a). In 1997, the government also introduced English into university entrance examinations called the Korean Scholastic Ability Test, thus making English proficiency a form of barrier to the attainment of a university education. This decision had a robust washback effect on the educational market at earlier levels. University education is strongly in demand as it provides a much better professional status, which has consequences on other spheres of life, such as chances of employment in middle-class jobs and marriage with individuals of similar status. The socioeconomic gap between high-status professionals and non-professionals is enormous. Thus, knowledge of English is an objective 'class marker' (Park & Abelmann, 2004). It symbolises 'personal competence, success, and socioeconomic status' (Chung & Choi, 2016: 284). It is thus not surprising that English competency is a desire of many ambitious middle-class parents who want to secure the intergenerational position of their family. Consequently, it leads to massive competition among individuals and boosts the private educational market.

Even though the Korean government has gradually lowered the age of starting early English education, due to which children start FL education at grade 3 of primary school, and has introduced the Teaching English through English (TETE) approach at secondary level, these measures have been regarded as insufficient. In practice, children start learning English earlier than that, either through private preschools or publicly subsidised preschools that all include English education in their curricula (Chung & Choi, 2016: 285). Additionally, there is a buoyant private educational market of English language teaching known as cram schools (*hagwon*) where children can learn English as an extracurricular activity after school as early as five years old, often taught by NESTs (Park, 2009). Equally popular is hiring a private tutor or even sending primary school children abroad, often with one parent or alone, so that they can learn the language in an immersion environment. Those who cannot afford to go abroad can choose one of the so-called English villages, a type of campsite that aims to imitate immersion environments while being situated in Korea. This educational market is estimated to be worth approximately 15 billion dollars (Park, 2009).

The example of Korea shows how top-down decisions have indirectly and in an unplanned manner impacted the educational market. No matter how much investment the government commits, it is considered insufficient at the bottom end of the market. Thus, although policy does not regulate FL education at pre-primary level, it is booming, to the moderate satisfaction and success of both parents and children, as shown in performance in international exams (Garton, 2014). Additionally, as Chung and Choi (2016) observe, top-down regulation negatively affects those who should be responsible for policy implementation, that is, teachers, as they often lack adequate language skills to teach efficiently, which in turn causes their burnout. As Chung and Choi (2016) call it, this policy overload may be a factor responsible for variability in the quality of very early FL teaching.

Likewise, in mainland China there is a fast-growing private market of pre-primary English education despite the fact that since the establishment of the country in the 1950s, 'Chinese education experienced a rollercoaster ride of changing policy directives in FL education' (Bolton & Graddol 2012: 4), with English being interchangeably ejected and revived in the curriculum in parallel to the sociopolitical situation or political direction of the country (Gil, 2016). However, in the 1990s, English regained its position as the major FL due to China's ambition to reform its economy and open up to the world. This was reflected in the issuance of *Guidelines for Vigorously Promoting the Teaching of English in Primary Schools* in 2001, which aimed to provide English education to all children from grade 3 upwards in city, suburban and rural areas. In some bigger cities such as Beijing, Shanghai and Guangzhou, English was already being taught in grade 1. In order to ensure high quality of language teaching, in 2003 the Ministry of Education introduced a standards-based curriculum for English teaching, revised in 2011, and now known as *English Curriculum Standards for Compulsory Education* (Gil, 2016). In order to secure adequate staff, a document titled *Guidelines for Improving the Quality of Undergraduate Teaching* was issued in 2001, which required that EMI instruction should be used for 5–10% of the entire instruction time at the tertiary level. As regards kindergarten level, English is not part of the curriculum, yet English lessons are provided in institutions of major cities by means of songs, games and toys (Cortazzi & Jin, 1996).

In addition, China's government has issued a number of strategies that could be described as soft policies to popularise learning English and strengthen the country's position on the international scene. Examples of such strategies, among others, include: organising English courses, in which 100 basic sentences were taught, in addition to broadcasting TV/radio programmes and sections in newspapers in English, to prepare the public for upcoming international events, such as the Asia Pacific Economic Cooperation (APEC) meeting in Shanghai in 2001. Similar sponsored activities for civil servants preceded the Beijing Olympic Games in 2008 (Gil, 2016).

However, this endorsement of English language learning within the last two decades has been questioned for fear of its negative effect on learning the mother tongue, that is, Chinese, particularly by kindergarten children. This opinion found its manifestation in the prohibition of teaching through English in kindergartens by the Shanghai Education Commission in 2004 under the penalty of subsequent nonacceptance of children by local primary schools. Even though teaching English at the pre-primary level is questioned nowadays, the language has an unquestionable position on the linguistic scene due to its utility in higher education, scholarship, media, business, tourism, literature and creative arts, and not knowing English could act as a barrier to educational and occupational opportunities. However, it is estimated that the percentage of Chinese people who use English daily is relatively low amounting to 7.3%, while those who use it occasionally constitute 23.3% (Wei & Su, 2012). What distinguishes China from, for example, South Korea is the fact that English is mainly taught in the educational system, for which the Chinese government has sufficiently provided. In addition, while not abandoning English, China acts to promote its language on the international scene, for example, through the establishment of Confucius Institutes and cooperation with universities, which may raise some interesting questions about the future of English language learning in that country as it regains its position as a world power (Gil, 2016).

Similarly, globalisation and internationalisation have inclined policymakers to deliberately place FL education on the agenda in South America, which often embraces children as young as five. Since the year 2000, different countries have regularly introduced legislation, educational programmes and initiatives to support FL learning from the beginning of schooling, or even in ECEC. As Banfi (2017: 14) puts it, 'foreign language skills....(in) recent years have seen the most remarkable expansion of coverage in the early years of primary school or even preschool'. Banfi (2017) enumerates educational projects that have been introduced in order to support language learning in various countries, including the programme *English Opens Doors* in Chile, started in 2003 with the aid of the British Council and aimed at providing language courses to teachers via summer workshops. The National Programme of Bilingualism 2004–2019 in Colombia was aimed at children starting primary school (age 5;0) to introduce certification and professional development of language teachers based on the CEFR scale. Additionally, De Mejia (2016) provides examples of projects in Mexico, such as the introduction in 2008 of the National Plan of English for Basic Education, which is the content and language integrated learning approach from kindergarten up to 15-year-old learners (middle school). In Argentina, in the capital city of Buenos Aires in particular, bilingual Spanish-English schools are popular, which use teams of Spanish-speaking (L1) and English-speaking (L2) teachers.

Enever (2019, 2020) portrays Uruguay as a model example of explicit and successful policy planning. It started with top-down legislation (the General Education Law. No. 18,437) in 2008, which aimed to provide equal learning opportunities to all children, irrespective of their place of living, that is, in both rural and urban areas. The government achieved its political aim first of all by equipping every child and teacher with a low-cost laptop and high-speed internet connection. This measure, called the Ceibal project, enabled access to video-conferencing classes in English, broadcast from the capital, Montevideo, or even from other distant countries (e.g. the United Kingdom). This compensated for the shortage of English teachers in Uruguay. At the same time, a platform with teaching resources with instructions on how to use them was set up as an additional endorsement of the local teachers. As a result of these measures, by 2017, 70% of pupils were evaluated to have achieved A2 level proficiency by grade 6. In 2017, the national curriculum reference framework (MCRN) was published in order to track learners' progression. Enever (2020) concludes the project is successful because it focuses on what is achievable and not aspirational and provides institutional support from the onset of project implementation through the publication of the MCRN.

Banfi (2015) attributes the popularity of mainly English language learning not only to policy borrowing, as evident in, for example, applying CEFR scales in measuring language development in Colombia, but also to the endorsement and activity of the British Council or US government, which sponsor educational projects retraining EFL teachers across various countries in South America or provide additional free FL instruction, often via online courses, as, for example, in the Ceibal English project in Uruguay or promote international certification.

A more complex situation can be found in Sub-Saharan Africa. ECEC education is generally less common, yet a steady increase in ECEC policies in various countries has been noted since 2002 (Mrutu *et al.*, 2016). Primary education is commonly conducted in the children's indigenous languages (Bunyi & Schroeder, 2017) . English provision usually starts in primary schools and aims to prepare learners for further education in this language, as EMI is promoted as a language of secondary instruction and university education to integrate learners from diverse ethnolinguistic backgrounds.

5.3 Early Language Learning Policy Implementation

It is an unquestionable fact that teachers play a pivotal role in the implementation of any policy at the micro level. It is dependent on them and their agency whether the goals of early FL policy are realised, that is, whether they provide an intrinsically motivating and language-awareness-raising experience to the children. Teachers need to show willingness to teach very young children and have sufficient knowledge of the target language and the appropriate methodology of teaching the FL, as discussed in Chapter 2.

Teacher agency manifests in their beliefs about early language learning and teaching. These can be shaped by common wisdom, tradition and education. Thus, teacher beliefs show teacher cognition about their subject and impact their practices. As Barcelos and Kalaja (2011: 282) put it, one can observe 'how beliefs develop, fluctuate and interact with actions, emotions, identities or affordances, and how they are constructed within the micro- and macro-political contexts of learning and teaching languages'. Thus, this definition encompasses the ecological view of beliefs, highlighting their interconnectedness with actions/practices and dynamics. Teachers can hold different beliefs in monolingual versus multilingual settings where languages are present in public spaces (cf. Putjata & Koster, 2023). Investigating pre-primary teachers' beliefs may be particularly relevant in contexts where there is an insufficiency of well-trained FL teachers who, therefore, are mainly driven by their own beliefs and teaching experience in their teaching practice. Alternatively, it may be essential to investigate how teachers translate policy recommendations into their daily practice. So far, only a few studies have been noted in that respect in contexts where English is taught as a FL. In a study of pre-primary language teacher beliefs, which was conducted prior to the 2014 reform and official implementation of the FL in the ECEC curriculum in Poland, Rokita-Jaśkow (2016) observed that the majority of pre-primary teachers still held to the popular belief that 'the earlier one starts learning, the better', or believed in the benefit of habituation to language, its sounds, words and syntax, thus expecting long-term pay-off of early exposure to the language. This belief, however, did not affect their teaching. The teachers did not aim to develop in their learners communicative ability in language use by speaking the target language themselves. On the contrary, they exhibited feelings of inadequacy in using the target language. They also showed little awareness of the objectives of teaching very young learners, resulting from a lack of training towards that goal and no connection between their beliefs and practices. Only in respect of intercultural awareness did teacher beliefs find moderate support (above 3.0 on a 5-point Likert-type scale). They were found to correlate with teacher practices, such as organising meetings with foreigners or organising art contests. These findings indicated little awareness of the goals of early FL instruction as stipulated in European policy documents, which could be attributed to a lack of training in early FL methodology as well as the relatively low prestige of the profession: most of the teachers studied were young and treated early FL teaching as a temporary occupation, being itinerant teachers.

In a different context, in Macau, Reynolds *et al.* (2021) conducted a qualitative study on beliefs held by pre-service language teachers in their third year of tertiary education, in which they uncovered existing beliefs about pre-primary language education with a view to modifying future teacher education preparation in Macau and possibly other Asian contexts. The identified beliefs concerned 'beliefs about classroom practice, EFL learners and learning, pedagogical knowledge, teaching, content, goals of language teaching, the role of teaching, subject, schooling, hearsay, self, learning to teach, and the teacher education program' (Reynolds *et al.*, 2021: 13), whereby beliefs about classroom practice, EFL learners and learning and pedagogical knowledge were most commonly held, whereas beliefs about self, learning to teach or the teacher education programme were mentioned only by a few students. In general, the beliefs identified seem to have been influenced by the participants' pedagogical content knowledge, obtained through instruction in earlier years of study, which manifested in their beliefs regarding the necessity of catering to children's well-being and socioemotional learning. However, since they did not have any prior instruction on how a FL is taught or acquired, they based their beliefs in that respect on their knowledge of how the first language is acquired. They emphasised the teacher's job, stating 'they should facilitate EFL learning by providing a "fun environment" in which learners are engaged in play-like behaviors' (Reynolds *et al.*, 2021: 11). Yet, other beliefs were unfounded and unsupported by second language acquisition research. The study's findings identified that the teachers had little knowledge of teaching English as an FL. It was also recognised that pre-service teachers' beliefs are shaped to a large extent by the educational programmes offered by institutions, which in consequence were treated by the researchers as an essential indication to modify courses of study of pre-service ECEC teachers by incorporating courses on language pedagogy.

In relation to the lack of professionalisation of FL teachers of young learners, Nazari *et al.* (2023) drew attention to the low status of EFL teachers of young learners in many other settings, Iran being a case in point. This is a result of varying demands from different elements of the educational ecology, thus causing tension and emotional labour that constitutes a threat to the teachers' emerging identity. One reason for this was the 'discursive alignment that they [the teachers] were expected to develop with YLEs [Young learners of English]. That is persistent behaviours of smiling, openness, and verbal agreement (...) because such behaviours did not necessarily match their internal feelings and understandings' (Nazari *et al.*, 2023: 6). A lack of adequate linguistic and pedagogical preparation to work with very young learners has been voiced in many settings outside Europe, where there is a huge demand for language teachers of young and very young learners (e.g. Alenezi, 2023; Bekleyen, 2011), which poses a major challenge to recruitment to the young learners' teaching profession.

These studies on teacher beliefs indicate that generalist ECEC teachers in various settings have little knowledge of the principles of language pedagogy and need adequate preparation that would enlighten them in this respect and help them to internalise the principles and goals of early FL teaching so that they could be implemented in their daily practice. Early FL teaching also requires professionalisation and adequate status so that it is conducted by dedicated professionals and not accidental itinerant teachers who build no relationship with the children nor invest in their own professional development. To empower teachers and give them more control, it is essential to provide adequate support to enable the achievement of policy objectives. This can be done through teacher development programmes, an example of which is the EAN project in Greece, aimed at teacher training for pre-primary English education (Alexiou, 2021, 2023) and often sponsored by the European Commission.

On a European level, policy guidelines are endorsed and further implemented by the European Centre of Modern Languages in Graz. Upon issuing the *Pre-Primary Policy Handbook* (European Commission, 2011), ECML issued an educational project, the outcome of which was *Pepelino. European Portfolio for Pre-Primary Educators* (Goullier et al., 2015). Like other examples for older learners and teacher trainees, the *Portfolio* is dedicated to pre-service and in-service ECEC teachers who wish to obtain additional qualifications to teach early FL. As a teacher training aid, it aims to raise teacher awareness of how languages are learnt by children and how cooperation with other stakeholders (e.g. parents, ECEC teachers) should be developed, using reflective practice as a significant teacher development technique. Furthermore, it specifies core areas and competencies that the efficient ECEC FL teacher should develop, such as:

I. 'Adopting appropriate behaviour. (Analysing and adapting how to talk to children; Responding positively to linguistic and cultural diversity).

II. Creating a favourable learning environment for children. (Taking account of the way in which young children acquire languages; Organising activities on the theme of languages and diversity).

III. Observing and supporting each child's development. (Taking children's individual needs into account. Supporting the linguistic development of children with other first languages).

IV. Cooperation. (Cooperating with the children's families; Working as a team.)'

(Goullier et al., 2015: 8)

Notably, the *Portfolio* is intended for use in both monolingual and multilingual settings, where children of diverse mother tongues can attain an additional FL. Thus a particular focus is placed on developing teacher intercultural and linguistic awareness to enable teaching of very young learners in multilingual settings.

At this point, it must be emphasised that the aim of retraining ECEC teachers to teach a FL is not unrealistic. Generalist teachers already have adequate psychopedagogical preparation, familiarity with child-appropriate teaching methodology and, above all, motivation to work with young learners. What they need is to learn to perform the same tasks in a FL. Considering that, at least in Europe, many secondary school graduates are obliged to finish school/university with at least a B2 level of language skills (Eurydice, 2023), new generations of ECEC teachers should be prepared to face this challenge. The changeability of teacher beliefs through training was also further confirmed in a study conducted among postgraduate ECEC teachers by means of the *Pepelino* portfolio indicators (Rokita-Jaśkow & Król-Gierat, 2021). Additionally, it should be observed that instead of striving for native-like mastery of a language, which was a pervading ideology for monolingual classrooms, ECEC teachers are nowadays required to meet the needs of children of various heritage languages, as multilingual pre-primary classrooms are also becoming a more frequent phenomenon in a globalised world due to migration (cf. Kirsch, 2018). Yet, this requirement may be challenging to meet by teachers who have been primarily educated to work in monolingual settings, and participation in training courses may not be sufficient to change their monolingual bias (Rokita-Jaśkow & Król-Gierat, 2021). For this reason ECML continues to issue projects which endorse ECEC teachers in recognising diversity in their classes and their understanding of how all children's languages can be made visible and included in the education system, also while learning another FL, as in the PALINGUI project (Birnie et al., 2023).

The *Portfolio* exemplifies a form of endorsement in teacher training, but it is also apparent that the goals of early FL teaching are specified at the macro-level. In the era of global governance in education, too rarely are local teachers given a voice that would allow them to use their expertise and tailor general programmes to local needs. Thus, their agency in preparing the course contents is severely limited by other agents of the macro- and mezo-system, such as government. Thus, teachers may find it challenging to identify with policy goals, or they may find it too difficult to implement the suggested solutions in their teaching situation as the level of financial subsidy or teaching conditions (e.g. large classrooms) do not facilitate this process. This is evident, for example, in South Korea, where the official legislature endorses very early FL teaching but the results of early FL teaching are regarded as inadequate, mainly due to inadequate teacher FL competencies.

Another factor that limits teacher agency in their course development derives from the hidden agendas of neoliberal rule. Since English is a global language and a desired competency, this boosts the educational market, thus prompting the publishing and production of materials for English teaching, including at pre-primary level. This involves publishing whole teaching/learning packages for very young learners that include course books, flashcards, toys, access to IT resources, classroom posters and so on. Even though the use of course books for very young learners has been discouraged by policymakers in many contexts, for example China, on the grounds that the children should be taught by the provision of meaningful, authentic play-based experiences (cf. OECD, 2020), they are widely issued in a free market. Although it is up to the teachers whether they use them, parents of children enrolled in fee-paying courses are often expected to buy them, which shows how early FL teaching has become a market that generates profit. Likewise, certified language exams are provided. For example, the Cambridge Key English test can be taken by children as young as six. Teacher training packages and fee-paying teacher development courses/workshops are also offered to fill the market niche.

The stakeholders involved in publishing severely limit and diminish teacher agency in that respect. In consequence, teachers become merely technicians following blindly the guidelines set by authors of the learning material instead of developing their own activities to specifically match the abilities and interests of the children they teach.

5.4 Access Policy and Equity

The terms 'equity' and 'equality' are often used interchangeably but somewhat wrongly. The former relates to the expectation of similar outcomes of achievement while the latter to equal learning opportunities at the onset of the educational path. As Enever (2020: 13) argues, equality may offer equal access to education but a prerequisite for facilitating equity in educational outcomes is ensuring an equal starting point for all learners.

Those countries that aim to regulate pre-primary FL learning through policy legislation fulfil the access policy as Kaplan and Baldauf (2005) distinguish it. FL instruction for all, particularly at the pre-primary level, is a very costly solution if it is to be effective, as it requires a number of well-educated, well-paid and motivated teachers, attractive teaching aids, small classrooms and so on. These, however, are rarely secured by local government. This observation brings to mind the notion of provision, that is, how policymakers provide adequate teacher education, curricula, materials and school financing to enable effective implementation. This mainly concerns settings other than Europe which have been educationally under-invested for a long time. Enever (2019) depicts several different primary language classrooms in India, Uruguay and China to show how the conditions in which language learning takes place differ. Class sizes can vary from 15 (Shanghai, China) to 46 (India). Teachers may speak a FL or may not speak it at all, may use communicative methodology (Shanghai), rely on choral repetition of single words (India) or rely on blended learning with the use of digital technologies (Uruguay). The frequency of instruction may also vary from one to five hours a week. Thus, it can be seen that while early language learning policy, at least at the European level, aims to be inclusive and to counteract the negative consequences of unequal access to this type of education, the implementation of such policies has been differently realised in various contexts, which *de facto* does not resolve the problem of a lack of equity/equality. Enever (2019: 10) points out that 'political, social and economic factors most often work against achieving and sustaining equity'. These mechanisms decide class sizes, availability of teaching materials, teacher competencies and so on, which all impact the final quality. Furthermore, Enever (2018) argues that inequality of educational opportunities concerning English achievement concerns school attendance as mediated by the place of living (urban-village), gender and the associated choice of educational paths and access to IT resources and internet connection.

Similarly, in Asian contexts, Butler (2015a) notes that language-in-education policy, instead of securing equal access to good quality FL education, widens the economic gap between learners (and families) of various socioeconomic status (SES). The introduction of English as an FL in consequential exams, as in South Korea, has initiated the competitiveness for achieving the highest scores. A performance advantage is secured in those exams by learning more and earlier, mainly in the private sector, such as cram (afternoon) schools, early study abroad programmes, technology-based learning and employment of NEST teachers. In China, even though the government opted to introduce a FL in grade 3 to guarantee equal learning opportunities, many higher SES parents, particularly in big cities, have opted to provide private FL education for their children, thus boosting the educational market (Butler, 2015a).

In Mexico, a programme called The Programa Nacional de Ingles (PRONI) has introduced a significant increase (400%) in the number of English lessons for children aged three to 10 in the public sector. Sayer (2018, 2019) provides examples of three primary schools located in different areas (rural, suburban and urban) to demonstrate the variability in quantity and quality based on the learners' social class. At first glance, teaching conditions varied considerably across the institutions: in the outer design (e.g. a wired fence in a lower-class public school vs. freshly painted walls in a middle-class school and a dedicated classroom in an affluent school), decoration (or lack of it) and classroom size (up to 45 students in a rural class). Regarding the quality of teaching, even though a similar quantity of contact hours was provided, the lessons differed in teaching methodology (copying words in rural schools vs. communicative methodology in middle-class schools vs. EMI in affluent schools), availability and variability of teaching materials, discipline and classroom management issues. A different teaching approach was adopted for working-class kids, which included rote learning, stamina, repetition and following mechanical procedures. For middle-class kids, the approach involved using templates to create dialogues with some creativity and improvisation within limits. In more affluent schools, knowledge was seen as more open to discovery, construction and meaning-making (Sayer, 2018). On the surface, providing English instruction to all students starting from primary grades appears to advance educational and linguistic equity. However, contrary to this overt goal, a hidden agenda of public education could be ascertained, the goal of which is to prepare students for monotonous and tedious jobs, which could be observed from the poor quality of education offered to working-class children who do not seem to be worthy of investment (Sayer, 2018, 2019). He acknowledges that massive programmes of teaching FLs in poor settings are costly as they require educated teachers and well-developed materials. For this reason, it is doubtful that they really 'open doors' and change children's educational and vocational opportunities. Nevertheless, he concludes that 'curriculum developers and language education policymakers have not addressed how exactly these English programs generate greater socioeconomic opportunities in real terms' (Sayer, 2019: 38).

The status of young learner teachers is still relatively low in various countries, and this impacts salary levels and, consequently, who teaches a FL to young and very young learners. Since FL education is only a part of a kindergarten's early childhood educational curriculum, two solutions are usually applied. The language teacher is either the itinerant language specialist, who travels from one institution to another, or a generalist teacher who switches to a FL for specific periods of daily routine. Specialist language teachers or NEST teachers are relatively rarely employed, usually in the private sector.

These examples demonstrate that early language learning policy can both regulate and deregulate the private pre-primary FL educational market. Political decisions are made to introduce early or very early FL instruction with the aim of providing equal learning opportunities. However, the diversity of provision, which frequently is very poor, does not guarantee equal outcomes. For this reason, many higher-SES parents following 'the earlier, the better' common belief want to secure high achievement through the best learning opportunities for their children. Thus, they seek opportunities for more and earlier FL learning instruction, often in the private market.

In consequence, very early FL (mainly English) education has become a commodity, another market niche, targeted with new learning materials such as learning packages (coursebooks, workbooks, associated toys, etc.), learning apps, educational software and other teaching materials (game boards, game cards, posters, storybooks, etc.). Consequently, due to global employment opportunities for NESTs and fluent NNESTs, the training of FL teachers becomes professionalised, usually by private institutions, if policy does not regulate the market. Such institutions usually offer numerous fee-paying training sessions for in-service teachers, ready-to-go curricula and teaching materials and, last but not least, employment opportunities (Tsui, 2020).

5.5 Evaluation Policies

There are no policy regulations for evaluating FLs at the pre-primary level. Standardised tests for the very young are already available (Wolf & Butler, 2017) or are being developed (De Ruiter et al., 2022) also for the purposes of conducting research studies. Their primary goal is to prove accountability, that is, the efficacy of teaching, to policymakers and other stakeholders involved in early FL learning, for example, research funding agencies. Accountability to parents as clients in the private sector is a motive for evaluating children's performance. In Poland this typically denotes preparing very young learners for an end-of-year show in which children perform English songs and recite chants to show parents what they have learnt. It also manifests itself in encouraging children to take a formal exam, preparation for which sets learners' long-term goals and boosts their instrumental motivation. However, little is written on the potential adverse effects of such testing on very young children's motivation and self-esteem. Such tests allow only one attempt and do not consider the dynamics of the child's overall linguistic development nor daily predispositions. They emphasise failure (not meeting standards) and thus mainly raise instrumental motivation for learning, which promotes reaching targets rather than engagement in the current learning situation (Nikolov & Timpe-Laughlin, 2021). Enever (2018) emphasises the possible negative washback effect of these exams on learner attitudes and motivation towards language learning, on curricula which instead of developing oracy and listening comprehension often focus on memorisation of lexis to be tested and on teachers, whose main objective is for learners to achieve high performance in those exams to prove their effectiveness as teachers.

To date, no formal assessment measures (akin to the PISA study for 15-year-olds) have been introduced to verify the effectiveness of very early teaching of a FL. The effectiveness of very early FL learning can therefore only currently be verified by research studies. One noteworthy empirical research study on the effects of early contact with English at pre-primary level on lower primary education was conducted in the Chinese context (Chen et al., 2022). The authors undertook a study in which they aimed to measure what kind of effect early English exposure had on the children's performance in both English and Chinese in the 1st and

3rd grades of primary school. In their analysis, they used data obtained from standardised tests in English and Chinese held annually at the end of each school year while controlling for 'children's age, gender, the mother's education level, the mother's level of English proficiency, family income, shared book reading time, and parental teaching of English to children' (Chen et al., 2022: 9). The findings revealed that students who started to learn English at pre-primary level were more likely to obtain highest scores on their English exam in elementary (Chen et al., 2022: 11) when they started learning it in grade three. This resulted from having much more exposure to English in terms of the cumulative number of lessons. Strikingly, a similar influence was observed in reference to the impact of early English education on scores in Chinese (i.e. the mother tongue), which was a finding indicating that FL learning can have a positive effect on first language learning and also dispelled doubts that early FL learning can have a negative impact on the development of the mother tongue. The child grows up bilingually and, in line with Bialystok's (2001) findings, the competency in each language corresponds to the amount of input provided in each of the languages.

Attitudes to learning English in elementary school were similarly found to be neutral or more positive among children who had earlier exposure to L2, which was probably the outcome of more supportive home environments and opportunities for authentic language use. It is noteworthy that in the sample of children attending were higher SES mothers who had higher education levels and a command of English that enabled them to provide additional language practice (cf. Chapter 3).

However, these results have to be treated with caution, as pre-primary teaching of English in China mainly takes place in the private sector; those who enrol in such classes usually possess a higher socioeconomic status which in turn has been found to generally correlate with higher academic achievement (Zhang et al., 2019; cf. Chapter 3). Moreover, the study was conducted in Shanghai, an international hub, where children already experience some exposure to English outside of formal classes, for example in the streets, via advertisements and commercials as well as available learning apps. Finally, the potential advantage of pre-primary FL learning was observed only in reference to the early years of elementary school learning. From this data, it cannot be stated that any advantage will continue over the remaining school years.

As regards testing young and very young learners, Nikolov and Timpe-Laughlin (2021) conducted an overview of research into formative and summative assessment among children aged 3–14, that is, also including pre-primary learners, spanning over the last three decades (since 1997). They observed that early research (around the year 2000) indicated considerable variability of early FL teaching contexts and lack of conceptualisation of clear learning goals. Instead, teachers focused mainly on 'providing anxiety–free, positive testing experiences' (Nikolov & Timpe-Laughlin, 2021: 7).

A decade later, a call for a shift in this approach was noted, advocating for more accountability and the setting of realistic targets for young learners to achieve (Johnstone, 2009). As a result, in a European context at least, attempts were made to align any assessment measures to CEFR as benchmarks (Nikolov & Timpe-Laughlin, 2021) and adjust self-assessment descriptors of ELP for young learners, which resulted in issuing the *European Portfolio* for very young learners (Goullier *et al.*, 2015) in selected countries, such as Spain, Poland, Switzerland, Germany and the Czech Republic (https://www.coe.int/en/web/portfolio/by-educational-sector).

Summative assessment/assessment of learning was introduced in order to compare the effectiveness of various educational programmes, for example comparing early and later starters' performance in school-leaving exams in Croatia (Mihaljević Djigunović & Vilke, 2000), Spain (Muñoz, 2006), Germany (Jaekel *et al.*, 2017), Denmark (Fenyvesi, 2020) or an international Early Language Learning in Europe (ELLiE) study (Enever, 2011). Most studies, except for the ELLiE study (Enever, 2011), focused on vocabulary and literacy as they are the easiest to measure and do not evaluate the skills that children would be most likely to show competency in, that is, listening and oral skills. Nikolov and Timpe-Laughlin (2021) conclude there is still a vast amount of research needed to design well-validated tests that would realistically measure achievable outcomes of young and very young learners who had learnt a FL with age-appropriate methodology. They point out that such tests should factor into account that children's performance undergoes fluctuations. Furthermore, they criticise the summative assessment on the grounds that there is little information on 'how stakeholders utilize them in children's interest' (2021: 30) and, in particular, the interests of learners from disadvantaged family backgrounds or with specific learning difficulties. They also raise doubts about ethical issues arising from such assessments, which potentially may concern children who are tired/sleepy and whose attention span is exceeded. They point out that children are vulnerable to criticism and failure; therefore, special care must be taken to avoid negative impact as testing itself, as well as its results, 'may interact with how children see themselves and how they are seen as individuals' (Nikolov & Timpe-Laughlin, 2021: 23). This is particularly disheartening if testing in language is consequential and given to 11–12-year-olds at a stage which determines children's future life chances. In contrast, similarly to Pinter and Kuchach (2021), they agree that small-scale research projects conducted in the classroom can contribute to improving children's learning outcomes, encapsulating assessment *for* learning.

To support this view, it is worth citing the viewpoint of the Organisation for Economic Co-operation and Development (2020: 20) on the principles of learning in ECEC, which should also encompass FL learning. The document states that:

> there is no trade-off between early learning and children's happiness or indeed from the child's perspective, between learning and play. Happy, healthy children are active and curious and enjoy the natural process of learning. These processes occur through interactions with family and other caregivers and through different types of play. Through these experiences children learn about and actively explore their world as they also develop their language and other cognitive skills, socioemotional skills, and physical skills. (Shuey & Kankaraś, 2018)

To recapitulate, global governance in education has an impact on evaluation policies, that is, it requires that long-term educational investment is supported by evidence of learner achievement in key exams. While such exams are mainly taken on completion of primary/lower-secondary education, they have a substantial impact on lower-level/age learners in the sense that they promote mainly instrumental motivation in learning and reaching learning targets and emphasise fear of failure. Privatising a large portion of the educational market is another reason that testing, although not justified by psychological research or child developmental patterns, is a pervasive educational procedure. Accountability to various stakeholders has outweighed the quality of day-to-day teaching practice, paying a disservice to billions of children worldwide.

5.6 Agency and Policy

Agency in language policy and planning denotes institutional 'capacity and power to act in the world, attributed to social organizations or institutions and individuals' (Glasgow & Bouchard, 2019: 2). In other words, agency in early language policy planning and implementation depends on the agency of stakeholders involved in the process, such as top governmental decision-makers at the macro-level, kindergarten head teachers as well as other agents such as publishers, private entrepreneurs and teacher education institutions at the meso-level and finally teachers at the micro-level. It is 'stakeholders' agency [that] takes shape in empowerment and participation in language policies and practices' (Krompák, 2023: 5). From this perspective, we can talk of *institutional* agency that states that 'actors are key in maintaining, creating or dismantling institutions, depending on a range of concerns, including personal and professional' (Glasgow & Bouchard, 2019: 4). We can also distinguish professional agency that relates to educators' willingness to implement change, new didactic solutions or who, on the contrary, resist proposed policy guidelines.

Zhao and Baldauf (2012) distinguish several types of people involved in policymaking:

- *People with power*, that is, those who hold office at governmental level and are involved in determining regulation;
- *People with expertise*, those possessing knowledge and competence in a particular area, in this case, for example, researchers specialising in early language acquisition and education, as well as trained educators;
- *People with influence*, for example, academics, writers, bloggers, journalists and so on who can impact society by, for example, promoting early language learning; and
- *People with interest*, ordinary people who may be involved in making decisions about early teaching and use of languages in their institutions, such as parents and kindergarten head teachers.

From this chapter, it is evident that governments in various settings readily introduce early language learning policies by issuing legislation in the hope that FL (mainly English) competencies will help citizens boost their country's economy in the global market. These decisions are mainly political, aimed at satisfying government's own ambitions and/or the aspirations of parents as voters. The opinions of academics who question the necessity of such an early start in low-exposure settings are rarely taken into account. Furthermore, in most contexts, except for Hong Kong, there is little tangible support from top decision-makers to realise these polices at the meso- and micro-levels, which means that government agency is limited only to legislation. This has several consequences. Firstly, without state support, implementation of policy is poor, which results in poor quality of teaching as apparent from oversized classes, inappropriate methodology, teacher unpreparedness and/or overload and burnout. Secondly, little involvement of the state leaves space for private institutions to fill the gap in the market. As in Poland or South Korea, numerous private kindergartens arise in response to parental demand and dissatisfaction with public institutions. Additional services, such as summer camps, and products are offered to satisfy demand. Consequently, the policies which were intended to create equal access to FL education instead boost the private market and widen the economic and educational gap between children of diverse socioeconomic backgrounds. Scholarly opinion does not seem to have sufficient strength to cut through the futility of these endeavours, which only suggests that the goals and possible outcomes of very early teaching of FLs in low-exposure situations need to be more strongly publicised.

Summary

The chapter describes the origins and directions of the early language learning policy in the EU, following Kaplan and Baldauf's (2005) framework of successful language-in-education policy planning. It is argued that the European policy serves as a background to introducing similar policies in other countries across the globe with an emphasis on the early introduction of English as a lingua franca. The rationale for this phenomenon is provided and exemplified by specimen countries, such as Poland, China, South Korea and selected countries in South America. Further, the chapter emphasises how the policies can guarantee equal access to learning opportunities. It draws attention to teacher beliefs and teacher preparation as a prerequisite for effective policy implementation. Finally, it critically draws on the issue of assessing very young learners as an attempt at policy evaluation. In conclusion, it pinpoints the role of the agency of top-level decision-makers and other stakeholders who promote and influence early language learning policies.

6 The Chronosystem

This chapter refers to the last element of Bronfenbrenner's model, that is, the issue of time and its role in the foreign language (FL) learning process. Time can be understood vertically and horizontally, that is, correspondingly as a critical moment in the child's life or as a length of time. The milestones in the very young child's development comprise joining a FL class and transition to primary education, where continuity of learning and literacy matter. The stage of beginning to learn a FL is discussed as utilising a 'window of opportunity' for language learning. The transition to primary education raises the issues of continuity and consistency of the teaching programmes and the potential benefits to very early starters.

6.1 A Very Early Start in an FL as Utilising 'a Window of Opportunity'

In line with ecological theory, language learning is an emergent process that may undergo ups and downs and accelerations and retardation of the process. A very early start in a FL does not necessarily lead to a higher level of language competence than that achieved by later starters, as language knowledge is not cumulative. Conversely, it is a lifelong process (Pfenninger *et al.*, 2023) where an early age is not the sole factor guaranteeing success in the whole ecology of learning (Pfenninger, 2017). However, many parents decide to enrol their young children in various forms of organised FL instruction even before they have acquired their mother tongue (i.e. below 3;0), thus succumbing to the popular view that 'the earlier [one starts learning a FL], the better'. The origins of this catchphrase in the light of selected research and possible outcomes of an early start in a FL are presented below.

The decision to sign a child up for early instruction may be dictated by the need to utilise a particular 'window of opportunity', a sensitive period (Seliger, 1978), that is, a time slot after which similar skill acquisition would not be possible. Psychologists distinguish several sensitive periods for different aspects of human development such as personality and cognition (Bornstein, 1987). In contrast, linguists have believed for a long time that multiple critical periods exist for the acquisition of different language areas (Seliger, 1978). Some may close as early as five or seven years old, that is, by the end of kindergarten. While this position in linguistic studies is broadly questioned nowadays, it is worth understanding the reasons underlying the formulation of these beliefs.

It is widely accepted that, particularly in the first two years of a child's life, the brain develops rapidly due to the creation of numerous neurological connections in response to external stimuli. If the connections are created early in life, they will be stronger and last longer. By age five nearly 90% of neural connections are established (Power & Schlaggar, 2017), which is compatible with the concept that the window of opportunity closes for a particular skill.

Sensitive periods have been distinguished for the child's overall sensory (hearing and vision), linguistic, motor, social (attachment, independence, cooperation), emotional (trust, impulse control) and cognitive (cause and effect, problem-solving) development. Even though many of these skills are developed later in life (up to puberty), this is when the earliest neural circuitry is formed. Thus, to fully realise a child's potential for growth, the child must receive appropriate care and nutrition in the family in its earliest years. Alternatively, high-quality institutional childcare is considered to be able to compensate for low-income family support (Zeanah *et al.*, 2011). However, to truly enable the child's growth, the institutional provision should be high quality (Zeanah *et al.*, 2011).

From this perspective, early exposure to a FL can be perceived as yet another experience, stimulating the child's growth cognitively (by enhancing memory and attention span), emotionally (by building a sense of pride and self-confidence through experiencing positive emotions) and socially (by inducing interaction with peers and the teacher). For this reason, social-emotional learning as an educational framework in early childhood education and care (ECEC) has recently gained enhanced attention and academic support (OECD, 2020). Children's linguistic development is supported by engaging them in early literacy skills, such as joint book reading, chanting, routines and so on, and providing them with language-rich input. Caregivers' rich quality of input and interactions result in children's development of larger vocabularies, proper syntax and pragmatic use which, in turn, transfer to ease in school learning.

As regards first language development, such sensitive periods have been long established. They relate to the acquisition of different language subsystems: phonology, that is, discrimination and articulation of sounds, should be developed between the ages of 6 and 12 months; syntax by the age of 4 months; and semantics by age 15 to 16 years (Ruben, 1997).

The sensitive period for language acquisition is associated with Lenneberg's (1967) Critical Period Hypothesis (CPH), which states that there is a critical period associated with puberty (up to 14 years of age) up to which language can be acquired easily by mere exposure to language. While the hypothesis was initially formulated for first language (L1) development, it has also attracted a proliferation of research into the possibility of its existence in early second language (L2) development, stating that there is an age after which it is impossible to learn the language implicitly or to achieve native-like proficiency in that language. Here, the findings of research conducted in naturalistic situations, that is, where the L2 was spoken in the environment, point to the purported advantage of earlier starters in syntax (DeKeyser, 2000; Johnson & Newport, 1989; Patkowski, 1980; Snow & Hofnagel-Höhle, 1978) and phonology (Asher & Garcia, 1969; Oyama, 1976), that is, rule-governed areas of language, and not so much in lexicon, the acquisition of which takes place throughout life and is directly related to its frequency in the linguistic input (Singleton, 1999). It must be noted, however, that except for a study by Snow and Hofnagel-Höhle (1978), which was conducted on immigrant children learning L2 Dutch in an immersion situation, other studies were typically conducted on young adults (university students) whose language performance in a test battery was correlated with their age of arrival in the host country, and consequently the length of exposure to the language, disregarding possible other sociocultural (e.g. family socioeconomic status [SES], family time and support in the L2 acquisition, literacy practices, etc.) and psychological (e.g. aptitude, personality) factors that may have played a role in attaining proficiency in the L2. For a significant length of time, the outcomes of the studies have been quoted by various stakeholders, including private entrepreneurs and key-decision policymakers (cf. Chapter 5) as an argument for starting FL learning as early as possible.

This approach was additionally supported by findings in neurolinguistics which, thanks to advanced technological inventions such as functional magnetic resonance imaging (fMRI) and positron emission tomography (PET), allows a better insight into the structure and functioning of the brain. The advantage of early starters over later learners can be attributed to the neurolinguistic development of the brain. Firstly, the CPH has been formulated in response to the findings of Penfield and Roberts' (1957) discovery of brain plasticity and its lateralisation, that is, specialisation of the two hemispheres of the brain where the left hemisphere is more responsible for language processing in the so-called Broca's and Wernicke's areas, responsible for speech production and speech comprehension, respectively. Concerning bilingual learners, it has been found that in the case of later L2 learners, adjacent yet slightly distinct areas for each language could be distinguished in Broca's area (Kim *et al.*, 1997), thus affecting the degree to which the L2 overlaps with L1, which could be relevant for later recall and use of L2. However, more recent research (Berken et al., 2016; Sulpizio et al., 2020) suggests that there is no evidence that there are distinct areas of the brain for diverse languages but that there is a shared neural network for both L1 and L2 and what can be observed is the variability in brain activation instead.

Secondly, it needs to be recognised, as posited by connectionist theories of language (Westermann, 2009) learning, that learning in neurolinguistic terms proceeds by training neural networks to respond to a particular stimulus, which takes place through repetition and reoccurrence of the same word (or another language element) in the environment. Creating neuron connections in the brain proceeds by communication between neuron cells via axons and dendrites, which combine an auditory/visual stimulus in the outside world and its representation in the brain. The more often a given word appears in the input the more easily it is retrieved. Axons are covered in the myelin sheath that facilitates the transfer of electric signals along the axons. Word memorisation and retrieval are most likely to occur in frequently trained networks. It is notable that, particularly up until the age of two, the brain undergoes rapid development due to the process of myelinisation of axons (Elman, 1993), which is why the very early period of life is regarded to be the most fertile period for rapid learning from novel experiences.

Some evidence for training neural networks comes from a study by Kuhl et al. (2005) on the acquisition of phonology, in which she observed that at seven months, children's discrimination abilities of native and non-native sounds differently predict future language abilities, that is, better sound discrimination of native language sounds predicted better language development in later life in several skills such as the number of words produced, the degree of sentence complexity and the mean length of utterance. However, no such correlation was observed for the discrimination of non-native sounds, that is, those children who could discriminate L2 sounds well at seven months did not necessarily show more proficient language abilities later in life. Moreover, the better the children were at recognising native language sounds at seven months the worse they were at recognising non-native sounds. She concluded that '[a]s native-language phonetic learning occurs, and neural networks become committed to the experienced acoustic properties, patterns that do not conform to those learned (such as those of a nonnative language) are no longer detected with equal accuracy' (Kuhl et al., 2005: 252). The networks stay flexible and continue to learn until the number and variability of occurrences of a particular vowel (like the /ɒ/ in pot) have produced a distribution that predicts new instances of the vowel; new instances then no longer significantly shift the underlying distribution. This view is consistent with connectionist accounts of critical period effects, such as Elman et al. (1996). According to this view, critical period phenomena arise not from a genetically determined change in learning capacity at a particular age but from entrenchment, which is the direct outcome of learning.

More recent neurolinguistics research shows that brain plasticity also allows for modification of its structure and density of grey matter thanks to language learning and other complex skills. Notably, it has been observed that if large volumes of language-related tasks are to be processed, the brain can restructure a particular language area (Mechelli *et al.*, 2004). Furthermore, language learning/bilingualism has been found to result in greater integrity of white matter, that is, thicker cortex, which enhances communication between different areas of the brain responsible for language processing regardless of the age of the learner (Pfenninger *et al.*, 2023); for example, neural circuits for lexis are spread all over the brain, as posited in the Dynamic Restructuring model (Pliatskias *et al.*, 2020 in Pfenninger *et al.*, 2023). These findings allow us to conclude that neuroplasticity is a lifelong process. For this reason, it would be unjustified to claim that there is a sharp decline in the ability to learn, which questions the justifiability of the CPH (Pfenninger *et al.*, 2023).

The evidence defying the CPH in the instructional setting comes from studies conducted in the primary classroom. The impact of Age of Onset (AoO) is usually investigated in relation to the *rate* of FL acquisition in its early stages and its *final* (or long-term) *attainment*.

Concerning rate, in formal settings younger learners typically have been shown to learn more slowly than older learners (Muñoz, 2006; Snow & Hofnagel-Höhle, 1978) due to less-developed cognitive abilities (such as working memory [WM] and attention) and a lack of elaborate memory strategies which facilitate memorisation. Therefore, the rate of FL acquisition among same-level/age children, including pre-primary learners (Sun *et al.*, 2016), depends on external factors, mainly the amount of FL exposure provided both in the ECEC and the family, rather than individual predispositions (cf. Chapter 1). In other words, those children who experience more contact with a FL and more frequently will eventually show better learning results. The children memorise the language forms frequently encountered in the input.

Regarding the final level of achievement, some researchers (Pfenninger *et al.*, 2023) argue that from the perspective of lifelong FL learning it is difficult to estimate when final attainment will occur. Thus, it is not easy to evaluate the potential benefits of an early start. However, when comparing learning achievement between those children who started to learn a FL early and those who started learning a FL in early adolescence, the earlier starters show a long-term advantage over later learners in certain areas, particularly regarding listening skills (Burstall *et al.*, 1975; García Mayo & García Lecumberri, 2003; Muñoz, 2006, 2008).

Furthermore, children who started learning a FL earlier usually perform better in the initial stages of formal learning of a FL when compared with children who have not received early instruction (Garcia Mayo &

Garcia Lecumberri, 2003; Jaekel *et al.*, 2017; Larson-Hall, 2008; Muñoz, 2006, 2008, 2011). However, this effect is not long-lasting, as older learners typically catch up or surpass earlier starters as FL learning progresses. Larson-Hall (2008) claims that these age effects are also visible in FL learners in low-input situations, that is, those exposed to a FL for less than four hours per week, but provided they have attained a certain level of language proficiency. Thus, previously acquired language input is likely to be the factor that gives an advantage to earlier starters, not chronological age.

In the same vein, the impact of FL learning in the ECEC is usually measured in the early primary school years. The results of these studies usually show an advantage for those children who have learnt a FL in the ECEC over those who have not at the beginning of learning a FL, which can be attributed to the cumulative language intake (Unsworth *et al.*, 2015). For example, in a study conducted in China, Chen *et al.* (2022) compared the results of children who obtained very early exposure to L2 English in ECEC with those who did not, at the onset of formal learning of L2 English at grade 3. They found that 'students with early childhood English learning experience have significantly higher chances of obtaining an A (the highest score) in both English and Chinese exams' (Chen *et al.*, 2022: 13). Additionally, contrary to parental and educationalist fears, children maintained positive attitudes towards English despite a two-year interval since learning English in ECEC. However, the authors recognised the facilitatory role of the family's higher SES, enabling the children to attend private and, most likely, high-quality early English instruction.

Similarly, measuring the effectiveness of intensive content and language integrated learning (CLIL) programmes in a Swiss context, Pfenninger (2022: 16) found that 'late starters (AoO year 9) in partial CLIL programs not only attain lower proficiency levels than earlier starters (AO years 5 and 7) by the end of primary school, they also show markedly different L2 trajectories'. She attributed this fact not only to the very early age of first exposure to a FL but also to the intensity of exposure (daily contact as opposed to a few hours a week) and the fact that such exposure got the children used to noticing the target language in their surroundings, most notably using mobile technology (apps on smartphones and tablets). However, she also recognised that the differences between pre-primary and primary starters reduced with time.

Erk (2025) asked 13-year-old primary school children themselves to take a retrospective look at their early FL experiences and to evaluate whether it is important to start learning a FL in the pre-primary years. Their answers showed a considerable variability and no statistically significant differences were found between children who started FL learning in the pre-primary and in the primary years, which the author attributed mainly to their current perception of their proficiency in the

FL. The children also indicated a number of problems (such as lack of continuity) which impacted their fluctuating motivation to learn a FL and achievement in mid-adolescent years. All these findings led the author to the conclusion that starting FL learning at pre-primary was not seen as necessary by the children themselves.

Singleton and Ryan (2004) argue in relation to the age factor that Cummins's (1978, 1979) distinction between CALP (cognitive/academic language proficiency) and BICS (basic interpersonal communication skills) is relevant. They claim that BICS and L1 competencies, such as accent, oral fluency and sociolinguistic competence, are very much context-embedded, as they rely on paralinguistic and situational cues and develop mainly implicitly through exposure to language. Meanwhile, CALP relies on linguistic cues in communication and thus is much more cognitively demanding and requires the development of some degree of metalinguistic awareness, which are skills facilitated by literacy, both in L1 and L2. Cummins (1979) believes the same distinction is valid in L2 and says that 'the older learners, whose CALP is better developed, would acquire cognitive/academic L2 skills more rapidly than younger learners; however, this would not necessarily be the case for those aspects of L2 proficiency unrelated to CALP (i.e. L2BICS)' (Cummins, 1979: 199ff in Singleton & Ryan, 2004: 89).

It is noteworthy, however, that child FL learning differs from L1 and L2 learning in the naturalistic setting. A child typically joins a kindergarten or other form of ECEC at 2;0 or 3;0 when they have already acquired their mother tongue. Suppose a child joins an institution in which the instruction is entirely conducted in an L2, as is the case of immigrant children in the host society. In that case, we may discuss bilingual L2 acquisition or sequential bilingualism (De Houwer, 2017). If a child joins a monolingual institution where instruction is conducted in the mother tongue, contact with the FL is granted up to a few times a week. In either case, the child can rely on rules and strategies already acquired for L1 as some transfer of learning can take place, yet the extent to which it is possible to derive the rules from L2 depends on the amount of exposure to that language. There is much less contact with a FL so the child has to rely mainly on cognitive predispositions (WM and other executive functions). For this reason, older children typically learn a FL faster than younger children (Birdsong, 2018).

For these reasons, an important milestone in children's FL development will be the onset of schooling and the development of literacy, which can accelerate language development and enhance the growth of metalinguistic awareness (Lieven & Tomasello, 2008). In light of the research mentioned above, the amount of FL input and intake provided is of importance, as the children's FL proficiency may be a key factor that will provide them with an advantage over later starters, provided that in the primary years they do not start learning from scratch but continue FL learning. Thus, the notion of continuity in primary school is addressed below.

6.2 FL Learning Continuity From Pre-Primary to Primary School

While teaching FLs to very young learners has become a widespread phenomenon in various settings (cf. Chapter 5), it is still mainly conducted on a private basis, that is, it is not regulated by educational policy. The main downside of this phenomenon is a lack of learning continuity in the transition from pre-primary to primary school where a FL can be taught from grade 1 or later, thus causing a gap in FL learning or its continuation in the private sector. As a result, at the beginning of obligatory FL instruction in primary school (or higher) a class may comprise both early and late-starting children, which increases language level heterogeneity. This situation may not be beneficial for any party. For one thing, teachers are obliged to follow the curriculum and usually teach a FL from scratch, which places children who started FL learning at pre-primary level in an advantageous position as they typically excel at language elements they have had a chance to learn previously. However, this may also cause a lack of challenge and boredom. In contrast, children who start FL learning in primary schools may find the learning pace too fast or feel intimidated by the earlier starting children's performance.

The transition from pre-primary to primary level has found little support in research except in a recent study by Letica Krevelj and Mihaljević Djigunović (2021). The authors enquired how different types of early foreign instruction at the pre-primary level may impact children's performance at the primary level, more precisely their motivation, attitudes, self-concept and strategic awareness. Informed by the results of a study conducted on 25 young learners and their parents, they found that in parents' opinions, the pre-primary learning experience had a beneficial effect on their children's later language learning. As regards the children, they generally held positive attitudes and motivation towards FL learning in pre-primary. However, they did not always regard English as a favourite subject in primary school, which the authors (Letica Krevelj & Mihaljević Djigunović, 2021) ascribed to the novelty of other school subjects catching children's interest. Children's motivation was observed to fluctuate over time. Thus, the authors concluded that children's motivation at pre-primary level did not appear to influence subsequent motivation at primary level, which was argued to be caused by a lack of coherence in methodology and continuity. However, those children who had learnt the language at pre-primary enjoyed FL learning from out-of-school exposure much more and showed more significant levels of reflectivity and self-awareness at primary level, which manifested in their ability to self-assess and express preferences. Regarding attitudes, children who had learnt the language earlier found it easier to learn at the primary level but with less enjoyment (motivation). Likewise, the pre-primary children's self-concept remained higher for the first two years of primary school while no strategic use could be mentioned, which was probably caused by the fact that they had acquired the language mainly implicitly.

All these findings show that pre-primary FL learners may not necessarily benefit from an early start, which may be caused by a lack of consistency in teaching curricula and continuity. This situation shows that there is space and need for the intervention of educational policy which can take place only if pre-primary FL learning is a part of the compulsory curriculum. As advocated by the Language Policy guidebook (European Commission, 2011) for EU member states, including FL learning in obligatory ECEC curricula would prevent these problematic issues. Following the European policy guidelines, Mihaljević Djigunović and Letica Krevelj (2021) contend that the advocated criteria of coherence (understood as 'structural integration' of educational levels, consistency of methodology and curricula) at the pre-primary level should be guaranteed. Additionally, they assert that continuity of learning the language started at pre-primary level should be secured at primary level so that the learner meets with challenges and thus sustains his learning motivation. Drawing on the overview of research findings on the transition from primary to secondary levels (e.g. Baumert *et al.*, 2020) in general education, they conclude that the essential elements facilitating successful transition are understanding the role of parents and teachers in the process and aligning the curricula at two stage levels so that they complement each other. In a nutshell, they propose, following Griebel and Niesel's (2006) arguments, that the transition process flows smoothly if there is close collaboration of all the agents involved, that is, parents, school educators and children. Additionally, they suggest that learners' motivation and resilience towards language learning may be the key factors facilitating or inhibiting smooth transition, which require further investigation.

6.3 Agency and Time

While time is too abstract a term to talk of its agency, the necessity of observing the relationship between time, temporality and agency has been highlighted by several scholars in sociology, for example Flaherty (2011), Emirbayer and Mische (1998), Elder (1994) and Giddens (1981). They argue that individuals' agency is embedded in temporal situations and can only be observed in its whole dimension over a specific period. Flaherty (2011) proposes that agency, time and temporality are related to one's determinism and self-determination to achieve specific goals. He observes that 'individuals purposefully construct lines of activity or social situations to create or inhibit diverse forms of temporal experience' (Flaherty, 2011: 11). There can be many dimensions of time, such as *duration*, *frequency*, *sequence* (that is, what precedes or follows a particular moment) and *allocation*, that is, setting aside time for a particular event (Flaherty, 2011).

Looking from this perspective at the process of pre-primary FL learning, the very early years may be seen by some parents as a critical juncture requiring action and allocation of time. The same momentum can inhibit or call to action other stakeholders involved in the process, most likely key decision-makers. Thus, the point at which FL instruction is started can be considered a trigger to agentic behaviours of other actors in the ecosystem, who will mobilise their efforts, not only in that given moment but also during subsequent learning experiences throughout the educational career, which illustrates the sequence dimension. Finally, the frequency dimension is relevant because it determines the visible results of early exposure to a FL during the pre-primary years.

To summarise, in relation to the question of whether it is worthwhile to teach FLs in pre-primary years, it is important to note that research does not support the idea that starting at a younger age is the most important factor. In fact, older children in primary years can learn more quickly and effectively. It is also important to recognise that language skills are not always cumulative and may fluctuate depending on external factors. However, early FL learning can be a valuable experience for a child's overall socioemotional and cognitive development but only if it is of high quality. It also seems to result in greater sensitivity to a FL in out-of-school settings in comparison with children starting at an older age. Therefore, it is essential for all those involved in a child's pre-primary FL education to focus on providing high-quality FL learning opportunities.

Summary

This chapter discusses two important stages that regulate the process of pre-primary FL learning. These are the start of FL instruction and the transition to primary education. In relation to the former, the chapter presents arguments for and against an early start based on neurolinguistics and classroom research findings. Regarding the latter, the chapter highlights the problems that arise due to a lack of continuity in FL learning.

Finally, the chapter briefly talks about the concept of agency in relation to the temporal dimension. It is essential to recognise that very early FL learning can be an enriching experience for a child's overall growth because they can learn more and faster. However, the child's knowledge of language may experience fluctuations depending on the external conditions of learning. Therefore, high-quality early FL teaching should be the focus of all the agents involved in the child's ecosystem from a lifelong learning perspective.

Concluding Remarks

The overall objective of this book was to present pre-primary foreign language (FL) learning in various ecologies (i.e. environments) around the globe. It can be seen that despite a lack of linguistic evidence for the necessity of a very early start in a FL (cf. Chapter 6), such programmes are implemented in the private and state sectors with a burgeoning popularity. The reason for such a very early start is the widespread belief that it will have a beneficial impact on overall linguistic competence in later life (Huang, 2016; Thieme et al., 2022) and will lead to attaining bilingual competence, notably in the lingua franca English, which in the era of the global economy is believed to open doors to participation in the worldwide economy. Remarkably, parents and policymakers endorse this stance in countries with limited access to the language in the public environment, thus prolonging the overall length of FL learning.

Looking at this phenomenon from an ecological perspective, one can clearly observe how the principles of van Lier's and Bronfenbrenner's theories fit the description of the very early FL learning process (cf. Figure C.1 below for an overview).

Firstly, it takes place in various contexts, that is, in early childhood education and care (ECEC), which comprises occasional and immersion types of instruction, in afternoon courses and at home with parental endorsement. Each of these contexts is characterised by a different frequency of FL contact and type of teaching-learning process, impacting the relationship between the very young child and the teacher. It is mainly through close emotional bonds that the children are willing to interact and absorb a FL, that is, a language that *is not* their tool of communication, as using it requires a solid cognitive effort. For this reason, teaching quality that is oriented towards securing a child's engagement and enjoyment of the process of learning is of primary importance, as only then can the child acquire language, which develops dynamically and unpredictably depending on the available input as well as the endorsement of other actors in the ecosystem.

In many publications (e.g. Bland, 2015; Schwartz, 2020), early second language learning is seen as a composite of overall linguistic

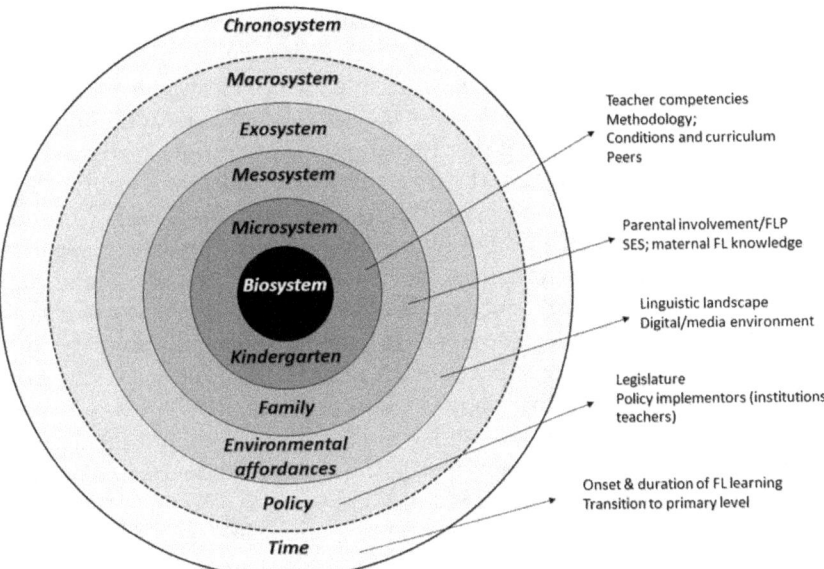

Figure C.1 Very early FL learning through the ecological lens

multicompetence, where different languages are acquired from birth throughout a lifetime. The extent to which each of these languages is mastered usually equals the amount of linguistic input obtained in each of these languages, in the family, in the ECEC and in the outside world. While language learning in formal contexts, which usually takes place from primary school years and is facilitated by literacy development, also aids in building linguistic competence, FL learning in the formal setting in the pre-primary years does not comply with the same principles as second language learning in naturalistic situations. Thus, there should be a clear delineation between second language learning, which takes place in the natural environment, and FL learning, which is mainly taught in the classroom (kindergarten, afternoon courses, etc.) and comprises minimal contact with a FL.

For one thing, very young children can be exposed to a foreign language, even in nursery, that is, below the age of 3;0, at a time when they still have not acquired their mother tongue. However, the input they receive is minimal, usually approximately one hour, up to a few hours a week among older children. Consequently, even if the children pick up a few foreign words, progress is slow; lexis must be continuously revised to prevent it from being forgotten. Children develop, first of all, oral comprehension skills, whereas production is limited to formulaic chunks and repetition of input from an adult or constitutes a cued recall (upon a picture cue in a book or a cartoon). With so little contact with a FL, the children are more likely to use it for nonlinguistic purposes, that is, to show off their knowledge of another language, rather than for authentic communication. Additionally, the children lack a communicative need to speak a FL, as usually all the children in the classroom and the teacher share the same mother tongue. This lack of authenticity and communicative need in FL use is what distinguishes FL development from second language development. For the same reasons, children rarely show agency in socialising with peers in a FL, except for pretend play (Mourão, 2014, 2018) as observed among bilingual children in naturalistic settings. The youngest children are still acquiring their mother tongue and may not have acquired certain concepts yet, which is another reason for their slowness in language development. It also has to be emphasised that given the same amount of input, not all children are able to benefit from it to the same extent, which may depend on inner predispositions such as attention span, working memory ability, temperament, experienced emotions (such as anxiety, enjoyment) and motivation levels. All of these issues were discussed in Chapters 1 and 2.

Secondly, while intraindividual ability among children varies, an even greater variability can be observed in the type of instruction offered to very young children as described in Chapter 2, which manifests in varied levels of teacher linguistic skills (native-speaker vs. language specialist vs. ECEC teacher), teachers' pedagogical and didactic preparation and their terms of employment, thus informing the extent to which they form an attachment to children and provide contact with a FL. These issues are related to the socioeconomic status (SES) of families as higher SES children typically have access to instruction of a higher quality, characterised by smaller groups, higher frequency of FL contact (content and language integrated learning [CLIL]-type), more authentic and meaningful learning tasks and better-qualified teachers. Thus, not all children benefit from FL instruction to the same extent, which calls for the adoption of a critical stance towards unequal learning opportunities.

Thirdly, there are cases of children who have demonstrated productive use of a FL in the pre-primary years. However, these were usually children of parents who were linguists themselves. Thus, the parents knew a FL at a higher proficiency level and were more knowledgeable about available FL resources and ways of scaffolding new meanings to facilitate their children's FL development. These were, in fact, cases where bilingual development of the child was a part of their family language policy. Parental involvement in their children's FL education, as shown in Chapter 3, seems to be a fundamental factor in supplying or complementing FL input. It is related to parental, and especially maternal, FL proficiency, often mediated by their educational level and SES. Parental involvement is particularly a means to realizing parents' goals and aspiration if they do not possess proficiency in a FL themselves.

Fourthly, parental endeavours are unsurprising if the family lives in a society where access to the FL is not present in the outer world and cannot be picked up by mere exposure to the linguistic landscape as part of the ecosystem, as discussed in Chapter 4. While access to the language of global reach, that is, English, is becoming easier via the internet, educational apps and so on, this is a resource that very young children should be using only to a limited extent. Their use should be regulated and mediated by parents in order not to impede their language development via extensive screen watching, as it may affect their attention span, metalinguistic reasoning and sociopragmatic skills, among others. Language, after all, is acquired through interaction with its users. There is also potential for providing opportunities for implicit FL acquisition in exposing literate children to subtitled TV. However, passive exposure to media seems to play a role in language acquisition once children have developed a level of metalinguistic awareness, which allows them to analyse the language input on their own. In the case of pre-primary learners, there is potential for implicit language acquisition in increasingly multilingual ECEC classrooms in certain settings (cf. Kirsch, 2018). It seems that if a FL is a language of instruction, as in CLIL/EMI-type of instruction, then it could also become a language of mutual interaction among children.

Fifthly, FL learning at the pre-primary level, either in the state or private sector, is promoted by macro forces, that is, either the educational market, which has identified in parental aspirations a market opportunity, or policymakers who attempt to both regulate the market as well as respond to parental demands. These issues are explored in Chapter 5. However, once early FL instruction is introduced, policymakers should ensure that teachers are adequately supported in its implementation, for example, additional training in the target language and teaching English to young learners (TEYL) methodology should be made available.

Finally, the issue of time is raised. Research results do not provide an unequivocal answer as to whether it is beneficial or not to start FL learning early. An extensive overview of studies on early language learning (Huang, 2016) shows that older learners have advantages over younger learners in the short and long term. Additionally, it has been found (Pfenninger & Singleton, 2017) that in an instructed setting, children who started FL learning very early may surpass older learners in the initial stages of FL learning. However, older learners soon catch up and can perform at the same level, if not a higher one. Brumen (2011) suggested that very young children should not start FL learning earlier than age 5;0, the age by which they should have mastered the conceptual system of their L1, if they are to enjoy early FL learning activities and not experience anxiety due to lack of comprehension.

In summary, from an ecological perspective, early language learning should be viewed as a dynamic and emergent process, made up of a combination of many affordances provided by the agents in the child's vicinity at the micro-, meso-, exo- and macro-levels. A child learner may flourish linguistically, or may not, depending on the quality of relationships they are engaged in, homecare quality, kindergarten instruction and teacher qualities. From a broader perspective, this also encompasses the sociocultural and sociopolitical situation of the country one lives in, as language learning by children can be endorsed or defied explicitly or implicitly by various affordances available in the environment and by policy measures. The affordances are provided if the actors involved in the process of early language learning show sufficient agency in language policy planning and its implementation.

Throughout the pages of this book, we have looked at different elements of the educational ecosystem within which early FL learning takes place while trying to answer the overarching question, that is, whose agency plays a role in early FL learning? Agency is a manifestation of policy construction and implementation. On a macro scale, it is educational authorities and institutions that create policies to promote or sustain the use of a particular language for the implementation of which teachers are specifically trained.

The social actors involved in language policy planning at micro-, meso- and macro-levels fulfil various roles. As Ball *et al.* (2011) indicate, these can be those of *narrators, entrepreneurs, outsiders, transactors, enthusiasts, translators, critics* and *receivers*. Following this taxonomy, it seems the macro-level agents, such as institutions, that put forward policy regulations fulfil the role of narrators and entrepreneurs as they select and initiate the focus of language policy. The meso-level actors, as represented by, for example, private entrepreneurs (owners of private kindergartens/language schools), material writers, course developers as well as, for example, blog writers and journalists, exploit the educational market in the role of outsiders and translators, as they mediate between macro- and micro-policy levels and formulate discourse (e.g. texts) on policy. Parents can also be entrepreneurs in language policy if they campaign to make early FL instruction available to their children. They can also act as outsiders who form partnerships with kindergartens and who, by participating in their children's early FL learning process, thus endorse policy implementation.

Teachers who work at the micro-level can act as *enthusiasts* who approach their teaching enthusiastically and imbue their teaching with age-appropriate FL methodology, as *transactors* who ensure that macro-level policies are implemented locally or as critics if they reject or resist policy implementation.

FL learners will act merely as *receivers* of the policy, as they depend on others to experience quality FL input. Thus their agency seems to be least visible and activated. As Çekaite (2020: 5) says, '[y]oung children's willingness and openness toward a new language is a complex matter that is not limited to the child's characteristics, but that is highly affected by the language policies, social relations, and learning ecologies of the educational institutions'.

Whose agency is it?

In answer to this overriding question, it is evident in respect of very early FL learning that parental agency comes to the fore, as it is parents who plan and provide for the early multilingual growth of their children and liaise with the educational institution in order to obtain additional support. However, this agency is nested in other elements of the ecosystem, first of all in the exo- and macrosystems that promote particular linguistic ideologies. Parents adopt these ideologies as they transfer into their children's cultural and socioeconomic advantage. Also, educational institutions play an important role in translating macro-policies at the micro-level, which can thus instil in children an interest in the FL in tandem with their parents.

Children as FL learners are mainly recipients of these agentic actions in an instructional setting. Thus, it is my belief that in contrast to Schwartz's (2018) proposal (which emphasises that in instructional settings language socialisation processes are an outcome of the interaction of parents, teachers *and children*), successful early FL learning is the outcome of agentic behaviours of all actors involved in the process *except* for the children's. Very young FL learners are hardly likely to use the FL in order to communicate with peers if they share the same mother tongue for they do not possess a communicative need. What they can initiate is pretend play, that is, imitating language and procedures from their English classes as shown by Mourão (2018) or inserting L2 words and chunks into L1 utterances (Rokita, 2006), which denotes metalinguistic function of language use and is where they demonstrate agency. Such use of language, however, does not lead to the development of novel sentences and is hardly ever used for communicative purposes. A child must acquire a certain critical amount of FL vocabulary and grammatical rules to be able to combine them into novel, meaningful FL utterances, which does not happen in limited-input situations. Also, very young children do not seem to be capable of using transfer from L1 as a strategy of building more complex utterances in a FL (Hopp *et al.*, 2019).

Potential direction of future research

The book aimed to encapsulate the current state of knowledge of pre-primary FL learning. It is self-evident that the teaching of FLs very early is expanding globally, despite two decades of research, which does not conclusively support the necessity of starting FL learning very early. Nevertheless, the diversity of learning contexts provides opportunities for further investigation from an ecological perspective. As Pfenninger (2022: 42) noted, 'it is important to take an ecological approach that simultaneously examines individual learners and their interdependence with spatial-temporal context so as to cope with the increasing complexity and diversity of language use in the 21st century'.

Firstly, in line with the ecological perspective, it is essential to investigate FL learning outcomes subject to environmental factors, such as the child's family and its distal characteristics. Additionally, the role of the exosystem should be considered in promoting particular languages and their presence in the sociocultural milieu. In this respect, comparative international studies would be of specific interest. Additionally, it would be worth investigating whether children of diverse first languages differently acquire target languages that may be typologically distant, and so differ much in phonology and structure, such as Chinese and English vs. English and other Indo-European languages. Indeed, there is also an underrepresentation of other FLs in pre-primary education; thus, prospectively, the same questions could be raised about other languages.

Secondly, it needs to be recognised that in many contexts worldwide, pre-primary classrooms are becoming more and more culturally and linguistically diverse, as pointed out by Kirsch (2018). While children obtain ECEC instruction in the dominant societal language, they may also be exposed to a FL. Thus, it would be interesting to find out how all these languages interact within the child's mind and the routes and outcomes of the prospective children's linguistic multicompetence.

Thirdly, there are many issues we would like to learn more about concerning children's reasoning and learning processes, in particular the impact of very early FL on the overall child's cognitive and emotional development. There are potential indications of an associated beneficial impact, particularly on the executive functions, as well as how emotional development impacts possible gains from a specified amount of language input. To explore this, one would need to investigate children's abilities using psychological tests, possibly in psycholinguistic laboratories, while ensuring safe and child-friendly conditions; thus, a closer collaboration between linguists and psychologists in this respect would be needed. Furthermore, the long-term effects of early FL contact in low-input situations are only speculative. Longitudinal research projects are required on the impact of pre-primary exposure to a FL at the onset of primary and later primary school years.

However, the call for more research in this area raises some objections of an ethical nature. In this respect, I agree with Nikolov and Timpe-Laughlin (2021), who are against testing preschool children on the grounds that the children may be given tasks that they may not be able to do well, which may have a detrimental effect on their learning as it 'may induce anxiety and take precious time away from learning activities' (Nikolov & Timpe-Laughlin, 2021: 30), particularly since FL learning is such a changeable and emergent process that few results will be generalisable. It seems, therefore, that no testing should be conducted on whole groups of preschool children. Still, ethical research should focus on testing children individually, employing non-intrusive observation and play-based methods so that they do not know they are being tested. These proposals run in tandem with Butler and Huang's (2023), Pinter's (2023) and Pinter and Kuchah's (2021) call for more research *with* very young learners while securing its ethicality. This can be done by obtaining the consent of parents and children, doing research in the presence of children in an environment that is familiar and friendly to them, approaching the children with respect and, as best practice, adopting techniques that resemble play as children's well-being should be prioritised. This also means that such research should preferably be conducted by individuals with whom the children are well acquainted. With such an increase in the early teaching of FLs and the availability of ethical research methods, we are bound to obtain a proliferation of informative research in the future.

References

Ager, D.E. (2001) *Motivation in Language Planning and Language Policy*. Multilingual Matters.

Ahn, S.-Y. and West, G.B. (2018) Young learners' portrayals of 'good English teacher' identities in South Korea. *Applied Linguistics Review* 9 (2–3), 225–248.

Aitchison, J. (2003) *Words in the Mind: An Introduction to the Mental Lexicon* (3rd edn). Blackwell.

Akdemir, A.S. (2017) eTwinning in language learning: The perspectives of successful teachers. *Journal of Education and Practice* 8 (10), 182–190.

Akmal, S., Masna, Y. and Nasution, L.A. (2021) Engaging to nurturing, English language teaching strategies and constraints for very young Muslim learners at kindergarten in ACEH. *Islam Futura* 21 (1), 46–62.

Albaladejo, S.A., Coyle, Y. and Roca De Larios, J. (2018) Songs, stories, and vocabulary acquisition in preschool learners of English as a foreign language. *System* 76, 116–128.

Alenezi, H., Ihmeideh, F.M. and Alshaboul, Y. (2023) Kindergarten teachers' challenges in teaching English as a foreign language to children. *International Journal of Early Years Education* 31 (3), 722–737.

Alexiou, T. (2009) Young learners' cognitive skills and their role in foreign language vocabulary learning. In M. Nikolov (ed.) *Early Learning of Modern Foreign Languages: Processes and Outcomes* (pp. 46–61). Multilingual Matters.

Alexiou, T. (2015) Vocabulary uptake from Peppa Pig. A case study of preschool EFL learners in Greece. In C. Gitsaki and T. Alexiou (eds) *Current Issues in Second/Foreign Language Teaching and Teacher Development. Research and Practice* (pp. 285–301). Cambridge Scholars Publishing.

Alexiou, T. (2021) Special issue. Innovations and trends in early foreign language context. *Research Papers in Language Teaching and Learning* 11 (1), 6–10.

Alexiou, T. (2023) Introducing English in preschool education in Greece: An overview of the EAN project. *The Asian Conference on Education 2022. Official Conference Proceedings* (pp. 1009–1018). IAFOR. https://doi.org/10.22492/issn.2186-5892.2023.77

Alexiou, T. and Vitoulis, M. (2014) iGeneration issues. Tracing preschoolers English receptive and productive vocabulary though interactive media. Mission impossible? In J. Enever, E. Lindren and S. Ivanov (eds) *Conference Proceedings from Early Language learning. Theory and Practice* (pp. 16–22). Umeå University.

Alexiou, T., Roghani, S. and Milton, J. (2019) Assessing the vocabulary knowledge of preschool language learners. In D. Prošić-Santovac and S. Rixon (eds) *Integrating Assessment into Early Language Learning and Teaching* (pp. 207–220). Multilingual Matters.

Ali, N.L., Hamid, M.O. and Moni, K. (2011) English in primary education in Malaysia: Policies, outcomes and stakeholders' lived experiences. *Current Issues in Language Planning* 12 (2), 147–166.

Alstad, G.T. (2020) Preparing teachers for early language education. In M. Schwartz (ed.) *Handbook of Early Language Education* (pp. 1–28). Springer.

Altman, C., Goldstein, T. and Armon-Lotem, S. (2018) Vocabulary, metalinguistic awareness and language dominance among bilingual preschool children. *Frontiers in Psychology* 23 (9), 1953.

American Montessori Society (2019) Introduction to Montessori method. https://amshq.org/ (accessed 29 August 2023).

Ardila, A. (1999) A neuropsychological approach to intelligence. *Neuropsychology Review* 9 (3), 117–136.

Arnau, J. (2000) Catalan immersion teachers: Principles of language teaching. *International Journal of Bilingual Education and Bilingualism* 3 (2), 79–100.

Aronin, L. and Singleton, D. (2012) Affordances theory in multilingualism studies. *Studies in Second Language Learning and Teaching* 2 (3), 311–331.

Asher, J.J. (1969) The total physical response approach to second language learning. *The Modern Language Journal* 53 (1), 3–17.

Asher, J. and Garcia, R. (1969) The optimal age to learn a foreign language. *Modern Language Journal* 53, 334–341.

Avello, D. and Muñoz, C. (2023) The development of receptive language skills from captioned video viewing in primary school EFL learners. *Education Sciences* 13 (5), 479.

Baddeley, A. (2000) The episodic buffer: A new component of working memory? *Trends in Cognitive Science* 1 (4), 417–423.

Baddeley, A.D. and Hitch, G. (1974) Working memory. *Psychology of Learning and Motivation* 8, 47–89.

Ball, S., Maguire, M., Braun, A. and Hoskins, K. (2011) Policy actors: Doing policy work in schools. *Discourse: Studies in the Cultural Politics of Education* 32 (4), 625–639.

Banegas, D.L. (2013) ELT through videoconferencing in primary schools in Uruguay: First steps. *Innovation in Language Learning and Teaching* 7 (2), 179–188.

Banfi, C. (2017) English language teaching expansion in South America: Challenges and opportunities. In L.D. Kamhi-Stein, G.D. Maggioli and L.C. de Oliveira (eds) *English Language Teaching in South America: Policy, Preparation and Practices* (pp. 13–30). Multilingual Matters.

Barcelos, A.M.F. and Kalaja, P. (2011) Introduction to beliefs about SLA revisited. *System* 39 (3), 281–289.

Barnes, J. (2008) Early trilingualism: The development of communicative competence in English alongside Basque and Spanish. In C. Perez-Vidal, M. Juan Garau and A. Bel (eds) *A Portrait of the Young in the New Multilingual Spain* (pp. 63–85). Multilingual Matters.

Baumert, J., Fleckenstein, J., Leucht, M., Köller, O. and Möller, J. (2020) The long-term proficiency of early, middle, and late starters learning english as a foreign language at school: A narrative review and empirical study. *Language Learning* 70, 1091–1135.

Beacco, J.-C. and Byram, M. (2007) *Guide for the Development of Language Education Policies in Europe: From Linguistic Diversity to Plurilingual Education* (rev edn). Council of Europe.

Becker, C. (2015) Assessment and portfolios. In J. Bland (ed.) *Teaching English to Young Learners. Critical Issues in Language Teaching with Children 3-12 year Olds* (pp. 261–278). Bloomsbury Academic.

Bekleyen, N. (2011) Can I teach English to children? Turkish preservice teacher candidates and very young learners. *Journal of Early Childhood Teacher Education* 32 (3), 256–265.

Bello-Rodzeń, I. (2016) Multilingual upbringing as portrayed in the blogosphere: On parent-bloggers' profile. *Theory and Practice of Second Language Acquisition* 2 (2), 27–46.

Ben-Zeev, S. (1977) The influence of bilingualism on cognitive strategy and cognitive development. *Child Development* 48, 1009–1018.

Berken, J.A., Gracco, V.L., Chen, J.K. and Klein, D. (2016) The timing of language learning shapes brain structure associated with articulation. *Brain Structure and Function* 221, 3591–3600.

Bernstein, L. (Producer) (1999) *Sesame English*. Sesame Workshop.

Bialystok, E. (2001) *Bilingualism in Development. Language, Literacy, and Cognition*. Cambridge University Press.

Bialystok, E., Majumder, S. and Martin, M.M. (2003) Developing phonological awareness. Is there a bilingual advantage? *Applied Psycholinguistics* 24 (1), 27–44.

Biedroń, A. and Véliz-Campos, M. (2021) Trainability of foreign language aptitudes in children. In J. Rokita-Jaśkow and A. Wolanin (eds) *Facing Diversity in Child Foreign Language Education* (pp. 39–53). Springer.

Bielicka, M. (2017) *Efektywność nauczania języka niemieckiego na poziomie przedszkolnym i wczesnoszkolnym w dwujęzycznych placówkach edukacyjnych w Polsce. [Effectiveness of Teaching German at Pre-primary and Lower Primary Levels in Bilingual Schools in Poland]*. Wydawnictwo Naukowe PWN.

Birdsong, D. (2018) Plasticity, variability and age in second language acquisition and bilingualism. *Frontiers in Psychology* 9.

Birnie, I., Musilova, D., Carre-Karlinger, C. and Schank, F. (2023) *Young Children's Language Learning Pathways*. Council of Europe, ECML.

Bland, J. (ed.) (2015) *Teaching English to Young Learners: Critical Issues in Language Teaching with 3-12-year-olds*. Bloomsbury.

Blewitt, P., Rump, K., Shealy, S. and Cook, S.A. (2009) Shared book reading: When and how questions affect young children's word learning. *Journal of Educational Psychology* 101, 294–304.

Block, D. (2014) *Social Class in Applied Linguistics*. Routledge.

Blondin, C., Candelier, M., Edelenbos, P., Johnstone, R., Kubanek-German, A. and Taeschner, T. (1998) *Foreign Languages in Primary and Pre-school Education*. CILT.

Bloom, P. (2000) *How Children Learn the Meanings of Words*. The MIT Press.

Bolton, K., and Graddol, D. (2012) English in China today. *English Today* 28 (3), 3–9.

Bornstein, M.H. (ed.) (1987) *Sensitive Periods in Development. Interdisciplinary Perspectives*. Psychology Press.

Bouchard, J. and Glasgow, G.P. (2019) *Agency in Language Policy and Planning. Critical Inquiries*. Routledge.

Bourdieu, P. (1991) *Language and Symbolic Power*. Polity Press.

Bourdieu, P. and Passeron, J.C. (2000 [1977]) *Reproduction in Education, Society and Culture*. Sage.

Bowerman, M. and Choi, S. (2003) Space under construction: Language-specific spatial categorization in first language acquisition. In D. Gentner and S. Goldin-Meadow (eds) *Language in Mind: Advances in the Study of Language and Thought* (pp. 387–427). Boston Review.

Brewster, J., Ellis, G. and Girard, D. (2002) *The Primary English Teacher's Guide*. Pearson.

Bronfenbrenner, U. (1979) *The Ecology of Human Development Experiments by Nature and Design*. Harvard University Press.

Broomfit, C., Moon, J. and Tongue, R. (eds) (1991) *Teaching English to Children. From Practice to Principle*. Collins ELT.

Brown, K.D. (2012) The linguistic landscape of educational spaces. Language revitalization and schools in southeastern Estonia. In D. Gorter, H.F. Marten, and L. Van Mensel (eds) *Minority Languages in the Linguistic Landscape* (pp. 281–298). Palgrave Macmillan.

Brown, R. (1973) Development of the first language in the human species. *American Psychologist* 28 (2), 97–106.

Browne, E. (2014) *Handa's Surprise*. Walker Books.

Brumen, M. (2011) The perception of and motivation for foreign language learning in preschool. *Early Child Development and Care* 181 (6), 717–732.

Bruner, J. (1983) *Child's Talk. Learning to Use Language*. W.W. Norton & Co.

Bunyi, G. and Schroeder, L. (2016) Bilingual education in Sub-Saharan Africa: Policies and practice. In O. García, A.M.Y. Lin and S. May (eds) Bilingual and Multilingual Education (pp. 1–18). Springer.

Burstall, C. (1975) Primary French in the balance. *Educational Research* 17, 193–198.

Butler, Y.G. (2015a) English language education among young learners in East Asia: A review of current research (2004–2014). *Language Teaching* 48 (3), 303–342.

Butler, Y.G. (2015b) Parental factors in children's motivation for learning English: A case in China. *Research Papers in Education* 30 (2), 164–191.

Butler, Y.G. (2018) Gaming and young learners. In S. Garton and F. Copland (eds) *The Routledge Handbook of Teaching English to Young Learners* (pp. 305–319). Routledge.

Butler, Y.G. (2022) Learning through digital technologies among pre-primary school children. Implications for their additional language learning. *Language Teaching for Young Learners* 4, 30–65.

Butler, Y.G. and Le, V.-N. (2018) A longitudinal investigation of parental social-economic status (SES) and young students' learning of English as a foreign language. *System* 73, 4–15.

Butler, Y.G. and Huang, B.H. (2023) *Research Methods for Understanding Child Second Language Development*. Routledge.

Butler, Y.G., Someya, Y. and Fukuhara, E. (2014) Online games for young learners' foreign language learning. *ELT Journal* 68 (3), 265–275.

Butler, Y.G., Sayer, P. and Huang, B. (2018) Introduction, social class/socioeconomic status and young learners of English as a global language. *System* 73, 1–3.

Byram, M. (2008) *From Foreign Language Education to Education for Intercultural Citizenship: Essays and Reflections*. Multilingual Matters.

Cameron, L. (2001) *Teaching Languages to Young Learners*. Cambridge University Press.

Campbell, R. and Sais, E. (1995) Accelerated metalinguistic (phonological) awareness in bilingual children. *British Journal of Developmental Psychology* 13, 61–68.

Campfield, D.E. (2021) Cognition and second language experience: How are executive function and second language acquisition related? In J. Rokita-Jaśkow and A. Wolanin (eds) *Facing Diversity in Child Foreign Language Education* (pp. 17–37). Springer.

Campfield, D.E. and Murphy, V.A. (2014) Elicited imitation in search of the influence of linguistic rhythm on child L2 acquisition. *System* 42, 207–219.

Campfield, D. and Murphy, V.A. (2017) The influence of prosodic input in the second language classroom: Does it stimulate child acquisition of word order and function words? *The Language Learning Journal* 45, 81–99.

Carbonara, V. (2019) Teaching Italian language in a bilingual kindergarten in Turkey: A framework for teacher training. In S. Zein and S. Garton (eds) *Early Language Learning and Teacher Education: International Research and Practice* (pp. 177–196). Multilingual Matters.

Carmel, R. (2022) Parents' discourse on English for young learners. *Language Teaching Research* 26 (1), 141–159.

Çekaite, A. (2020) Early language education and language socialization. In M. Schwartz (ed.) *Handbook of Early Language Education* (pp. 1–23). Springer.

Cenoz, J. (2004) Teaching English as a third language: The effect of attitudes and motivation. In C. Hoffman and S. Ytsmea (eds) *Trilingualism in Family, School and Community* (pp. 202–218). Mutlilingual Matters.

Černa, M. (2015) Pre-primary second language education in Slovakia and the role of teacher training programmes. In S. Mourão and M. Lourenço (eds) *Early Years Second Language Education. International Perspectives on Theory and Practice* (pp. 165–176). Routledge.

Chen, S., Zhao, J., de Ruiter, L., Zhou, J. and Huang, J. (2022) A burden or a boost: The impact of early childhood English learning experience on lower elementary English and Chinese achievement. *International Journal of Bilingual Education and Bilingualism* 25, 1212–1229.

Choi, N., Kang, S., Cho, H. and Sheo, J. (2019) Promoting young children's interest in learning English in EFL context: The role of mothers. *Education Sciences* 9 (1), 46.

Choi, N., Kim, T., Kiaer, J. and Morgan-Brown, J. (2020) Mothers' educational beliefs and preschoolers' English learning attitudes: The mediating role of English experiences at home. *Sage Open* 10 (4).

Christison, M., Krulatz, A. and Sevinç, Y. (2021) Supporting teachers of multilingual young learners: Multilingual Approach to Diversity in Education (MADE). In J Rokita-Jaśkow and A. Wolanin (eds) *Facing Diversity in Child Foreign Language Education* (pp. 271–289). Springer.

Christophe, A. and Dupoux, E. (1996) Bootstrapping lexical acquisition: The role of prosodic structure. *The Linguistic Review* 13 (3–4), 383–412.

Christophe, A., Dupoux, E., Bertoncini, J. and Mehler, J. (1994) Do infants perceive word boundaries? An empirical study of the bootstrapping of lexical acquisition. *Journal of Acoustical Society of America* 95, 1570–1580.

Chung, J. and Choi, T. (2016) English education policies in South Korea: Planned and enacted. In R. Kirkpatrick (ed.) *English Language Education Policy in Asia*. Springer.

Clark, E.V. (1993) *The Lexicon in Acquisition*. Cambridge University Press.

Clark, E.V. (2003) *First Language Acquisition*. Cambridge University Press.

Coady, J.A. and Aslin, R.N. (2004) Young children's sensitivity to probabilistic phonotactics in the developing lexicon. *Journal of Experimental Child Psychology* 89, 183–213.

Coelho, D., Andrade, A.I. and Portugal, G. (2018) The 'Awakening to Languages' approach at preschool: Developing children's communicative competence. *Language Awareness* 27 (3), 197–221.

Collaborative for Academic, Social, and Emotional Learning (CASEL) (2013) *2013 Guide: Effective Social and Emotional Learning Programs: Preschool and Elementary School Edition*. CASEL. https://files.eric.ed.gov/fulltext/ED581699.pdf (accessed 15 January 2024).

Cole, N.L. (2024) How sociologists define human agency. Retrieved from https://www.thoughtco.com/agency-definition-3026036

Cook, V.J. (1991) The poverty of the stimulus argument and multi-competence. *Second Language Research* 7 (2), 103–117.

Cortazzi, M. and Jin, L. (1996) English teaching in China. *Language Teaching* 29, 61–80.

Cortés Pascual, A., Moyano Muñoz, N. and Quílez Robres, A. (2019) The relationship between executive functions and academic performance in primary education: Review and meta-analysis. *Frontiers in Psychology* 10, 449759.

Cortina-Pérez, B. and Andúgar, A. (2021) Exploring the ideal foreign language teacher profile in Spanish preschools: Teacher education challenges. *Teachers and Teaching* 27, 713–729.

Cortina-Pérez, B. and Otto, A. (2022) Special issue: Researching foreign languages at pre-primary education. *Porta Linguarum* 7.

Cortina-Pérez, B., Andúgar, A., Álvarez-Cofiño, A., Corral, S., Martínez-León, N. and Otto, A. (2022) *Addressing Future Challenges in Early Language Learning and Multilingual Education*. Dykinson.

Coste, D., Moore, D. and Zarate, G. (2009) *Plurilingual and Pluricultural Competence*. Council of Europe.

Council of Europe (1998) Recommendation no. R (98) 6 of the Committee of Ministers to member states concerning modern languages, Jan, 2024. https://rm.coe.int/16804fc569accessed15

Council of Europe (2006) *Plurilingual Education in Europe. 50 Years of International Cooperation*. ECML.
Council of Europe (2019) Council recommendation of 22 May 2019 on high-quality early childhood education and care systems. https://op.europa.eu/es/publication-detail/-/publica tion/38e20eca-876b-11e9-9f05-01aa75ed71a1/language-en/format-HTML/source-120618859 (accessed 2 May 2024).
Council of Europe (2020) *Common European Framework of Reference for Languages, Learning, Teaching, Assessment – Companion Volume*. Council of Europe Publishing.
Cowan, N. (1997) The development of working memory. In N. Cowan (ed.) *The Development of Memory in Childhood* (pp. 163–199). Psychology Press/Erlbaum.
Coyle, Y. and Gómez Gracia, R. (2014) Using songs to enhance L2 vocabulary acquisition in preschool children. *ELT Journal* 68 (3), 276–285.
Coyle, Y. and Férez Mora, P.A. (2018) Learning a second language in pre-school: Using dramatized stories as a teaching resource. *Didáctica. Lengua y Literatura* 30, 73–85.
Crabbe, D. (2003) The quality of language learning opportunities. *TESOL Quarterly* 37 (1), 9–34.
Crosnoe, R., Leventhal, T., Wirth, R.J., Pierce, K.M., Pianta, R.C. (2010) Family socioeconomic status and consistent environmental stimulation in early childhood. *Child Development* 81 (3), 972–987.
Crystal, D. (2003) *English as a Global Language*. Cambridge University Press.
Cummins, J. (1978) Bilingualism and the development of metalinguistic awareness. *Journal of Crosscultural Psychology* 9, 131–149.
Cummins, J. (1979) Linguistic interdependence and the educational development of bilingual children. *Review of Educational Research* 49 (2), 222–251.
Curdt-Christiansen, X.L. (2016) Conflicting language ideologies and contradictory language practices in Singaporean multilingual families. *Journal of Multilingual and Multicultural Development* 37 (7), 694–709.
Curdt-Christiansen, X.L. and Wang, W. (2018) Parents as agents of multilingual education: Family language planning in China. *Language, Culture and Curriculum* 31 (3), 235–254.
Curriculum Development Council (China) (2006) *Guide to the Pre-primary Curriculum*. Government Printer.
d'Ydewalle, G. and Van de Poel, M. (1999) Incidental foreign-language acquisition by children watching subtitled television programs. *Journal of Psycholinguistic Research* 28 (3), 227–244.
Dalton-Puffer, C. (2011) Content-and-language integrated learning: From practice to principles? *Annual Review of Applied Linguistics* 31, 182–204.
Darling, N. (1999) *Parenting Style and Its Correlates*. ERIC Digest.
De Houwer, A. (2017) Bilingual language acquisition. In P. Fletcher and B. MacWhinney (eds) *The Handbook of Child Language* (pp. 219–250). Blackwell.
De Keyser, R.M. (2000) The robustness of critical period effects in second language acquisition. *Studies in Second Language Acquisition* 22 (4), 499–533.
de Mejía, A.-M. (2016) Early childhood bilingual education in South America. In V. Murphy and M. Evangelou (eds) *Early Childhood Education in English for Speakers of Other Languages* (pp. 43–56). British Council.
De Ruiter, L.E., Wen, P. and Chen, S. (2022) The assessment of Chinese children's English vocabulary-A culturally appropriate receptive vocabulary test for young Chinese learners of English. *Frontiers in Psychology* 13, 769415.
de Villiers, J.G. (1985) Learning how to use verbs: Lexical coding and the influence of the input. *Journal of Child Language* 12 (3), 587–595.

De Wilde, V. and Eyckmans, J. (2017) Game on! Young learners' incidental language learning of English prior to instruction. *Studies in Second Language Learning and Teaching* 7 (4), 673–694.

Deuchar, M. and Quay, S. (2000) *Bilingual Acquisition*. Oxford University Press.

Dickinson, D.K. and Tabors, P.O. (1991) Early literacy: Linkages between home, school and literacy achievement at age five. *Journal of Research in Childhood Education* 6 (1), 30–46.

Döpke, S. (1992) *One Parent, One Language: An Interactional Approach*. John Benjamins.

Dörnyei, Z. (2009) *The Psychology of Second Language Acquisition*. Oxford University Press.

Dulay, H. and Burt, M. (1973) Should we teach children syntax? *Language Learning* 23, 245–258.

Duncan, G.J., Dowsett, C.J. and Classens, A. (2007) School readiness and later achievement. *Developmental Psychology* 43, 1428–1446.

Durlak, J.A., Weissberg, R.P., Dymnicki, A.B., Taylor, R.D. and Schellinger, K.B. (2011) The impact of enhancing students' social and emotional learning: A meta-analysis of school-based universal interventions. *Child Development* 82, 405–432.

Edelenbos, P., Johnstone, R. and Kubanek, A. (2006) *The Main Pedagogical Principles Underlying the Teaching of Languages to Very Young Learners. Languages for the Children of Europe. Published Research, Good Practice & Main Principles*. (Final report of the EAC 89/04, Lot 1 study). European Commission.

Elder, G.H. (1994) Time, human agency, and social change: Perspectives on the life course. *Social Psychology Quarterly* 57 (1), 4–15.

Elman, J. (1993) Learning and development in neural networks: The importance of starting small. *Cognition* 48, 71–99.

Elman, J.L., Bates, E.A., Johnson, M.H., Karmiloff-Smith, A., Parisi, D. and Plunkett, K. (1996) *Rethinking Innateness: A Connectionist Perspective on Development*. The MIT Press.

Emirbayer, M. and Mische, A. (1998) What is agency? *American Journal of Sociology* 103 (4), 962–1023.

Enever, J. (2007) Yet another early-start languages policy in Europe: Poland this time! *Current Issues in Language Planning* 8, 208–221.

Enever, J. (2011) *ELLiE. Early Language Learning in Europe*. British Council.

Enever, J. (2018) *Policy and Politics in Global Primary English*. Oxford University Press.

Enever, J. (2019) Looking beyond the local. Equity as a global concern in Early Language Learning. *AILA Review* 32, 10–35.

Enever, J. (2020) Global language policies. Moving English up the educational escalator. *Language Teaching for Young Learners* 2 (2), 162–191.

Epstein, J.L. (1996) New connections for sociology and education: Contributing to school reform. *Sociology of Education* 69, 6–23.

Erk, M. (2021) Diversity in EELL: Matters of context and contact. In J. Rokita-Jaśkow and A. Wolanin (eds) *Facing Diversity in Child Foreign Language Education* (pp. 75–98). Springer.

Erk, M. (2025) Children's voices on starting English at the primary vs. pre-primary level. In M. Nikolov and S. Letica Krevelj (eds) *Early Foreign Language Learning and Teaching: Evidence Versus Wishful Thinking* (pp. 184-200). Multilingual Matters.

Erk, M. and Pavičić Takač, V. (2021) Teacher target language input and young learners' aural comprehension of English. *ExELL* 9 (1), 1–25.

Ervin-Tripp, S.M. (1974) Is second language learning like the first? *TESOL Quarterly* 8 (2), 111–127.

Esteve-Gibert, N. and Muñoz, C. (2021) Preschoolers benefit from a clear sound-referent mapping to acquire nonnative phonology. *Applied Psycholinguistics* 42 (1), 77–100.

European Commission (1995) *White Paper on Education and Training. Teaching and Learning towards the Learning Society*. European Commission. https://op.europa.eu/en/publication-detail/-/publication/d0a8aa7a-5311-4eee-904c-98fa541108d8/language-en (accessed 15 January 2024).

European Commission (2002) *Barcelona Presidency Conclusions*. European Commission. https://ec.europa.eu/invest-in-research/pdf/download_en/barcelona_european_council.pdf (accessed 15 January 2024).

European Commission (2006) *Lifelong Learning Programme 2007–2023*. European Commission. https://eur-lex.europa.eu/eli/dec/2006/1720/oj (accessed 15 January 2024).

European Commission (2011) *Language Learning at Pre-primary School Level: Making it Efficient and Sustainable. Policy Handbook*. European Commission. https://education.ec.europa.eu/document/commission-staff-working-paper-language-learning-at-pre-primary-level-making-it-efficient-and-sustainable-a-policy-handbook (accessed 15 January 2024).

European Education and Culture Executive Agency, Eurydice (2023) *Key Data on Teaching Languages at School in Europe, 2023 Edition*. Publications Office of the Euroepan Union.

European Parliament (2000) Lisbon presidency conclusions. https://www.europarl.europa.eu/summits/lis1_en.htm (accessed 15 January 2024).

Faitaki, F. and Murphy, V.A. (2023) Using theatre to improve English as an additional language learners' communication skills. In B. Cortina-Pérez, A. Andúgar, A. Álvarez, S. Corral, N. Martínez and A. Otto (eds) *Addressing Future Challenges in Early Language Learning and Multilingual Education* (pp. 141–148). Dykinson.

Fan, X. and Chen, M. (2001) Parental involvement and students' academic achievement: A meta-analysis. *Educational Psychology Review* 13, 1–22.

Fenson, L., Dale, P.S., Reznick, J.S., Bates, E., Thal, D.J., Pethick, S.J., Tomasello, M., Mervis, C.B. and Stiles, J. (1994) Variability in early communicative development. *Monographs of the Society for Research in Child Development* 59 (5), i–185.

Fenyvesi, K. (2020) English learning motivation of young learners in Danish primary schools. *Language Teaching Research* 24 (5), 690–713.

Fernández-Fernández, R. and López-Fuentes, A.V. (2023) Promoting intercultural competence through children's literature. In A. Otto and B. Cortina-Pérez (eds) *Handbook of CLIL in Pre-primary Education* (pp. 441–456). Springer.

Fisch, S., Rosemarie, M., Truglio, T. and Cole, C.F. (1999) The impact of Sesame Street on preschool children: A review and synthesis of 30 years' research. *Media Psychology* 1 (2), 165–190.

Flaherty, M.G. (2011) *The Textures of Time, Agency and Temporal Experience*. Temple University Press.

Fleta, T. (2019) From research on child L2 acquisition of English to classroom practice. In J. Rokita-Jaśkow and M. Ellis (eds) *Early Instructed Second Language Acquisition: Pathways to Competence* (pp. 57–79). Multilingual Matters.

Fleta Gouillen, T. (2018) Scaffolding discourse skills in pre-primary L2 classrooms. In M. Schwartz (ed.) *Preschool Bilingual Education. Agency in Interactions between Children, Teachers, and Parents* (pp. 283–312). Springer.

Fogle, L.W. (2012) *Second Language Socialization and Learner Agency: Adoptive Family Talk*. Multilingual Matters.

Fojkar Dagarin, M. and Skubic, D. (2017) Pre-service preschool teachers' beliefs about foreign language learning and early foreign language teaching in Slovenia. *CEPS Journal* 7, 85–104.

Forey, G., Besser, S. and Sampson, N. (2016) Parental involvement in foreign language learning: The case of Hong Kong. *Journal of Early Childhood Literacy* 16 (3), 383–413.

Freudenstein, R. (ed.) (1979) *Teaching Foreign Languages to the Very Young*. Pergamon Press.

Galambos, S.J. and Hakuta, K. (1988) Subject-specific and task-specific characteristics of metalinguistic awareness in bilingual children. *Applied Psycholinguistics* 9, 141–162.

Galambos, S.J. and Goldin-Meadow, S. (1990) The effects of learning two languages on levels of metalinguistic awareness. *Cognition* 34, 1–56.

García, O. (2009) *Bilingual Education in the 21st Century: A Global Perspective.* John Wiley & Sons.

García Mayo, M.P. and García Lecumberri, M.L. (eds) (2003) *Age and the Acquisition of English as a Foreign Language.* Multilingual Matters.

Garton, S. (2014) Unresolved issues and new challenges in teaching English to young learners: The case of South Korea. *Current Issues in Language Planning* 15, 201–219.

Garton, S. and Copland, F. (eds) (2019) *The Routledge Handbook of Teaching English to Young Learners.* Routledge.

Gass, S. (2018) *Input, Interaction and the Second Language Learner* (2nd edn). Routledge.

Gass, S.M. and Mackey, A. (2007) Input, interaction, and output in second language acquisition. In B. Vanpatten and J. Williams (eds) *Theories in Second Language Acquisition* (pp. 175–200). LEA.

Gathercole, S.E., Willis, C. and Baddeley, A.D. (1991) Differentiating phonological memory and awareness of rhyme, reading and vocabulary development in children. *British Journal of Psychology* 82, 387–406.

Genesee, F. (1989) Early bilingual development, one language or two? *Journal of Child Language* 16, 161–179.

Gerken, L., Jusczyk, P.W. and Mandel, D.R. (1994) When prosody fails to cue syntactic structure: 9-month-olds' sensitivity to phonological versus syntactic phrases. *Cognition* 51 (3), 237–265.

Ghosn, I.-K. (2022) *Teaching English to Young Arabic Speakers. Assessing the Influence of Instructional Materials, Narratives and Cultural Norms.* Bloomsbury.

Giannakopoulou, A. (2021) Care and language pedagogy in preschool education from a distance: A teacher-parent synergy. *Research Papers in Language Teaching and Learning* 11, 53–65.

Giddens, A. (1981) Agency, institution, and time-space analysis. In K. Knorr-Cetina and A.V. Cicourel (eds) *Advances in Social Theory and Methodology. Toward an Integration of Micro- and Macro-Sociologies* (pp. 161–174). Routledge.

Gifford, C., Walsh, V. and Weiner, E. (Producers) and Chialtas, G.S. (Director) (2000) *Dora the Explorer.* Nickelodeon Productions.

Gil, J. (2016) English language education policies in the People's Republic of China. In R. Kirkpatrick (ed.) *English Language Education Policy in Asia* (pp. 49–90). Springer.

Glasgow, G.P. and Bouchard, J. (2019) Introduction. In J. Bouchard and G.P. Glasgow (eds) *Agency in Language Policy and Planning. Critical Inquiries* (pp. 1–21). Routledge.

Gohar, A.G. (2017) The impact of a proposed interactive e-book on developing English language skills of kindergarten children. *International Journal of Internet Education* 16 (1), 1–33.

Goriot, C., Broersma, M., McQueen, J.M., Unsworth, S. and van Hout, R. (2018) Language balance and switching ability in children acquiring English as a second language. *Journal of Experimental Child Psychology* 173, 168–186.

Gorter, D. and Cenoz, J. (2024) *A Panorama of Linguistic Landscape Studies.* Multilingual Matters.

Goullier, F., Carré-Karlinger, C. and Orlova, N. (2015) *European Portfolio for Pre-primary Educators. The Plurilingual and Intercultural Dimension.* ECML.

Graddol, D. (2010) The ET column. Will Chinese take over from English as the world's most important language? *English Today* 26 (4), 3–4.

Griebel, W. and Niesel, R. (2006) Co-constructing transition into kindergarten and school by children, parents and teachers. In H. Fabian and A.-W. Dunlop (eds) *Transitions in the Early Years: Debating Continuity and Progression for Young Children in Early Education* (pp. 64–75). Routledge.

Grigorenko, E.L., Sternberg, R.J. and Ehrman, M.E. (2000) A theory-based approach to the measurement of foreign language learning ability. The canal-F theory and test. *Modern Language Journal* 84 (3), 390–405.

Griva, E. and Sivropoulou, R. (2009) Implementation and evaluation of an early foreign language learning project in kindergarten. *The Early Childhood Journal* 37 (1), 79–87.

Grolnick, W.S. (2016) Parental involvement and children's academic motivation and achievement. In W.C. Liu, J.C.K. Wang and R.M. Ryan (eds) *Building Autonomous Learners* (pp. 169–183). Springer.

Grolnick, W.S. and Slowiaczek, M.L. (1994) Parents' involvement in children's schooling: A multidimensional conceptualization and motivational model. *Child Development* 65, 237–252.

Grolnick, W. S. and Marbell, K. (2009) Parenting. *Encyclopaedia of Human Relationships* 3, 1207–1210.

Guevara, D.C. and Ordoñez, C.L. (2012) Teaching English to very young learners through authentic communicative performances. *Colombian Applied Lingusitics Journal* 14, 9–27.

Haman, E. (2003) Early productivity in derivation. A case study of diminutives in the acquisition of Polish. *Psychology of Language and Communication* 7, 37–56.

Hamid, M.O. (2010) Globalisation, English for everyone and English teacher capacity: Language policy discourses and realities in Bangladesh. *Current Issues in Language Planning* 11 (4), 289–310.

Hickey, T. and Cainín, Ó. (2001) First language maintenance and second language acquisition of a minority language in kindergarten. In M. Almgren, A. Barreña, M.-J. Ezeizabarrena, I. Idiazabal, and B. MacWhinney (eds) *Research on Child Language Acquisition* (pp. 137–150). Cascadilla Press.

Hillyard, S. (2015) Rhythmic patterns in stories and word order production (adjective + noun) in four-year-old EFL learners. In V.A. Murphy and M. Evangelou (eds) *Early Childhood Education in English for Speakers of Other Languages* (pp. 279–292). British Council.

Hirsh-Pasek, K., Kemler Nelson, D.G., Jusczyk, P.W., Cassidy, K.W., Druss, B. and Kennedy, L. (1987) Clauses are perceptual units for young infants. *Cognition* 26 (3), 269–286.

Hoff, E. (2006) How social contexts support and shape language development. *Developmental Review* 26, 55–88.

Hoff, E. and Laursen, B. (2019) Socioeconomic status and parenting. In M.H. Bornstein (ed.) *Handbook of Parenting: Biology and Ecology of Parenting* (pp. 421–447). Routledge.

Hood, M., Conlon, E. and Andrews, G. (2008) Preschool home literacy practices and children's literacy development. A longitudinal analysis. *Journal of Educational Psychology* 100, 252–271.

Hopp, H., Steinlen, A., Schelletter, C. and Piske, T. (2019) Syntactic development in early foreign language learning: Effects of L1 transfer, input, and individual factors. *Applied Psycholinguistics* 40 (5), 1241–1267.

Hosseinpour, V., Sherkatolabbasi, M. and Yarahmadi, M. (2015) The impact of parents' involvement in and attitude toward their children's foreign language programs for learning English. *International Journal of Applied Linguistics and English Literature* 4 (4), 175–185.

Hu, G. and McKay, S.L. (2012) English language education in East Asia: Some recent developments. *Journal of Multilingual and Multicultural Development* 33 (4), 345–362.

Huang, B.H. (2016) A synthesis of empirical research on the linguistic outcomes of early foreign language instruction. *International Journal of Multilingualism* 13 (3), 257–273.

Huttenlocher, J., Vasilyeva, M., Cymerman, E. and Levine, S. (2002) Language input and child syntax. *Cognitive Psychology* 45 (3), 337–374.

ICEPELL Consortium (2022) *The ICEGuide: A Handbook for Intercultural Citizenship Education through Picturebooks in Early English Language Learning.* CETAPS, NOVA FCSH.

Iluk, J. and Jakosz, M. (2017) Storytelling and its effectiveness in developing receptive skills among children. *Studia Linguistica Universitatis Iagellonicae Cracoviensis* 134 (4), 337–352.

Ioannou-Georgiou, S. (2015) Early language learning in Cyprus: Voices from the classroom. In S. Mourão and M. Lourenço (eds) *Early Years Second Language Education* (pp. 95–108). Routledge.

Jaekel, N., Schurig, M., Florian, M. and Ritter, M. (2017) From early starters to late finishers? A longitudinal study of early foreign language learning in school. *Language Learning* 67, 631–664.

Jagatić, M. (1993) Are available teaching time and the number of pupils important factors? In M. Vilke and Y. Vrhovac (eds) *Children and Foreign Languages* I (pp. 45–71). Faculty of Philosophy, University of Zagreb.

Jalkanen, J. (2009) Language proficiency and age-appropriate methodology at the English Kindergarten of Kuopio. In M. Nikolov (ed.) *The Age Factor and Early Language Learning* (pp. 97–118). De Gruyter Mouton.

Javorsky, A. and Thurlow, C. (eds) (2010) *Semiotic Landscapes. Language, Image, Space.* Bloomsbury.

Jia, C.W., Ismafairus, A.H.A. and Malin, A.J. (2018) Working memory from the psychological and neurosciences perspectives: A review. *Frontiers in Psychology* 9, 401.

Jin, L., Zhou, J., Hu, X., Yang, X., Sun, K. and Zhao, M. (2016) *Researching the Attitudes and Perceived Experiences of Kindergarten Learners of English and their Parents in China.* British Council.

Jensen, S.H. (2017) Gaming as an english language learning resource among young children in Denmark. *CALICO Journal* 34 (1), 1–19.

Johnson, J.S. and Newport, E.L. (1989) Critical period effects in second language learning: The influence of the maturational state on the acquisition of ESL. *Cognitive Psychology* 21, 60–99.

Johnson, P., Kessler, T., Santomero, A.C. (Producers) and Sheridan, M. (Director) (1996) *Blue's Clues.* Nick Jr Productions.

Johnstone, R. (2009) An early start: What are the key conditions for generalized success? In J. Enever, J. Moon and U. Raman (eds) *Young Learner English Language Policy and Implementation: International Perspectives* (pp. 31–42). Garnet Education.

Kachru, B. (1992) World Englishes: Approaches, issues and resources. *Language Teaching* 25, 1–14.

Kagan, J. (1999) The role of parents in children's psychological development. *Pediatrics Springfield* 104, 164–167.

Kalaycı, G. and Öz, H. (2018) Parental involvement in English language education: Understanding parents' perceptions. *International Online Journal of Education and Teaching (IOJET)* 5 (4), 832–847.

Kang, H.D. (2012) Primary school English education in Korea: From policy to practice. In B. Spolsky and Y. Moon (eds) *Primary School English-Language Education in Asia: From Policy to Practice* (pp. 59–82). Routledge.

Kapa, L.L. and Colombo, J. (2014) Executive function predicts artificial language learning. *Journal of Memory and Language* 76, 237–252.

Kaplan, R.B. and Baldauf, R.B. (2005) Language-in-education policy and planning. In E. Hinkel (ed.) *Handbook of Research in Second Language Teaching and Learning* (pp. 1013–1034). Lawrence Erlbaum.

Karoulla-Vrikki, M. and Vrikki, M. (2014) Early English language learning in Cyprus: Parental perceptions of identity and intelligibility. In B. O'Rourke, N. Bermingham and S. Brennan (eds) *Opening New Lines of Communication in Applied Linguistics. Proceedings of the 46th Annual Meeting of the British Association of Applied Linguistics* (pp. 219–229). Scitsiugnil Press.

Kemler Nelson, D.G., Hirsh-Pasek, K., Jusczyk, P.W. and Wright-Cassidy, K. (1989) How the prosodic cues in motherese might assist language learning. *Journal of Child Language* 16, 55–68.

Kiaer, J., Morgan-Brown, J.M. and Choi, N. (2021) *Young Children's Foreign Language Anxiety: The Case of South Korea*. Multilingual Matters.

Kim, K., Relkin, N., Lee, K.M., Hirsch, J. (1997) Distinct cortical areas associated with native and second languages. *Nature* 388, 171–174.

King, K. and Fogle, L. (2006) Bilingual parenting as good parenting: Parents' perspectives on family language policy for additive bilingualism. *International Journal of Bilingual Education and Bilingualism* 9 (6), 695–712.

King, K., Fogle, L. and Logan-Terry, A. (2008) Family language policy. *Language and Linguistics Compass* 2, 907–922.

Kirkgöz, Y. (2007) Language planning and implementation in Turkish primary schools. *Current Issues in Language Planning* 8 (2), 174–191.

Kirsch, C. (2018) Young children capitalising on their entire language repertoire for language learning at school. *Language, Culture and Curriculum* 31 (1), 39–55.

Kirsch, C. (2021) Practitioners' language-supporting strategies in multilingual ECE institutions in Luxembourg. *European Early Childhood Education Research Journal* 29 (3), 336–350. https://doi.org/10.1080/1350293X.2021.1928721.

Kirsch, C. and Mortini, S. (2023) Engaging in and creatively reproducing translanguiging practices with peers: A longitudinal study with three-year-olds in Luxembourg. *International Journal of Bilingual Education and Bilingualism* 26 (8), 943–959.

Kiss, C. (2009) The role of aptitude in young learners' foreign language learning. In M. Nikolov (ed.) *The Age Factor and Early Language Learning* (pp. 253–276). Mouton de Gruyter.

Kiss, C. and Nikolov, M. (2005) Developing, piloting, and validating an instrument to measure young learners' aptitude. *Language Learning* 55 (1), 99–150.

Kokla, N. (2016) Dora the explorer. A TV character or a preschoolers' foreign language teacher? *Selected Papers of the 21st International Symposium on Theoretical and Applied Linguistics (ISTAL 21)* (pp. 666–683). Aristotle University of Thessaloniki.

Kolb, A. and Brunsmeier, S. (2019) Extensive reading in primary EFL: Can story apps do the trick? In J. Rokita-Jaśkow and M. Ellis (eds) *Early Instructed Second Language Acquisition: Pathways to Competence* (pp. 153–167). Multilingual Matters.

Komorowska, H. (2014) Analyzing linguistic landscapes. A diachronic study of multilingualism in Poland. In A. Otwinowska and G. De Angelis (eds) *Teaching and Learning in Multilingual Contexts: Sociolinguistic and Educational Perspectives* (pp. 19–31). Multilingual Matters.

Korosidou, E., Griva, E. and Pavlenko, O. (2021) Parental involvement in a program for preschoolers learning a foreign language. *International Journal of Research in Education and Science* (IJRES) 7 (1), 112–124.

Kramsch, C. (2020) *Language as Symbolic Power*. Cambridge University Press.

Krompák, E. (2023) Commentary on the special issue "Language policies and practices in early childhood education, perspectives across European Migration Societies". Agency in language policies and practices: A response to multilingual early childhood education and care. *International Journal of Multilingualism* 20 (4), 1404–1413.

Krompák, E., Fernández-Mallat, V. and Meyer, S. (eds) (2022) *Linguistic Landscapes and Educational Spaces*. Multilingual Matters.

Krulatz, A., Neokleous, G. and Dahl, A. (eds) (2022) *Theoretical and Applied Perspectives on Teaching Foreign Languages in Multilingual Settings: Pedagogical Implications*. Multilingual Matters.

Kubler, A. (2001) *Head, Shoulders, Knees, and Toes...* Child's Play.

Kubota, R. (1998) Ideologies of English in Japan. *World Englishes* 17, 295–307.

Kuhl, P.K., Conboy, B.T., Padden, D., Nelson, T. and Pruitt, J. (2005) Early speech perception and later language development: Implications for the "critical period". *Language Learning and Development* 1 (3–4), 237–264.

Kuppens, A.H. (2010) Incidental foreign language acquisition from media exposure. *Learning, Media and Technology* 35, 65–85.

Lambelet, A. and Berthele, R. (2019) Difficulty and ease in learning foreign languages at the primary school level: General learning ability, language aptitude, or working memory? In Z.E. Wen, P. Skehan, A. Biedroń, S. Li, and R. Sparks (eds) *Language Aptitude, Advancing Theory, Testing, Research and Practice* (pp. 99–122). Routledge.

Landry, R. and Bourhis, R.Y. (1997) Linguistic landscape and ethnolinguistic vitality: An empirical study. *Journal of Language and Social Psychology* 16 (1), 23–49.

Langé, G. and Lopriore, L. (eds) (2014) *Esperienze di insegnamento di lingue straniere nella Scuola dell'Infanzia: Rapporto sulla rilevazione effettuata nel novembre 2014.* MIUR – Direzione Generale per gli Ordinamenti scolastici e la Valutazione del Sistema Nazionale di Istruzione. https://www.istruzione.it/allegati/2015/INFAN-ZIA_Lingue_Straniere_Rapporto_Monitoraggio_Dicembre%202014.pdf (accessed 15 January 2024).

Larson-Hall, J. (2008) Weighing the benefits of studying a foreign language at a younger starting age in a minimal input situation. *Second Language Research* 24 (1), 35–63.

Lau, C. (2020) English language education in Hong Kong: A review of policy and practice. *Current Issues in Language Planning* 21 (5), 457–474.

Laufer, B. (2017) From word parts to full texts. Searching for effective methods of vocabulary learning. *Language Teaching Research* 21 (1), 5–11.

Lee, M.W., Kim, H. and Moon-sub, H. (2021) Language ideologies of Korean mothers with preschool-aged children: Comparison, money, and early childhood English education. *Journal of Multilingual and Multicultural Development* 42 (7), 637–649.

Lefever, S.C. (2010) English skills of young learners in Iceland, "I started talking English when I was 4 years old. It just bang... just fall into me". Paper presented at the Menntakvika Conference, Reykjavik. https://hdl.handle.net/1946/7811

Lenneberg, E.H. (1967) *Biological Foundations of Language*. Wiley.

Leśniewska, J. and Pichette, F. (2014) Songs vs. stories: Impact of input sources on ESL vocabulary acquisition by preliterate children. *International Journal of Bilingual Education and Bilingualism* 19, 18–34.

Letica Krevelj, S. and Mihaljević Djigunović, J. (2021) Transition from pre-primary to primary level. A neglected variable in EFL learning. *The European Journal of Applied Linguistics and TEFL* 10 (2), 79–101.

Li, S. (2015) The associations between language aptitude and second language grammar Acquisition. A meta-analytic review of five decades of research. *Applied Linguistics* 36 (3), 385–408.

Lieven, E. and Tomasello, M. (2008) Children's first language acquisition from a usage-based perspective. In P. Robinson and N.C. Ellis (eds) *Handbook of Cognitive Linguistics and Second Language Acquisition* (pp. 168–196). Routledge.

Lim, L., Pakir, A. and Wee, L. (eds) (2010) *English in Singapore: Modernity and Management*. Hong Kong University Press.

Lindgren, E. and Muñoz, C. (2013) The influence of exposure, parents, and linguistic distance on young European learners' foreign language comprehension. *International Journal of Multilingualism* 10 (1), 105–129.

Little, S. (2019) 'Is there an app for that?' Exploring games and apps among heritage language families. *Journal of Multilingual and Multicultural Development* 40 (3), 218–229.

Lo Bianco, J., Jones, S. and Loh, J. (2021) English language education in Singapore: Research, practice & implications. *Asia Pacific Journal of Education* 41 (4), 635–640.

Łockiewicz, M., Sarzała-Przybylska, Z. and Lipowska, M. (2018) Early predictors of learning a foreign language in preschool – Polish as a first language, English as a foreign language. *Frontiers in Psychology* 9.

Loranc-Paszylk, B. (2019) Parental perceptions of bilingual primary schools in Poland: The (added) value of English. In J. Rokita-Jaśkow and M. Ellis (eds) *Early Instructed Second Language Acquisition: Pathways to Competence* (pp. 175–190). Multilingual Matters.

Lourenço, M., Andrade, A.I. and Sá, S. (2018) Teachers' voices on language awareness in pre-primary and primary school settings: Implications for teacher education. *Language, Culture and Curriculum* 31 (2), 113–127.

Łuniewska, M., Wójcik, M., Kołak, J., Mieszkowska, K., Wodniecka, Z. and Haman, E. (2022) Word knowledge and lexical access in monolingual and bilingual migrant children. Impact of word properties. *Language Acquisition* 29 (2), 135–164.

Luo, W. (2007) A collaborative model for teaching EFL by native and non-native English-speaking teachers. *The Journal of Asia TEFL* 3, 41–58.

Malinowski, D. (2008) Authorship in the linguistic landscape. A multimodal-performative view. In E. Shohamy and D. Gorter (eds) *Linguistic Landscape: Expanding the Scenery* (pp. 107–125). Routledge.

Marecka, M., Szewczyk, J., Jelec, A., Janiszewska, D., Rataj, K. and Dziubalska-Kołaczyk, K. (2018) Different phonological mechanisms facilitate vocabulary learning at early and late stages of language acquisition. Evidence from Polish 9-year-olds learning English—CORRIGENDUM. *Applied Psycholinguistics* 39 (1), 257–257.

Mayer, R.E. (2001) *Multimedia Learning*. Cambridge University Press.

McElwee, J. (2015) Introducing French to pre-primary children in the north-east of England. In S. Mourão and M. Lourenço (eds) *Early Years Second Language Education. International Perspectives on Theory and Practice* (pp. 109–119). Routledge.

Mechelli, A., Crinion, J., Noppeney, U., O'Doherty, J., Ashburner, J., Frackowiak, R.S. and Price C. J. (2004) Structural plasticity in the bilingual brain. *Nature* 431, 757.

Mifsud, C.L. and Vella, L.A. (2020) Early language education in Malta. In M. Schwartz (ed.) *Handbook of Early Language Education*. Springer.

Mihaljević Djigunović, J. (1993) Investigation of attitudes and motivation in early foreign language learning. In M. Vilke and Y. Vrhovac (eds) *Children and Foreign Languages* (pp. 45–71). University of Zagreb.

Mihaljević Djigunović, J. (2009) Impact of learning conditions on young FL learners' motivation. In M. Nikolov (ed.) *Early Learning of Modern Foreign Languages: Processes and Outcomes* (pp. 75–89). Multilingual Matters.

Mihaljević Djigunović, J. (2015) Individual differences among young EFL learners: Age- or proficiency-related? A look from the affective learner factors perspective. In J. Mihaljević Djigunović and M. Medved Krajnović (eds) *Early Learning and Teaching of English. New Dynamics of Primary English* (pp. 10–36). Multilingual Matters.

Mihaljević Djigunović, J. and Vilke, M. (2000) Eight years after: Wishful thinking vs facts of life. In J. Moon and M. Nikolov (eds) *Research into Teaching English to Young Learners* (pp. 66–86). Pécs University Press.

Mihaljević Djigunović, J. and Letica Krevelj, S. (2021) From preprimary to primary learning of English as a foreign language. Coherence and continuity issues. In M. Schwartz (ed.) *Handbook of Early Language Education*. Springer.

Milosavljevic, M. and Reynolds, B.L. (2024) The effectiveness of comprehension-based visual arts instruction and production-based flashcard instruction in young English language learners' vocabulary acquisition and retention. *Studies in Second Language Learning and Teaching* 14, 1–28.

Miyake, A. and Shah, P. (eds) (1999) *Models of Working Memory. Mechanisms of Active Maintenance and Executive Control*. Cambridge University Press.

Montero Perez, M.M. (2020) Incidental vocabulary learning through viewing video. The role of vocabulary knowledge and working memory. *Studies in Second Language Acquisition* 42 (4), 749–773.

Mortimore, L. (2023) A framework for developing Social and Emotional Learning (SEL) in pre-primary CLIL. In A. Otto and B. Cortina-Pérez (eds) *Handbook of CLIL in Pre-primary Education* (pp. 631–637). Springer.

Mourão, S. (2014) Taking play seriously in the pre-primary English classroom. *ELT Journal* 68 (3), 254–264.

Mourão, S. (2015) The potential of picturebooks with young learners. In J. Bland (ed.) *Teaching English to Young Learners. Critical Issues in Language Teaching with Children 3-12 Year Olds* (pp. 199–217). Bloomsbury Academic.

Mourão, S. (2018) Play and peer interaction in a low-exposure foreign language-learning programme. In M. Schwartz (ed.) *Preschool Bilingual Education* (pp. 313–342). Springer.

Mourão, S. (2021) English as a foreign language in ECEC: Itinerant teachers of English and collaborative practices for an integrated approach. *European Early Childhood Education Research Journal* 29 (3), 455–471.

Mourão, S. and Lourenço, M. (eds) (2015) *Early Years Second Language Education. International Perspectives on Theory and Practice*. Routledge.

Mourão, S. and Ferreirinha, S. (2016) Report: Early language learning in pre-primary education in Portugal. Associação Portuguesa de Professores de Inglês. https://run.unl.pt/handle/10362/124669 (accessed 15 January 2024).

Mourão, S. and Ellis, G. (2020) *Teaching English to Pre-primary Children. Educating Very Young Children*. Ernst Klett Sprachen GmbH.

Mrutu, N., Rea-Dickins, P., Bakuza, F., Walli, S. and Pence, A. (2016) Beyond ABC: The complexities of early childhood education in Tanzania. In V. Murphy and M. Evangelou (eds) *Early Childhood Education on English for Speakers of Other Languages* (pp. 91–112). British Council.

Muñoz, C. (ed.) (2006) *Age and the Rate of Foreign Language Learning*. Multilingual Matters.

Muñoz, C. (2008) Symmetries and asymmetries of age effects in naturalistic and instructed L2 learning. *Applied Linguistics* 29 (4), 578–596.

Muñoz, C. (2011) Input and long-term effects of starting age in foreign language learning. *International Review of Applied Linguistics in Language Teaching* 49 (2), 113–133.

Muñoz, C. and Tragant, E. (2023) English at the end of primary school: Explanatory factors. In E. Tragant and C. Muñoz (eds) *Ten Years of English Learning at School* (pp. 29–68). Palgrave Macmillan.

Murphy, V.A. (2014) *Second Language Learning in the Early School Years Trends and Contexts*. Oxford University Press.

Murphy, V.A. and Evangelou, M. (eds) (2016) *Early Childhood Education in English for Speakers of Other Languages*. British Council.

Murphy, V., Evangelou, M., Goff, J. and Tracz, R. (2016) European perspectives on early childhood education and care in English for speakers of other languages. In V. Murphy and M. Evangelou (eds) *Early Childhood Education in English for Speakers of Other Languages* (pp. 57–74). British Council.

Nazari, M., Karimi, M.N. and De Costa, P. (2023) Emotion and identity construction in teachers of young learners of English. An ecological perspective. *System* 112, 102972.

Neuman, S.B., Wong, K.M., Flynn, R. and Kaefer, T. (2019) Learning vocabulary from educational media. The role of pedagogical supports for low-income preschoolers. *Journal of Educational Psychology* 111 (1), 32–44.

Ng, C.L.P. (2016) Primary school English reform in Japan: Policies, progress and challenges. *Current Issues in Language Planning* 17 (2), 215–225.

Ng, M.L. (2013) Pedagogical conditions for the teaching and learning of English as a foreign language in Hong Kong kindergartens. *English Teaching and Learning* 37 (3), 1–35.

Ng, M.L. (2015) Difficulties with team teaching in Hong Kong kindergartens. *ELT Journal* 69 (2), 188–197.

Nguyen, C. (2019) 'Everyone thinks that I just need to know a few words and sing some songs to teach English to the kids': Primary school English language teachers struggled for their professional legitimacy. *Teacher Development* 23 (2) 174–191.

Nguyen, T.M.H. (2011) Primary English language education policy in Vietnam: Insights from implementation. *Current Issues in Language Planning* 12 (2), 225–249.

Nikolov, M. (1999) 'Why do you learn English?' 'Because the teacher is short.' A study of Hungarian children's foreign language learning motivation. *Language Teaching Research* 3 (1), 33–56.

Nikolov, M. and Mihaljević Djigunović, J. (2006) Recent research on age, second language acquisition, and early foreign language learning. *Annual Review of Applied Linguistics* 26, 234–260.

Nikolov, M. and Mihaljević Djigunović, J. (2011) All shades of every color. An overview of early teaching and learning of foreign languages. *Annual Review of Applied Linguistics* 31, 95–119.

Nikolov, M. and Mihaljević Djigunović, J. (2023) Studies on pre-primary learners of foreign languages, their teachers, and parents. A critical overview of publications between 2000 and 2022. *Language Teaching* 56 (4), 451–477.

Nikolov, M. and Lugossy, R. (2021) A critical overview of research methods used in studies on early foreign language education in pre-schools. In M. Schwartz (ed.) *Handbook of Early Language Education*. Springer.

Nikolov, M. and Timpe-Laughlin, V. (2021) Assessing young learners' foreign language abilities. *Language Teaching* 54 (1), 1–37.

OECD (2018) *Education at a Glance 2018: OECD Indicators*. OECD Publishing.

OECD (2020) Why early learning and child well-being matter. *Early Learning and Child Well-Being. A Study of Five-year-Olds in England, Estonia, and the United States.* OECD Publishing.

Olpińska-Szkiełko, M. (2013) Bilinguale Kindererziehung. Ein Konzept für den Polnischen Kindergarten. *Studia Naukowe IKSI UW*. https://portal.uw.edu.pl/documents/7732735/0/ SN+8+Magdalena+Olpi%C5%84ska-Szkie%C5%82ko+-+Bilinguale+Kindererziehung.pdf (accessed 4 January 2024).

Olszewska, A.I., Coady, M. and Markowska-Manista, U. (2022) Language planning, linguistic imperialism, and English language teacher education in post-Soviet Poland. A literature review. In L. McCallum (eds) *English Language Teaching, Theory, Research and Pedagogy* (pp. 51–67). Springer.

Otto, A. and Cortina-Pérez, B. (eds) (2023) *Handbook of CLIL in Pre-primary Education*. Springer.

Oyama, S. (1976) A sensitive period for acquiring a non-native phonological system. *Journal of Psycholinguistic Research* 5, 261–285.

Padial-Ruz, R., García-Molina, R. and Puga-González, E. (2019) Effectiveness of a motor intervention program on motivation and learning of English vocabulary in preschoolers. A pilot study. *Behavioral Sciences* 9 (8).

Paivio, A. (1986) *Mental Representations. A Dual-Coding Approach*. Oxford University Press.

Pamuła, M., Rzyska, J. and Dobkowska, M. (2007) *Moje pierwsze portfolio językowe dla dzieci od 3 do 6 lat. [My First Language Portfolio for Children Aged 3-6]*. CODN.

Park, H. (2008) Home literacy environments and children's reading performance: A comparative study of 25 countries. *Educational Research and Evaluation* 14 (6), 489–505.

Park, J.-K. (2009) 'English fever' in South Korea. Its history and symptoms. *English Today* 25 (1), 50–57.

Park, S.-J. and Abelmann, N. (2004) Class and cosmopolitan striving, Mother's management of English education in South Korea. *Anthropological Quarterly* 77, 645–672.

Patkowski, M. (1980) The sensitive period for the acquisition of syntax in a second language. *Language Learning* 30, 449–472.

Pattemore, A. and Muñoz, C. (2020) Learning L2 constructions from captioned audio-visual exposure: The effect of learner-related factors. *System* 93, 102303.

Pearson, B., Fernandez, S., Lewedeg, V. and Oller, D. (1997) The relation of input factors to lexical learning by bilingual infants. *Applied Psycholinguistics* 18 (1), 41–58.

Pesch, A. (2021) Semiotic landscapes as constructions of multilingualism – A case study of two kindergartens. *European Early Childhood Education Research Journal* 29 (3), 363–380.

Pfenninger, S.E. (2017) Not so individual after all. An ecological approach to age as an individual difference variable in a classroom. *Studies in Second Language Learning and Teaching* 7 (1), 19–46.

Pfenninger, S. (2022) Emergent bilinguals in a digital world: A dynamic analysis of long-term L2 development in (pre)primary school children. *International Review of Applied Linguistics in Language Teaching* 60 (1), 41–66.

Pfenninger, S.E. and Singleton, D. (2017) *Beyond Age Effects in Instructional L2 Learning: Revisiting the Age Factor*. Multilingual Matters.

Pfenninger, S.E. and Singleton, D. (2019) Making the most of an early L2 starting age. *Language Teaching for Young Learners* 1 (2), 111–138.

Pfenninger, S., Festman, J. and Singleton, D. (2023) *Second Language Acquisition and Lifelong Learning*. Routledge.

Philipson, R. (2003) *English Only Europe? Challenging Language Policy*. Routledge.

Piaget, J. (1926/2012) *The Language and Thought of the Child*. Routledge.

Piaget, J. (1953) *The Origins of Intelligence in Children*. Basic Books.

Pinter, A. (2006) *Teaching Young Language Learners*. Oxford University Press.

Pinter, A. (2011) *Children Learning Second Languages*. Palgrave Macmillan.

Pinter, A. (2016) Opportunities to learn and practise English as an L2 in parent–child conversations. *Classroom Discourse* 7 (3), 239–252.

Pinter, A. (2023) *Engaging Children in Applied Linguistics Research*. Cambridge University Press.

Pinter, A. and Kuchah, K. (eds) (2021) *Ethical and Methodological Issues in Researching Young Language Learners in School Contexts*. Multilingual Matters.

Pirchio, S., Taeschner, T., Colibaba, A.C., Gheorghiu, E. and Zacharová, Z.J. (2014) Family involvement in second language learning: The Bilfam project. In S. Mourão and M. Lourenço (eds) *Early Years Second Language Education. International Perspectives on Theory and Practice* (pp. 204–217). Routledge.

Pliatsikas, C., DeLuca, V. and Voits, T. (2020) The many shades of bilingualism: Language experiences modulate adaptations in brain structure. *Language Learning* 70, 133–149.

Power, J.D. and Schlaggar, B.L. (2017) Neural plasticity across the lifespan. *Wiley Interdisciplinary Reviews, Developmental Biology* 6 (1), e216.

Premack, D. and Woodruff, G. (1978) Does the chimpanzee have a theory of mind? *Behavioral and Brain Sciences* 1 (4), 515–526.

Priestley, M., Biesta, G.J.J. and Robinson, S. (2015) Teacher agency: What is it and why does it matter? In R. Kneyber and J. Evers (eds) *Flip the System. Changing Education from the Bottom Up* (pp. 1–11). Routledge.

Prošić-Santovac, D. (2017) Popular video cartoons and associated branded toys in teaching English to very young learners. A case study. *Language Teaching Research* 21 (5), 568–588.
Prošić-Santovac, D. and Radović, D. (2018a) Children's vs. teachers' and parents' agency: A case of a Serbian-English bilingual preschool model. *Language, Culture and Curriculum* 31 (3), 289–302.
Prošić-Santovac, D. and Radović, D. (2018b) Separating the languages in a bilingual preschool: To do or not to do? In M. Schwartz (ed.) *Preschool Bilingual Education: Agency in Interactions between Children, Teachers, and Parents* (pp. 27–56). Springer.
Prošić-Santovac, D. and Rixon, S. (eds) (2019) *Integrating Assessment into Early Language Learning and Teaching*. Multilingual Matters.
Protassova, E. (2018) Longing for quality: Experiences of Finnish-Russian bilingual kindergarten in Finland. In M. Schwartz (ed.) *Preschool Bilingual Education* (pp. 135–162). Springer.
Puimège, E. and Peters, E. (2019) Learners' English vocabulary knowledge prior to formal instruction. The role of learner-related and word-related variables. *Language Learning* 69 (4), 943–977.
Purić, D., Vuksanović, J. and Chondrogianni, V. (2017) Cognitive advantages of immersion education after one year. Effects of amount of exposure. *Journal of Experimental Child Psychology* 159, 296–309.
Putjata, G. and Koster, D. (2023) 'It is okay if you speak another language, but…': Language hierarchies in mono-and bilingual school teachers' beliefs. *International Journal of Multilingualism* 20 (3), 891–911.
Qi, G.Y. (2016) The importance of English in primary school education in China: Perceptions of students. *Multilingual Education* 6 (1), 1–18.
Ratner, N.B. and Gleason, J.-B. (1993) *Psycholinguistics*. Academic Press.
Reynolds, B.L., Liu, S., Ha, X.V., Zhang, X. and Ding, C. (2021a) Pre-service teachers learning to teach English as a foreign language to preschool learners in Macau: A longitudinal study. *Frontiers in Psychology* 12, 720660.
Reynolds, B.L., Liu, S., Milosavljevic, M., Ding, C. and McDonald, J. (2021b) Exploring pre-service pre-primary EFL teacher beliefs about teaching English to very young learners: A Macau case study. *Sage Open* 11 (4).
Rice, M., Huston, A., Truglio, R. and Wright, J. (1990) Words from "Sesame Street". Learning vocabulary while viewing. *Developmental Psychology* 26, 421–428.
Robinson, P., Mourão, S. and Kang, N.J. (2015) *English Learning Areas in Preschool Classrooms: An Investigation of their Effectiveness in Supporting EFL Development*. British Council. https://www.teachingenglish.org.uk/sites/teacheng/files/pub_English%20learning%20areas%20in%20pre-primary%20classrooms.pdf (accessed 15 January 2024).
Roehr-Brackin, K. and Tellier, A. (2019) The role of language analytic ability in children's instructed second language learning. *Studies in Second Language Acquisition* 41 (5), 1111–1131.
Roh, T.R.D. and Lee, Y.-A. (2018) Teacher repetition as an instructional resource for classroom interaction. Three pedagogical actions in kindergartens in an EFL context. *System* 74, 121–137.
Rokita, J. (2006) Code-mixing in early L2 lexical acquisition. In J. Arabski (ed.) *Crosslinguistic Influences in the Second Language Mental Lexicon* (pp. 177–190). Multilingual Matters.
Rokita, J. (2007) *Lexical Development in Early L2 Acquisition*. Kraków Pedagogical University Press.
Rokita-Jaśkow, J. (2010) Fostering artificial bilingualism: An ambiguous decision, ambiguous results. In J. Leśniewska and M. Jodłowiec (eds) *Ambiguity and the Search for Meaning* (pp. 269–280). WUJ.

Rokita-Jaśkow, J. (2013a) *Foreign Language Learning at Pre-primary Level. Parental Aspirations and Educational Practice*. Kraków Pedagogical University Press.

Rokita-Jaśkow, J. (2013b) Socioeconomic status and parental involvement as cognitive and affective factors fostering very young learners' second language development. In E. Piechurska-Kuciel and E. Szymańska-Czaplak (eds) *Language in Affect and Cognition* (pp. 189–204). Springer.

Rokita-Jaśkow, J. (2014) Using storybooks as a catalyst for negotiation of meaning and enhancing speaking among very young learners of L2: Evidence from a case study. In M. Pawlak and E. Waniek-Klimczak (eds) *Issues in Teaching, Learning and Testing Speaking in a Second Language* (pp. 205–217). Springer.

Rokita-Jaśkow, J. (2015a) Parental visions of their children's future as a motivator for an early start in a foreign language. *Studies in Second Language Learning and Teaching* 5 (3), 455–472.

Rokita-Jaśkow, J. (2015b) Is foreign language knowledge a form of capital passed from one generation to the next? In E. Piechurska-Kuciel and M. Szyszka (eds) *The Ecosystem of the Foreign Language Learner: Selected Issues* (pp. 153–168). Springer.

Rokita-Jaśkow, J. (2016) Kindergarten teachers' beliefs about the goals of very early FL instruction and their classroom practices: Is there a link? In M. Pawlak (ed.) *Classroom-Oriented Research* (pp. 135–150). Springer.

Rokita-Jaśkow, J. (2019) Parental involvement in very early L2 acquisition. In J. Rokita-Jaśkow and M. Ellis (eds) *Early Instructed Second Language Acquisition: Pathways to Competence* (pp. 191–205). Multilingual Matters.

Rokita-Jaśkow, J. (2022) Teaching foreign languages at the pre-primary level in a monolingual Setting: The case of Poland. *Porta Linguarum* 5, 31–42.

Rokita-Jaśkow, J. and Pamuła-Behrens, M. (2019) Policy and practice in early foreign language learning: The case of Poland. In J. Rokita-Jaśkow and M. Ellis (eds) *Early Instructed Second Language Acquisition: Pathways to Competence* (pp. 11–25). Multilingual Matters.

Rokita-Jaśkow, J. and Król-Gierat, W. (2021) Preparing teachers of Early Childhood Education to teach a foreign language: The PEPELINO portfolio in practice. *Issues in Early Education* 52 (1), 153–169.

Romaine, S. (2000) *Bilingualism* (2nd edn). Wiley-Blackwell.

Roos, J. and Nicholas, H. (2019) Using young learners' language environments for EFL learning. Ways of working with linguistic landscapes. *AILA Review* 32, 91–11.

Ruben, R.J. (1997) A time frame of critical/sensitive periods of language development. *Acta oto-laryngologica* 117 (2), 202–205.

Ruiz de Zairobe, Y. (2023) CLIL in pre-primary education. Trends, challenges and future directions. In A. Otto and B. Cortina-Pérez (eds) *Handbook of CLIL in Pre-primary Education* (pp. 631–637). Springer.

Sanvictores, T. and Mendez, M.D. (2022) *Types of Parenting Styles and Effects On Children*. StatPearls Publishing.

Sayer, P. (2018) Does English really open doors? Social class and English teaching in public primary schools in Mexico. *System* 73, 58–70.

Sayer, P. (2019) The hidden curriculum of work in English language education: Neoliberalism and early English programs in public schooling. *AILA Review* 32 (1), 36–63.

Schaffer, H.R. (2004) *Introducing Child Psychology*. Blackwell.

Scheffler, P. (2015) Introducing very young children to English as a foreign language. *International Journal of Applied Linguistics* 25 (1), 1–22.

Scheffler, P. and Domińska, A. (2018) Own-language use in teaching English to preschool children. *ELT Journal* 72 (4), 374–383.

Scheffler, P., Jones, C. and Domińska, A. (2021) The Peppa Pig television series as input in pre-primary EFL instruction. A corpus-based study. *International Journal of Applied Linguistics* 31 (1), 3–17.

Schmidt, R.W. (1990) The role of consciousness in second language learning. *Applied Linguistics* 11, 129–158.
Schönpflug, U. (2001) Bilingualism: Cognitive aspects. In N.J. Smelser and P.B. Baltes (eds) *International Encyclopedia of the Social & Behavioral Sciences* (pp. 1171–1175). Pergamon.
Schwartz, M. (ed.) (2018) *Preschool Bilingual Education. Agency in Interactions between Children, Teachers, and Parents.* Springer.
Schwartz, M. (2020) *Handbook of Early Language Education.* Springer.
Schwartz, M. (2023) Language-conducive strategies to enhance communication in the CLIL pre-primary classroom. In A. Otto and B. Cortina-Pérez (eds) *Handbook of CLIL in Pre-primary Education* (pp. 343–354). Springer.
Schwartz, M. and Deeb, I. (2018) Toward a better understanding of the language conducive context. An ecological perspective on children's progress in the second language in bilingual preschool. *International Journal of Bilingual Education and Bilingualism* 24, 481–499.
Scollon, R. and Scollon, S.W. (2003) *Discourses in Place. Language in the Material World.* Routledge.
Segers, E. and Verhoeven, L. (2003) Effects of vocabulary training by computer in kindergarten. *Journal of Computer Assisted Learning* 19, 557–566.
Seliger, H. (1978) Implications of a multiple critical periods hypothesis for second language learning. In W.C. Ritchie (ed.) *Second Language Acquisition Research. Issues and Implications* (pp. 11–19). Academic Press.
Seo, Y. (2023) The role of home language environment and parental efforts in children's English development in an EFL context. *Journal of Multilingual and Multicultural Development*, 1–15.
Shankar, P. and Gunashekar, P. (2016) Early childhood education in English in India. In V. Murphy and M. Evangelou (eds) *Early Childhood Education on English for Speakers of Other Languages* (pp. 75–90). British Council.
Shuey, E. and Kankaraš, M. (2018) The power and promise of early learning. *OECD Education Working Papers* No. 186.
Singleton, D. (1999) *Exploring the Second Language Mental Lexicon.* Cambridge University Press.
Singleton, D. and Ryan, L. (2004) *Language Acquisition: The Age Factor.* Multilingual Matters.
Snow, C.E. and Hoefnagel-Höhle, M. (1978) The critical period for language acquisition: Evidence from second language learning. *Child Development* 49 (4), 1114–1128.
Song, J.J. (2011) English as an official language in South Korea. Global English or social malady? *Language Problems and Language Planning* 35, 35–55.
Sopata, A. (2009) *Erwerbsteheoretische und glottodidaktische Aspekte des Fruehen Zweitspracherwerbs Sprachentwicklung der Kinder im naturlichen und schulischen kontext.* UAM.
Sparks, R.L. (2022) *Exploring L1-L2 Relationships: The Impact of Individual Differences.* Multilingual Matters.
Sparks, R. and Ganschow, L. (1993) The effects of multisensory structured language instruction on native language and foreign language aptitude skills of at risk high school foreign language learners. A replication and follow up study. *Annals of Dyslexia* 43, 194–216.
Sparks, R.L., Patton, J. and Luebbers, J. (2019) Individual differences in L2 achievement mirror individual differences in L1 skills and L2 aptitude. Crosslinguistic transfer of L1 to L2 skills. *Foreign Language Annals* 52, 255–283.
Spolsky, B. (2004) *Language Policy.* Cambridge University Press.
Statista (2023) Internet penetration rate in the European Union from 2019 to 2022, by country. https://www.statista.com/statistics/1246141/eu-internet-penetration-rate/ (accessed 5 May, 2024).

Statista (2024) Countries with the largest digital populations in the world as of January 2023. https://www.statista.com/statistics/262966/number-of-internet-users-in-selected-countries/ (accessed 5 May 2024).

Stoel-Gammon, C. (2011) Relationships between lexical and phonological development in structure. *The Linguistic Review* 13, 383–412.

Suh, S., Kim, S.-W. and Kim, N.-J. (2010) Effectiveness of MMORPG-based instruction in elementary English education in Korea. *Journal of Computer Assisted Learning* 26, 370–378.

Sulpizio, S., Del Maschio, N., Fedeli, D. and Abutalebi, J. (2020) Bilingual language processing: A meta-analysis of functional neuroimaging studies. *Neuroscience & Biobehavioral Reviews* 108, 834–853.

Sun, H. and Ng, E. (2021) Home and school factors in early English language education. *Asian Pacific Journal of Education* 4, 657–672.

Sun, H., de Boot, K., Steinkrauss, R. (2014) A multiple case study on the effects of temperamental traits in Chinese preschoolers learning English. *International Journal of Bilingualism*, 1–23.

Sun, H., Steinkrauss, R., Tendeiro, J. and de Bot, K. (2015) Individual differences in very young children's English acquisition in China. Internal and external factors. *Bilingualism, Language and Cognition* 19, 550–566.

Sun, H., Steinkrauss, R., van der Steen, S., Cox, R. and de Bot, K. (2016) Foreign language learning as a complex dynamic process: A microgenetic case study of a Chinese child's English learning trajectory. *Learning and Individual Differences* 49, 287–296.

Sundqvist, P. (2016) Gaming and young language learners. In F. Farr and L. Murray (eds) *The Routledge Handbook of Language Learning and Technology* (pp. 446–455). Routledge.

Swain, M. (1985) Communicative competence. Some roles of comprehensible input and comprehensive output in its development. In S. Gass and C. Madden (eds) *Input in Second Language Acquisition* (pp. 235–253). Newbury House.

Sylven, L.K. and Sundqvist, P. (2012) Gaming as extramural English L2 learning and L2 proficiency among young learners. *ReCALL* 24, 302–321.

Szabó, T. (2015) The management of diversity in schoolscapes. An analysis of Hungarian practices. *Apples – Journal of Applied Language Studies* 9 (1), 23–51.

Szpotowicz, M. and Szulc-Kurpaska, M. (2009) *Teaching English to Young Learners*. PWN.

Szramek-Karcz, S. (2016) The success of non-native bilingualism in Poland. *Applied Linguistics. Angewandte Linguistik* 17 (2), 93–102.

Tao, L., Marzecová, A., Taft, M., Asanowicz, D. and Wodniecka, Z. (2011) The efficiency of attentional networks in early and late bilinguals. The role of age of acquisition. *Frontiers in Psychology* 2, 123.

Teng, M.F. (2023) Effectiveness of captioned videos for incidental vocabulary learning and retention: The role of working memory. *Computer Assisted Language Learning*, 1–28.

Thieme, A.-M., Hanekamp, K., Andringa, S., Verhagen, J. and Kuiken, F. (2022) The effects of foreign language programmes in early childhood education and care: A systematic review. *Language, Culture and Curriculum* 35 (3), 334–351.

Toumpaniari, K., Loyens, S., Mavilidi, M.F. and Paas, F. (2015) Preschool children's foreign language vocabulary learning by embodying words through physical activity and gesturing. *Educational Psychology Review* 27, 445–456.

Tragant, E. (2006) Language learning motivation and age. In C. Muñoz (ed.) *Age and the Rate of Foreign Language Learning* (pp. 237–268). Multilingual Matters.

Tsui, A. (ed.) (2020) *English Language Teaching and Teacher Education in East Asia. Global Challenges and Local Responses*. Cambridge University Press.

UNESCO (1999) Records of the general conference. https://unesdoc.unesco.org/ark/48223/pf0000118514 (accessed 31 October 2023).
Unsworth, S., Persson, L., Prins, T. and de Bot, K. (2015) An investigation of factors affecting early foreign language learning in the Netherlands. *Applied Linguistics* 36 (5), 527–548.
Unsworth, S., Brouwer, S., de Bree, E. and Verhagen, J. (2019) Predicting bilingual preschoolers' patterns of language development: Degree of non-native input matters. *Applied Psycholinguistics* 40, 1189–1219.
Urmeneta, C.E. and Unamuno, V. (2008) Languages and language learning in Catalan schools: From the bilingual to the monolingual challenge. In C. Hélot and A.-M. de Mejía (eds) *Forging Multilingual Spaces: Integrated Perspectives on Majority and Minority Bilingual Education* (pp. 228–255). Multilingual Matters.
van Lier, L. (2004) *The Ecology and Semiotics of Language Learning. A Sociocultural Perspective*. Kluwer Academy.
van Lier, L. (2010) The ecology of language learning. Practice to theory, theory to practice. *Procedia Social and Behavioral Sciences* 3, 2–6.
Vićević Ivanović, S., Košuta, N. and Patekar, J. (2021) A look into young learners' language learning strategies: A Croatian example. *Training, Language and Culture* 5 (3), 83–96.
Vilke, M. (1976a) The age factor in the acquisition of foreign languages. *Rasegna Italiana di Linguistica Aplicada* 2/3, 179–190.
Vilke, M. (1976b) Implications of the age factor on the process of acquisition of an L2. *SRAZ* 41–42, 87–104.
Vygotsky, L.S. (1978) *Mind in Society. The Development of Higher Psychological Processes*. Harvard University Press.
Vygotsky, L. (1985) *Thought and Language* (2nd edn). MIT Press.
Waddington, J. (2021) Rethinking the "ideal native speaker" teacher in early childhood education. *Language, Culture and Curriculum* 35 (1), 1–17.
Waddington, J., Bernal, S.C. and Jofré, C.S. (2018) Creating and evaluating a foreign language area in an early childhood setting. *European Early Childhood Education Research Journal* 26 (3), 334–346.
Waite-Stupiansky, S. (2022) Jean Piaget's constructivist theory of learning. In L.E. Cohen and S. Waite-Stupiansky (eds) *Theories of Early Childhood Education* (pp. 3–18). Routledge.
Washington-Nortey, P.M., Zhang, F., Xu, Y., Chen, C.C. and Spence, C. (2020) The impact of peer interactions on language development among preschool English language learners: A systematic review. *Early Childhood Education Journal* 50, 49–59.
Wati, S. (2016) Parental involvement and English language teaching to young learners: Parents' experience in Aceh. *Proceeding of International Conference on Teacher Training and Education* 1 (1), 527–533.
Wei, R. and Su, J. (2012) The statistics of English in China. *English Today* 28 (3), 10–14.
Weigel, D., Martin, S. and Benett, K. (2006) Contributions of the home literacy environment to preschool-aged children's emerging literacy and language skills. *Early Child Development and Care* 176, 357–378.
Weitz, M., Pahl, S., Flyman, A., Mattsson, A., Buyl, A. and Kalbe, E. (2010) The Input Quality Observation Scheme (IQOS): The nature of L2 input and its influence on L2 development in bilingual preschools. In K. Kersten, A. Rohde, C. Schelletter and A. Steinlen (eds) *Bilingual Preschools* (pp. 5–44). Wissenschaftlicher.
Wen, Z.E. (2016) *Working Memory and Second Language Learning: Towards an Integrated Approach*. Multilingual Matters.
Wen, Z.E. (2019) Working memory as language aptitude. In Z.E. Wen, P. Skehan, A. Biedroń, S. Li, and R. Sparks (eds) *Language Aptitude, Advancing Theory, Testing, Research and Practice* (pp. 187–214). Routledge.

Westermann, G., Ruh, N. and Plunkett, K. (2009) Connectionist approaches to language learning. *Linguistics* 47 (2), 413–452.

Wilden, E. and Porsch, R. (2020) Teachers' self-reported L1 and L2 use and self-assessed L2 proficiency in primary EFL education. *Studies in Second Language Learning and Teaching* 10 (3), 631–655.

Wilder, S. (2014) Effects of parental involvement on academic achievement: A meta-synthesis. *Educational Review* 66 (3), 377–397.

Williams, G. (2010) *The Knowledge Economy, Language and Culture*. Multilingual Matters.

Winston, J. (2022) *Performative Language Teaching in Early Education. Language Learning through Drama and the Arts for Children 3–7*. Bloomsbury Academic.

Wolf, M. and Butler, Y.G. (eds) (2017) *English Language Proficiency Assessments for Young Learners*. Routledge.

Wong, K.M. and Samudra, P.G. (2021) L2 vocabulary learning from educational media, extending dual-coding theory to dual-language learners. *Computer Assisted Language Learning* 34 (8), 1182–1204.

Wong Fillmore, L. (1979) Individual differences in second language acquisition. In C.J. Fillmore, D. Kemplar and W.S-Y. Wang (eds) *Individual Differences in Language Ability and Language Behavior* (pp. 203–228). Academic Press.

Wood, D. (1998) *How Children Think and Learn* (2nd edn). Wiley-Blackwell.

Wouters, P., van Nimwegen, C., van Oostendorp, H. and van der Spek, E.D. (2013) A meta-analysis of the cognitive and motivational effects of serious games. *Journal of Educational Psychology* 105 (2), 249–265.

Wu, X. (2003) Intrinsic motivation and young language learners. The impact of the classroom environment. *System* 31, 501–517.

Xia, J. and Gao, X. (2022) Parental involvement in Chinese preschool children's mobile-assisted foreign language learning. *Porta Linguarum*. https://doi.org/10.30827/portalin.vi.23840.

Yashima, T. (2002) Willingness to communicate in a second language. The Japanese EFL context. *Modern Language Journal* 86, 54–66.

Yelland, G.W., Pollard, J. and Mercuri, A. (1993) The metalinguistic benefits of limited contact with a second language. *Applied Psycholinguistics* 14, 423–444.

Yeung, S.S., Siegel, L.S. and Chan, C.K. (2013) Effects of a phonological awareness program on English reading and spelling among Hong Kong Chinese ESL children. *Reading and Writing* 26 (5), 681–704.

Yeung, S. S., Ng, M.-l., & King, R. B. (2016) English vocabulary instruction through storybook reading for Chinese EFL kindergarteners: Comparing rich, embedded, and incidental approaches. *The Asian EFL Journal* 18(2), 89–112.

Yeung, S.S., Ng, M., Qiao, S. and Tsang, A. (2020) Effects of explicit L2 vocabulary instruction on developing kindergarten children's target and general vocabulary and phonological awareness. *Reading and Writing* 33, 671–689.

Zeanah, C.H., Berlin, L.J. and Boris, N.W. (2011) Practitioner review: Clinical applications of attachment theory and research for infants and young children. *Journal of Child Psychology and Psychiatry, and Allied Disciplines* 52 (8), 819.

Zein, S. (2021) Introduction to early language learning policy in the twenty-first century. In S. Zein and M.R. Coady (eds) *Early Language Learning Policy in the 21st Century* (pp. 1–37). Springer.

Zein, S. and Garton, S. (eds) (2019) *Early Language Learning and Teacher Education: International Research and Practice*. Multilingual Matters.

Zhang, X., Hu, B., Ren, L. and Zhang, L. (2019) Family socioeconomic status and Chinese children's early academic development. Examining child-level mechanisms. *Contemporary Educational Psychology* 59, 101729.

Zhao, S. and Baldauf, R.B. (2012) Individual agency in language planning: Chinese script reform as a case study. *Language Problems and Language Planning* 36, 1–24.

Subject Index

Access policy 101, 115
Affect 31, 33, 38
   Affective 50, 61, 98, 99, 102
Affordances 3, 7, 59, 77, 79, 84, 88, 90, 94, 111, 137, 138
Age of Onset 128
Agency 5–8, 29, 37, 122, 123, 138, 139
   Agency of landscape 94
   Child agency 6, 78, 94, 136
   Institutional agency/Agency of institutions 96, 121
   Parental agency 7, 60, 67, 68, 77, 78, 139
   Teacher agency 5, 31, 48, 58, 59, 111, 115
   Temporal agency 132, 133
Aptitude 6, 9, 19, 20, 24, 25, 27, 29, 30, 33, 126
Argentina 110
Aspirations 1, 7, 60, 61, 66–70, 73, 76, 79, 82, 85, 97, 122, 137
Assessment 21, 33, 40, 45, 83, 104, 118–120
Attention 18–23, 25–26, 29–30, 32, 36, 42, 46, 62, 78, 88, 120, 125, 128, 136–137
Attitude 31, 62, 83, 106

Basic Interpersonal Communication Skills (BICS) 130
Beliefs 3, 7, 51, 62, 66, 68, 73, 77, 79, 82, 85, 111–114
Bilingual kindergartens 36, 37, 54, 56, 84
Biosystem 6, 9, 29, 30

Capital (linguistic /symbolic) 60, 67, 69, 76, 77, 82
Chile 89, 109
China 109, 115, 116, 119, 123, 129
Chronosystem 8, 124
CLIL 36, 38, 39, 129, 136, 137
Code-mixing 15–17, 38, 41, 53
Cognitive Academic Language Proficiency (CALP) 130
Coherence 131, 132
Common European Framework of Reference for Languages (CEFR) 52, 104, 110, 120
Continuity 8, 72, 98, 99, 100, 103, 124, 131, 132, 133
Critical Period Hypothesis (CPH) 126, 128
Croatia 2, 55, 58, 89, 90, 120,
Curriculum 5, 33, 35–38, 50, 52, 56, 85, 96, 99, 101–104, 106–108, 110, 111, 117, 131, 132

Discourse 4, 7, 17, 18, 21, 41, 42, 47, 52, 53, 54, 56, 58, 59, 63, 73, 74, 78, 85, 87, 94, 138
Discourse strategies 4, 21, 47, 53, 54, 56, 63, 74
Diversity 3–5, 44, 94, 97–99, 102, 104, 113, 117, 139, 140
Dual Language Learners (DLL) 90, 91

Early Childhood Education and Care (ECEC) 36, 61, 96, 125, 134
Ecology 3, 4, 30, 52, 112, 124
English as an Additional Language (EAL) 43

English Language Area (ELA) 57–59
English-Medium Instruction (EMI) 84, 104
Equity 99, 103, 115–117
European Centre for Modern Languages (ECML) 45
European Language Policy (ELP) 7, 97
European Union (EU) 80, 97, 98, 104
Evaluation 32, 44, 54, 99, 101, 101, 118, 121, 123
Executive functions 6, 9, 22, 23, 24, 29, 30, 61, 130, 140
Exosystem 7, 79, 85, 94, 140
Expanding Circle 80
Explicit learning/teaching 92, 95, 110
Extramural 70, 90, 95

Family Language Policy (FLP) 62, 63, 67, 136
First Language (L1), 1, 9, 15, 37, 56, 60, 112, 113, 119, 125, 126, 140

Games 5, 32, 39, 40, 46, 47, 57, 65, 74, 88, 89, 92, 93, 94, 102, 109
Gaming 90, 92–95
Globalisation 79–81, 83, 88, 96, 97, 104, 105, 109
Greece 100, 101, 113

Identity 5, 14, 36, 68, 69, 77, 81, 99, 103, 112
Ideologies 61, 66, 69, 73, 77, 83, 85, 96, 97, 139
Implicit learning/teaching 6, 19, 20, 25, 39, 40, 42, 54, 77, 87–90, 94, 137
Incidental 39, 40, 65, 89, 92, 95
Inclusive 38, 56, 87, 116
Individual differences 4, 20
Intercultural awareness 44, 45, 111
Intrinsic motivation 31, 33, 36, 44, 65

Japan 49, 82, 83, 89, 92, 105, 106

Language planning/ language-in-education 68, 96, 97, 101, 104, 116, 123
Language policy 7, 8, 37, 38, 62, 63, 67, 96, 97, 100–102, 121, 132, 136, 138

Learning apps 117, 119, 129, 137
Lexicon 10, 11, 15, 16, 23, 27, 55, 87, 126
Linguistic imperialism 97
Linguistic landscape 7, 79, 81, 83, 85, 94, 137
Long-term memory 21, 22, 29, 40

Macrosystem 96, 139
Mobile-assisted language learning (MALL) 65, 66
Mesosystem 60
Metalinguistic awareness 6, 9, 25, 33, 88, 130, 137
Microsystem 6, 31, 59, 61
Model of human development 5, 30
Multimodal, multimodality 40, 46, 63, 71, 85

Native English-Speaking Teacher (NEST) 49, 51, 116, 117
Neoliberalism 79, 81, 84, 96

Parental FL proficiency 73
Parental involvement 73, 74, 76, 77, 78, 136
Parenting (style) 60–62, 66–68, 70, 77, 78
Partnership 70, 71, 138
Peers 29, 32, 57, 59, 90, 99, 125, 136, 139
Phonological awareness 18, 19, 25–29, 36, 41, 42, 46, 63
Poland 2, 37, 48, 51, 56, 67, 68, 82, 83, 88, 90, 100, 101, 103, 111, 118, 120, 122, 123
Policy handbook 99, 102, 113
Policy implementation 96, 108, 111, 123, 138
Portfolio 45, 113, 114, 120
Portugal 48, 57
Pragmatics 9, 60, 87
Pretend play 14, 18, 43, 47, 58, 74, 136, 139
Prosody, prosodic 10, 12, 28, 42

Scaffolding 15, 18, 39, 40, 53, 63–65, 74, 91, 93, 95, 136
Schoolscapes 85, 87, 94
Screen media 46, 47, 88

Second Language Acquisition (SLA) 51, 112
Semantic mapping 10
Socioeconomic Status (SES) 60, 73, 107, 116, 119, 126, 136
Socioemotional learning 38, 39, 48, 112
South Korea 37, 56, 57, 67, 68, 75, 82, 83, 94, 96, 105–107, 109, 114, 116, 122, 123
Song 37, 42, 46, 57, 86
Spain 35, 37, 52, 79, 89, 90, 100, 101, 120
Storybook 39, 40, 42, 43, 57, 71, 72
Storytelling 28, 39, 40–42, 71
Syntax 9–13, 17, 65, 87, 111, 125, 126

Teaching English to Young Learners (TEYL) 1, 52, 103, 137
Technology 39, 47, 59, 89, 100, 116, 129
Temperament 20, 25, 29, 136
Total Physical Response (TPR) 32
Transition 8, 70, 124, 131–133

Uruguay 110, 115, 116

Well-being 22, 36, 38, 56, 66, 112, 141
Working memory 6, 9, 22, 25, 92, 93, 95, 123, 136

Zone of Proximal Development (ZPD) 14, 90

Author Index

Alexiou, Thomai 2, 24, 26, 46, 47, 91, 113

Bronfenbrenner, Urie 8, 30

Butler, Yuko Goto 2, 46, 47, 49, 62, 69, 75–77, 83, 89, 92, 93, 106, 107, 116, 118, 141

Enever, Janet 2, 62, 73, 101, 103, 104, 105, 110, 115, 116, 118, 120

Mihaljević Djigunović, Jelena 2, 3, 32, 33, 120, 131

Mourão, Sandie 1, 2, 35, 39–41, 48, 50, 57, 63, 136, 139

Muñoz, Carmen, 1, 20, 40, 47, 73, 89, 90, 120, 128, 129

Nikolov, Marianne 2, 3, 24, 31, 32, 38, 1180120, 140

Piaget, Jean 13, 14, 39

Prošić-Santovac, Danijela 16, 17, 21, 34, 37, 43, 47, 50, 56, 64, 74, 91

Rokita-Jaśkow, Joanna 2, 36, 41, 48, 49, 51, 64, 67–71, 73–76, 82, 84, 97, 101–103, 111, 114

Sun, He 16, 20, 25, 74, 76, 128

Van Lier, Leo 3–6, 34, 52, 56, 85, 86

For Product Safety Concerns and Information please contact our EU Authorised Representative:

Easy Access System Europe

Mustamäe tee 50

10621 Tallinn

Estonia

gpsr.requests@easproject.com